Kwasi Wiredu

Chief Editor
Dr. Munguci D. Etriga, AJ

Kwasi Wiredu
Thoughts

Conference proceedings from Tangaza University

Preface by
Munguci D. Etriga, AJ

Domuni-Press

2024

THIS BOOK IS PUBLISHED
BY DOMUNI-PRESS
RESEARCH COLLECTION

Philosophy

ISSN: 2999-2508
ISBN: 978-2-36648-211-9
© DOMUNI-PRESS, January 2024

TANGAZA UNIVERSITY COLLEGE
The Catholic University of Eastern Africa
P.O. Box 15055– 00509 Langata Nairobi
Tell: 020-2379048/0722-204724

INSTITUTE OF PHILOSOPHY

Tangaza University College is a Catholic institution of higher learning. Started in 1986 in Nairobi -Kenya, the college hosts three schools: School of Theology, School of Education; and School of Arts and Social Sciences. The School of Theology is the biggest Catholic Philosophical and Theological centre in Africa, with students and lecturers from over 40 countries and approximately 100 Religious and or Missionary Institutes/Orders. The University is distinguished for academic excellence, service orientation and a commitment to social transformation under the motto: *Teaching Minds, Touching Hearts, Transforming Lives.* Tangaza Institute of Philosophy, which is one of the four institutes in the School of Theology, holds an annual International Philosophy Conference on the feat day of St. Thomas Aquinas – the Institute's patron. The year 2023's conference was dedicated to honour Professor Kwasi Wiredu, a foremost postcolonial African philosopher, who passed on the previous year.

Preface and Acknowledgments

On January 6, 2022, Professor Kwasi Wiredu, a foremost protagonist of post-colonial African philosophy, died at the age of 90. A great scholar, professor and humanist, his contributions to scholarly development, not just to Africa but to the universal pool of human knowledge, is exceptional.

Tangaza University (TU), through the Institute of Philosophy, decided that its annual international philosophy day 2023 be in honour of Wiredu's philosophical contribution. Accordingly, the symposium articles and presentations herein are designed to highlighting the significance of Wiredu's thoughts. I've been fortunate to chair the Symposium Steering Committee (SSC) that organizes the event. I was thus privileged to receive lots of articles, first as abstracts and later as presentations, from various respected researchers who donated some of their valuable time towards this course. This book is the fruit of their reflections.

On behalf of the SSC, therefore, I register my profound gratitude to the various contributors who made it possible for the TU to honour such a great and industrious philosopher. Indeed, not all articles contributed and presented found space in this production of Conference Proceeding 2 due to the limited volume accorded to it. Nonetheless, all the contributors within and without the publication are duly appreciated. The Institute is equally thankful to the TU, particularly through the offices of the DVC Research and Extension (DVCRE), and DVC Academics and Students Life (DVCASL), for rendering the needed support towards the realization of this project. Finally, to you the reader of the book, may you find something of value and inspiration!

Thanks.

Munguci D. Etriga, AJ
Nairobi, 2023

Kwasi Wiredu and the Development of Contemporary Philosophy in Africa

Prof. Oriare Nyarwath, Department of Philosophy and Religious Studies
University of Nairobi, oriare.nyarwath@uonbi.ac.ke

Abstract

This paper examines Kwasi Wiredu's contribution to the development of contemporary philosophy in Africa. Wiredu is one of the founding fathers of contemporary African philosophy. And his philosophical thought and works emerge from the background in which issues had been raised concerning meaning, nature and role of African philosophy. Wiredu's conception of African philosophy is informed by at least three historical movements in Africa; the precolonial thought systems, the colonial thought system and the advent of alien cultures and religions. The encounters of these systems create in an African an ambivalent culture, conceptual formulations and philosophy in particular. For colonial enterprise to succeed in establishing itself and dominating Africans, it had to fraudulently deprive precolonial African thought systems and knowledge of rationality and worth. The colonial encounter and subsequent spread of alien religions and cultures witnessed the imposition in Africa of foreign cultures, values, religions, philosophy and knowledge. All this are a mark of colonial mentality and enslavement of Africans. Contemporary philosophy has, in the view of Wiredu, as one of its tasks, the liberating of Africans from these colonial trappings as well as helping create conducive conditions of existence in contemporary Africa. African philosophy, therefore has to be critical of both our traditional values and values that have come from outside. This critical engagement would enable contemporary Africa to retain and develop the best of its traditions as well as borrow the best from outside. Contemporary African philosophy therefore has to be a synthesis of traditional African and modern philosophies.

Introduction

In this work I would like to outline, what in my view, is Kwasi Wiredu's idea of African philosophy and the background from which contemporary African philosophy emerges. Kwasi Wiredu (3 October 1931 – 6 January 2022) is a Ghanaian philosopher. He is one of the founding fathers of contemporary African philosophy and therefore one of the most influential figures in contemporary African philosophy. For those who have attempted to study or read contemporary African philosophy know that there have been a lot of controversies and contestations related to the meaning, nature and methodologies in African philosophy; but that is how philosophy is, and should be. It is not anything negative. When one reads works in African philosophy, of course, one would likely come across the contributions of Kwasi Wiredu to the emergence and development of contemporary African philosophy. I intend, in this work, to confine myself to sketching out the various resources and sources; according to Wiredu, of contemporary African philosophy.

Contemporary African Philosophy

Contemporary African philosophy emerges from the convergence of several historical currents; the precolonial African thought system that persists into the colonial period and can still be referred to as indigenous thought system, then there is the colonial thought system that characterizes the colonial era in Africa. The arrival and spread of alien religions such as Christianity and Islam can be considered as integral part of the colonial current. However, when we talk of contemporary African philosophy, it does not mean that there was no philosophy in African prior to the colonization of Africa, or the introduction of western philosophy in Africa. There was philosophy in Africa. Many scholars in the area of African Philosophy have tried to trace back the history of African philosophy beyond the contemporary African philosophy, and some scholars as far back before the colonial era. Many people forget that even prior to the colonization of Africa there was philosophy in Africa. There are several works that have been published on precolonial African philosophy. One of the excellent works in this area is *African Philosophy: The Pharaonic Period, 2780-330 B.C.* (2004) by Theophile Obenga that traces the history of African philosophy as far back as up to 330 BC that is as far back as the time of Aristotle. And he has done a very nice work about African philosophy in the pharaonic period. Other works in this area include *Stolen Legacy* by George G. M. James (1954), *The African Origin of Civilization: Myth or Reality* by Cheikh Anta Diop (1974), *Black Athena: The Afroasiatic Roots of Classical Civilization* by Martin Bernal (Vol. 1, 1987, Vol. 2, 1991, Vol. 3, 2006), and *Introduction to African Civilizations* by John G. Jackson. Many people tend to associate philosophy in African with the advent of the colonial era in Africa. But we recognize that before colonization of Africa, there was philosophy, and therefore the advent of the colonization in Africa resulted in the convergence of two currents; that is, colonization that comes with its own set of values and institutions and existent pre-colonial African thought system with its institutions and philosophy. The concurrence of these trends creates problematics for the development of contemporary African philosophy. So when we talk of contemporary African philosophy, we must look at it from that troubled background. Contemporary African philosophy therefore emerges and develops as an integration not only of the two historical currents; the colonial thought system and the pre-existing African thought system that persists through the colonial era and can still be referred to as indigenous thought system, but also incorporating postcolonial philosophical discourse in Africa. The mergence of these historical currents was well articulated by Kenyan political theorist Ali Mazrui in his work *The Africa: A Triple Heritage* (1986) in which he discusses the encounter and merging of the African traditional heritage, the colonial heritage and, western heritage characterized by, for instance, the Christian and Islamic heritage. This was also observed by Kwame Nkrumah in his book *Consciencism: Philosophy and ideology for Decolonization* (1964). But the fact is that these different heritages once we have encountered them, they become part and parcel of us. Our identity is formed by these experiences. So, there is no way we can escape their impact. We can only navigate through them and see what we are supposed to do. The convergence has created and imposed on Africans a lot of conceptual categories that result into philosophical, cultural and religious issues. And according to Wiredu, we need to critically interrogate colonially imposed conceptual categories of thought. Wiredu argues that uncritical assimilation of these foreign concepts or categories of thought would rightly constitute what he calls mental colonization. Wiredu has addressed some of these concepts just to illustrate the breadth and depth of our conceptual colonization. It is important that we look at some of the solutions Wiredu has advanced or proposed. The strategies for conceptual decolonization would be critical examination of all the foreign imposed categories of thought as well as critical examination of our own precolonial indigenous conceptual categories of thought.

Understanding colonialism in Africa, as is the case everywhere else colonialism was experienced, is complex and interesting. It can be debated whether indeed it ended with the so-called political independence of various African countries which is marked by Africans replacing colonizers simply by taking the reins of running the various social institutions, or whether colonialism still continues in Africa. Colonialism is indeed a complex phenomenon with several dimensions that include physical occupation and domination, mental and even spiritual domination. Mental and spiritual dimensions are more interesting because they are psychological and once they take root or hold, they become self-generating. The self-generation due to mental and spiritual colonization means that now Africans spearhead the perpetuation of their own colonization. And this is the very reason that makes mental and spiritual colonization more dangerous since they easily create the illusion of independence in the absence of physical domination. This seems to be the case in Africa where the physical exit of colonizers is seen as independence. Colonial religions and education systems focused more on mental and spiritual colonization. But this realization also means that effective liberation and independence for Africans has to focus on these dimensions as well, that is, mental and spiritual decolonization. For colonialism to establish itself and take control of Africa, it has partly to disparage / denigrate the African person and African thought systems but more so the thought systems that existed before the advent of African colonization. It had to create room for itself by disparaging and denigration our pre-colonial thought system. To this extent, colonialism inculcated in Africans an inferiority complex and the attitude of often considering non-Africans as superior to them in many ways; an attitude which extends to foreign cultures (products, values and practices). Actually once an inferiority complex, which is part of mental colonization has been established in Africans, then Africans tend to consider foreigners and foreign culture as more superior and more admirable. One can just look around and would see that pervasive attitude of Africans towards foreigners and foreign products, yet many Africans do not realize that that is an issue they should take seriously. Even things that appear as simple as naming of a child is still resiliently problematic. For instance, our Television contents, at least in Kenya, are more foreign than local, and I believe it is the same in several African countries. Many public universities in Africa are increasing acquiring Confucius Institutes which do not seem to be designed for cultural exchanges between China and respective African countries but to spread Chinese language and culture, and finally create Chinese cultural influence in these countries. Apart from China, there are several institutes and centres in public universities in several African countries meant to spread foreign languages and cultures. This you cannot find in a non-colonized society. To most of us Africa, it looks very normal. These are the things, though we take them lightly, they are vehicles for perpetuating foreign influences. Many researchers in several African institutions and universities tend to believe that if they publish their research findings and books in foreign countries, outside Africa, then that in itself necessarily ensures high quality of their publications. But this is not necessarily true. The belief is just a manifestation of colonized mentality. Furthermore, such publications hardly find their way back to Africa where the researches were done and where that knowledge in needed most. They also tend to be too expensive to be afforded by many people in Africa. Curricula, particularly, that of philosophy and religious studies in many African universities that I'm familiar with, are still heavily foreign and colonial both in their content and approach. There is need to decolonize most curricula in our universities. That does not mean that they should not contain contents of global nature and interest. Especially in philosophy and religious studies, it is still important to study world philosophical and religious systems to enrich comparative and intercultural knowledge. But more focus and emphasis should be put on African orientation to various disciplines in our universities, and even in the whole of our education system.

Inferiority complex often leads to lack of or less belief in oneself, one's worth and one's capacities. Thus one tends to look to and depend on outside for the solution to one's many problems. And if you look at African today, you would see the entrenchment of inferiority complex. Africans seems to be in a dilemma, they seem to be in a fix, they don't know which way or direction to go, they do not even know what they are capable of doing to be really independent. Thus inferiority complex tends to make people who have it to look to and depend on outside for the solutions to their own problems. Africa is one of the riches, if not the riches, continents in valuable natural resources in the world, yet Africa remains the poorest continent in the world. Whay is Africa unable to generate knowledge and technology that would enable it to harness its natural resources and develop food security, industrialization and good governance? One can easily find the answer to this question in inferiority complex and dependency syndrome created by colonization. Yet we should remember that the main goal of colonization was and is economic exploitation and domination of the colonized regions. This fact makes it difficult for the foreign imperial powers to easily let Africa be independent in the strict sense of the term since they would want to continue dominating and exploiting resources of Africa. It would seem like Africa, in the absence of military might, needs cunny and wisdom to outmanoeuvre the imperial foreign powers still operating in African under various guises. But such an undertaking would require political leaders who are visionary, patriotic and statesmen; the very leadership qualities that have become rare, if not lacking, in political leadership across Africa today. The crisis in political leadership in Nigeria exemplified by Chinua Achebe some years back in his book *The Trouble with Nigeria* (1983), seems to persist not only in Nigeria, but also reflects the general political situation in Africa. Achebe talks of the need for visionary leadership who have the ability and willingness to rise to the responsibility of leadership and challenge of personal example (Achebe 1983, 1-3). A responsible leader must not only be the embodiment of the needs and aspirations of the people he or she leads, but must also have the vision, ability and willingness to lead his or her people to the desired common good which is used here to include enabling or provision of the basic human needs. However, to the contrary, the political leadership across Africa seem to be as cruel and oppressive of the citizens as the neo-colonizers, or seem to be in cahoots with neo-colonizers.

The main goal of colonialism is domination and economic exploitation of the colonized regions. The other aspects of colonialism such as colonial culture and technology are just to serve this primary goal of resource exploitation. V. Y. Mudimbe aptly explains the colonial process that produces just the right kind of people for colonization (Mudimbe 1988, 1), the people who are mentally colonized and therefore would always look up to the colonizer as superior and for guidance. This consequently result into the psychology of dependency of the colonized on the colonizer and patronage by the colonizer. Frantz Fanon has succinctly articulated this psychology of dependency and patronage (Fanon 1967, 31-32). Fanon believes that the white people who believe that they are inherently superior to black people are as idiotic as the black people who believe that they are inherently inferior to white people, and both require liberation from their idiocy (Fanon 1967, 7).

African independent struggles, virtually all over Africa, seem to have missed out on this vital aspect of colonization, that is, economic independence, which should have been the ultimate goal of the independence struggles. The consequence of missing out on this means that African independent struggles focused and continue to focus on what is not the primary root of colonization. Oruka argues that social freedom or liberty must be understood as ability and opportunity one has in a given society to fulfill human needs (Oruka 1996, 51-53) that can be economic, political, intellectual, cultural, religious and sexual. However, to enjoy all the other needs requires economic need and freedom. Thus economic need and freedom becomes more primary to the rest of the human needs (Oruka 1996, 87-122). However, due to apparent lack of adequate understanding of the concept of social freedom, virtually all African freedom fighters, sought political freedom at the expense of economic freedom, not realizing that enjoyment of political freedom and the other freedoms depends on economic freedom. Cunningly, colonial regimes in Africa scuttled the development of consciousness of freedom within Africans by propagating the myth that Africa was long already underdeveloped before its colonialization, and that is indeed the reason why it fell to colonialism, hence, if anything, colonialism was meant to develop Africa (Oruka 1996, 89). Though as a result of not developing adequate consciousness of freedom, Africans missed out on achieving actual independence, and they remain colonized to date. The paradox is that even today no African political leadership or government seems to have understood this fundamental idea of social freedom. They should have focused on economic independence as a priority, instead they focused on, as their primary, political independence. May be Kwame Nkrumah, the first president of independent Ghana, was mistaken when he is reported to have said that "seek ye first political kingdom and all else will be added unto thee" (Oruka 1996, 88). Unfortunately, African countries sought first political independence but they have never gotten economic independence. Nkrumah and other African freedom fighters of that period thought that if they get political independence then, as a consequent, they will be economically independent. Without having economic independence, one cannot get or adequately have the other independences (political, cultural, intellectual, religious and sexual freedoms), and this is what we see in the world today. Let us take a case just to illustrate my point. Look at what Russia does today to her neighbouring countries Ukraine and others, due to its greater economic power! It just invaded and tried to take over Ukraine. And look at the economic power employed in the war between Russia and Ukraine by all the parties involved in the war! It is clear that today, economic power, rules the world. If you do not have powerful weapons and you cannot make them then you are not free and cannot be free. Worse still if one is weak but have abundant valuable natural resources as the case in Africa today. Anybody more powerful can just walk into your home or territory

IN HONOUR OF KWASI WIREDU

and occupy your territory. African political independence has not yet yielded economic and cultural independence after more than fifty years, and the end of this is not foreseeable in the near future. Africa should focus on being economically independence above, if it hopes to be politically and culturally independent.

Due to lack of economic independence, Africa continues to be manipulated politically and culturally by countries that are economically powerful. We often see more powerful foreign countries like America imposing their values and cultures on Africans, as currently is demonstrated by the practice of lesbian, gay, bisexual, transgender and queer (LGBT). I am not saying that LGBTQ is sinful, evil or immoral. That is a different issue. But Africans should be able or left alone to decide on how to deal with such important matters of culture and life, of course, on condition that Africans take seriously matter of human life and dignity. But it should not be forced on Africans with the threat of die economic consequences if they do not swallow it down their throat. Politics in Africa is still manipulated and controlled, to a large extent, by foreign powerful countries that have interest in African economic resources. They try to make sure that government in place serve their interest even if it does not serve the interest of its citizens. So, they influence the general elections in Africa especially of the presidents and consequently influence the policies of governments constituted by these presidents. Presidency is still more powerful in many African countries. Practice of democracy and constitutionalism is necessary for good governance. But democracy and constitutionalism have become honorific terms. So, to practice them requires embracing the spirit of democracy and constitutionalism, which apparently is lacking in Africa. Therefore, the common talk of democratically and constitutionally elected governments makes very little sense or no sense in Africa. The very idea of democracy requires that it is seen to work in at least two areas, in the election of office holders and in the act of governance. But in Africa there is virtually no credible election, especially of presidents, conducted in the spirit of democracy where the will and choice of the majority prevails. Apparently, the elections are always manipulated either by the deep state or by foreign dominant powers. On democratic governance, by this I mean governing on behalf of citizens, many African governments are not democratic in this sense. Otherwise, Africans would not be that poor in the face of massive natural resources the countries have. They would even be enjoying basic social services. Yet their leaders seem to be filthy rich. Maybe the failure of democratic practice in Africa should not be taken to mean the failure of the Western model of democracy, liberal democracy, in Africa. Many have argued that the Western liberal democracy has not worked well in Africa (Oduor 2022). Wiredu's proposal of democracy based on the principle of consensus (Wiredu 1996, 184-190) as opposed to majoritarian democracy which ignores the interest and rights of the minority, maybe be interpreted to to demonstrate the limit of liberal democracy as practiced in Africa. But on the other hand, it can be argued that Africans as a whole have not faithfully attempted to practice liberal democracy as it should be practice, according to the spirit of democracy. Rigging elections or looting public resources to enrich few members of ruling class is far from being democratic.

We are witnessing in Africa continuation of the scramble for its economic resources with more foreign powers that were not in the previous scrambles joining in the current scramble such as America, Russia, China, India and many more. The current scramble can be titled the third scramble for Africa whereas the first scramble was in the 1880s particularly marked by the partitioning of Africa (1885-1914). However, even after Africa got the so-called political independence, many foreign powers continued the exploitation of African resources but to operating under such organizations as World Bank, IMF and other non-governmental organizations of which they have greater control. This marked the second scramble for Africa. Though these organizations still operate in African, but apparently with no intention to see the real independence and development of Africa.

The third scramble is more interesting because we see more foreign powers are joining and not forcing themselves onto Africans, but Africans are inviting them to come as trading partners. However, the trading agreements are not on equal or fair terms. This is what mental and spiritual colonization do. Now it is Africans inviting these foreign powers to come and exploit the economic resources of Africa. Unlike the first scramble marked by the partitioning of Africa and the second a scramble characterized by the creation and operations of non-governmental organization such as World Bank and IMF that may appear well-intentioned but are essentially colonial in their actual intentions and operations especially in Africa where they advance loans and fiscal advice that are in essential to the advantage of the dominant and controlling members of those organization; the current (third scramble) is marked by African governments inviting the foreign powers to come and exploit African economic resources. This is what mental colonization and inferiority complex finally result into. If African countries were indeed truly independent by now they should have developed the technical knowhow to exploit and process its various natural resources which are the envy and cause of manipulation by many foreign countries.

Wiredu and African Philosophy

It is from this complex colonial background that Wiredu's idea and role of philosophy, but more so, his idea of conceptual decolonization, become very key because it is fundamental to the general decolonization of Africa; cultural decolonization, political decolonization and economic decolonization. We need to understand why we are focusing more on conceptual decolonization which, in a simple language, is mental decolonization.

The convergence of African indigenous thought systems, colonial thought system and postcolonial heritage creates in Africa an ambivalent personal identity and culture. This is inevitable since we are a product of our past experiences. The colonial system imposed on Africans not only Western values and cultures but also basic categories of thought or concepts that were particular to their tradition. Uncritical assimilation of these concepts and continued use of them would constitute mental colonization. Wiredu has addressed some of these concepts to demonstrate the disparity in their formulations in relation to African conceptual formulations traceable from their indigenous thought systems and analyses of indigenous languages. Some of these contestable concepts include Personhood, God, religion, truth, justice, death and religious narratives of original creation. Basic to these concepts, I think is, personhood or self. How the self is conceptualized determines the nature and goals of virtually all the social institutions, for instance, marriage and family, religion, politics, economics, education and culture in general. For instance, it is contestable whether the pervasive or dominant libertarian conception of human self as an isolated or unencumbered self is consistent with conceptions found among various African cultures. Taking, for the purposes of illustration, what is seen as the typical African conception of the self/person called *Ubuntu,* a conception of the self as necessarily socially encumbered. Imagine, if this conception were to take root in Africa and become pervasive, the social institutions and the structure of our communities would probably be different. There are several important recent researches and publications on this worldview dominant in Africa such as *Ubuntu and Personhood* (2018), *Ubuntu and the Reconstitution of Community* (2019), *Ubuntu and the Everyday* (2018). Yet, this ubuntu worldview has direct bearing on our conception and understanding of religion and belief in life after death, responsibility both moral and legal, and many others. For instance, criminal responsibility would not be put solely on an individual since an individual is seen as a web or relations, but would be seen in terms of relations that directly shape and influence and individual action. Consequently, punishment would not be meted out only to the individual, but the individual would be dealt with taking cognizance that he or she exist in a web of relationship. Let us just think of a result of libertarian conception of self as an unencumbered, a criminal will be punished as individual; and supposing the individual is imprisoned. So many other innocent people related to the person imprisoned such as spouse, child or parents are "punished" or subjected to lots of inconveniences due to the imprisonment yet due to the conception of self as isolated, and all these people are not considered in meting out punishment.

Contemporary African philosophy has therefore foreseeable tasks among others, the liberation of Africans from mental colonization through conceptual clarifications. This would help greatly in Africans developing self-belief and creating values that would serve their interest. In relation to the mode of liberation and development of genuine African philosophy, two schools of thought initially emerged. On the one hand, was the view that African philosophy is indigenous philosophy and should have no influences from the legacy of colonial Western philosophy. This view became known as particularist school. However, on the other hand, was the other view that African philosophy cannot ignore the other influences existent in Africa because there are some norms and values which are universal, and therefore apply across cultures. This school of thought became known as universalist school. This created in the early development of contemporary African two dominant schools of ethnophilosophical school and universalist school or what D, A. Masolo would prefer to call conceptual pragmatist school (Masolo 1994, 44,233). Wiredu's position reconciles these two schools of though. He believes that there are cultural universal and particulars (*Cultural Universals and Particulars* (1996). To Wiredu contemporary African philosophy has to get the best from indigenous philosophy as well as best techniques of modern philosophy of the Western heritage. African philosophy cannot remain traditional. It has to be modern if it is to address contemporary challenges in Africa. Critical analysis becomes very vital in the development of contemporary African philosophy (Wiredu 1980, ix-xi).

For traditional philosophies to be useful in modern times Wiredu advocates critical approach to avoid possible evils he calls anachronism, authoritarianism and supernaturalism (Wiredu 1980:1-6). These are beliefs and practices that subtly habour absolutism which is a hindrance to creativity and modernization. Of course, belief in absolutism is philosophically problematic. It is this belief that informs Wiredu controversial epistemological theory that truth is nothing but a considered opinion (Wiredu 1980, 111-123). We have to critically engage our traditional cultures in order not to cling on practices that have become outdated and cannot serve our modern needs simply because they are part of our heritage. But again, we should not reject certain values or things simply because they have foreign origin.

The fact that much of our traditional cultures and philosophies were mostly written down by colonial anthropologists, calls for critical examination and analysis because of possible incorrect presentation due to ignorance or deliberate distortion as part of disparaging African mental capacities and its cognitive products. Colonial anthropologist used many concepts in reference to African realities that have different connotations from African conceptions. For instance concepts such as bride price instead of bride wealth, tribe instead of nation, witchdoctor instead of healer, ancestor worship as opposed to ancestor veneration, sin as opposed to evil, soul as the essence of human person; all this tend to have connotations different from many African conceptions. Though there is good amount of ideas or concepts we can get from these writings as intellectual heritage of our people that are important for contemporary African philosophy. Therefore contemporary African philosophy needs to interrogate these kinds of colonial writings about Africa in order to attain conceptual clarifications.

Much of African traditional philosophies still exist as oral traditions. Therefore, our oral traditions still constitute much of thoughts and ideas of many of our people. Wiredu like Odera Oruka recognizes that contemporary African philosophy needs also to tap on the enormous resources that seem to lie with still many individual Africans who are not able to write their own thoughts. Many of these people are repositories of both individual and collective knowledge and wisdom. Some of these people have interesting views and perspectives on various realities and issues in life that when they are philosophically engaged, their thoughts documented and analyzed, would constitute an integral part of contemporary African philosophy. Their thoughts and views are likely to stimulate interesting philosophical debates for a long time, even for many generations to come (Wiredu 1996, 116-117).

Proverbs and folklores as part of our oral traditions are still valuable sources of our traditional wisdom and philosophies. Though their original creators are lost in the many generations that have passed, they definitely originated from the minds of individuals. When carefully analyzed, the proverbs and folklores, reveal underlying insightful conceptions of reality or human nature of philosophical status. Contemporary African philosophy cannot ignore these forms of oral traditions (Wiredu 1996, 155).

Language is also an area of great significance in conceptual understanding and clarification. Through language, concepts, meanings and ideas are transmitted among people. In African there is pervasive and significant use of colonial languages, for example, English, French, Portuguese, Arabic, Spanish, Italian, and some others. Many more are likely to take root in African like Chinese Russian and Indian. Language is both universal and particular, since it carries universal concepts and ideas that are particular to a culture. In many African countries, the colonial or foreign languages are the media of instruction in institutions of learning which means many concepts of foreign origin are uncritically transmitted to the learners, or even among the researchers such as ourselves here. But to carry our diligent conceptual analyses and clarification, we need to be competent in the understanding of our indigenous languages so that we may carry out effective conceptual comparisons and clarification. This is likely also to elicit interesting conceptual comparisons that are likely to help in making informed rational choices on which concepts to use. It is important to mention at this junction one of the pioneer philosophical works in indigenous languages, *Listening to Ourselves: A Bilingual Anthology of African philosophy* (2013). This anthology edited by Chike Jeffers involves philosophical papers written in six different African indigenous languages, Dholuo, Gikuyu, Akan, Igbo, Wolof and Amharic.

Of course we cannot just dismiss these metropolitan languages. Some of them are going to be here in African for a long time, if not forever. Given the ethnic structure of many of our countries currently, with several ethnic languages in one country, it might not make much sense to try to eliminate the metropolitan languages which are spoken in the whole country across ethnic groups.

Just like it is not possible to get rid of the colonial languages from many of countries, so is the case with our modern institutions of learning and curricula. May be the best approach would be to appropriate what is rationally of value from them. Despite the fact that much of our educational curricula are still heavily colonial, it is interesting that many people even among African philosophers still do not seem to understand the full import of such a scenario. Concepts of apparent foreign origin become problematic to understand. If we take for instance the concept of African philosophy just for the purpose of illustration. There are many Africans practitioners of philosophy, writing and teaching philosophy particularly in the areas they hardly associate with African philosophy such as logic, metaphysics, epistemology, philosophy of mathematics, philosophy of science and philosophy of social science, who still do not realize that they are indeed engaged in African philosophy. Because, I imagine, that some of them still have a narrow conception of African philosophy by which they do not consider such branches of philosophy as also possible legitimate branches of African philosophy. Contemporary African philosophy also needs people who are experts in every branch of philosophy including logic, metaphysics, epistemology, philosophy of mathematics, philosophy of science, and philosophy of social science. Contemporary African philosophy needs to appropriate modern development in philosophy regardless of the origin of that development, because that is the nature knowledge, it entails lending and borrowing.

Conclusion

Wiredu has made significant contribution to the emergence and development of contemporary African philosophy. He not only defended Africans by debunking the colonial mythical discourse on Africa that was intended to deprive Africans of both philosophy and humanity; but he also demonstrated the trajectories that postcolonial African philosophy should take. He has critically and beautifully illustrated how contemporary African philosophy should integrate its repositories of indigenous philosophies and resources of modern philosophy.

He not only attempted successfully to integrate indigenous philosophical knowledge with modern techniques of philosophy, but also illustrated how intercultural and cross-cultural philosophy can be fruitfully conducted through his contributions on cultural universals and particulars. In this, Wiredu demonstrates how African philosophers can deal with philosophical issues particular to Africa as well as global philosophical issues.

Wiredu's antithetical stance against continued colonization of Africa is well articulated in his idea of conceptual decolonization. This is not just a call to take our indigenous cultures and languages seriously in order to understand our traditional conceptual categories of thoughts, that in essence would enable us to competently engage in all sorts of conceptual comparisons and make rational choices on concepts that we use to describe and interpret our realities; but also liberates postcolonial African philosophy from colonial conceptual trappings and lays solid foundation for contemporary African philosophy.

Bibliography

ACHEBE, C., 1983. *The Trouble with Nigeria*. Nairobi: Heinemann educational Books Ltd.

BERNAL, M., 1987. *Black Athena: The Afroasiatic Roots of Classical Civilization*, vol. 1. New Brunswick, NJ: Rutgers University Press.

DIOP, C. A,. 1974. *The African Origin of Civilization: Myth or Reality*. New York: Lawrence Hill & Company.

FANON, F., 1967. *Black Skin, White Masks*. New York: Grove Press.

HOUNTONDJI, P. J., 1996. *African Philosophy: Myth and Reality*, 2nd edition. Bloomington: Indiana University Press.

JACKSON, J. G., 2001. *Introduction to African Civilizations*. New York: Kensington Publishing Corp.

James, G. G. M., 1992. *Stolen Legacy*. Trenton: Africa World Press.

Jeffers, C., ed. 2013. *Listening to Ourselves: A Multilingual Anthology of African Philosophy*. Albany: State University of New York State (SUNY) Press.

MASOLO, D. A., 1994. *African Philosophy in Search of Identity*. Bloomington and Indianapolis: Indiana University Press.

MUDIMBE, V. Y., 1988. *The Invention of Africa: Gnosis. Philosophy and the Order of Knowledge.* Bloomington and Indianapolis: Indiana University Press.

OBENGA, T., 2004. *African Philosophy: The Pharaonic Period: 2780 - 330 BC.* Popenguine, Senegal: Per Ankh.

ODUOR, R. M. J., ed. 2022. *Africa Beyond Liberal Democracy: In Search of Context-Relevant Models of Democracy for the Twenty-First Century.* Lanham: The Rowman & Littlefield Publishing Group.

ORUKA, H. O., 1996. *Philosophy of Liberty,* 2nd edition. Nairobi: Standard Textbooks Graphics and Publishing.

ORUKA, H. O., 1997. *Practical Philosophy in Search of an Ethical Minimum.* Nairobi: East African Educational Publishers.

ORUKA, H. O., ed. 1991. *Sage Philosophy: Indigenous Thinkers and Modern Debate on African Philosophy.* Nairobi: African Centre for Technology Studies (ACTS) Press.

OGUDE, J., ed. 2018. *Ubuntu and Personhood.* Trenton, N. J: Africa World Press.

OGUDE, J., ed. 2019. *Ubuntu and the Reconstitution of Community.* Bloomington: Indiana University Press.

OGUDE, J., and Unifier Dyer, eds. 2019. *Ubuntu and the Everyday.* Trenton, N.J: Africa World Press.

WIREDU, K., 1996. *Cultural Universals and Particulars: An African Perspective.* Bloomington and Indianapolis: Indiana University Press.

WIREDU, K., 1980. *Philosophy and an African Culture.* Cambridge: Cambridge University Press.

Conceptual Decolonization: Wiredu's Seminal Work

Munguci D. Etriga, AJ, Director Tangaza Institute of Philosophy, Nairobi-Kenya, and Part-time Lecturer at Apostles of Jesus Institute of Philosophy and Theology (AJIPT), Nairobi-Kenya, tualupublications@gmail.com

Abstract

Today there is no dispute that great deals of production of materials exist in African scholarly tradition in general, and in philosophy in particular. Like in any philosophical tradition punctuated with historical figures who changed trajectories of scholarly production through their seminal ideas, Africa's philosophic tradition is marked with historical figures. While it is not within my competence to nominate such figures, certainly when this history will be properly and or comprehensively documented, the one name that will stand epic for changing the trajectory of postcolonial African philosophy is Kwasi Wiredu. It is, therefore, my argument in this paper that: (i) Wiredu changed the trajectory of post-colonial African philosophy through his work of *Conceptual Decolonization*, (ii) Conceptual decolonization is a seminal idea not just in African philosophy, but in all scholarly work in Africa and beyond, (iii) Wiredu never gets the honour he truly deserves.

Key Words: Wiredu, Decolonization, Conceptualization, Domain, Impact.

Introduction

Current scholarly production in African philosophy has come of age, from oral to scripted tradition through denials and affirmations, often characterized by acrimonious debates. A lot can be said about this debate but for the purpose of this paper, I will limit my scope to *Conceptual Decolonization*. Like any other philosophical traditions, African philosophy is punctuated by ideas that have greatly influenced and altered the trajectories of its philosophical discourses. The appearance of *Conceptual Decolonization* four decades ago is one such an idea. It is a brainchild of Kwasi Wiredu from Ghana. He is the protagonist who did not only initiate this idea in philosophy but belaboured to nurture it through lectures, books, articles, conferences, symposia and interviews. This paper examines conceptual decolonization within the context of Wiredu's more general thoughts in philosophy to highlight its seminal nature, particularly in African scholarship. The following is the paper's structure: Contextualization, Wiredu's notion of conceptual decolonization, the Domain of conceptual decolonization, and the Impact of conceptual decolonization.

Contextualization

For a better grasp of the notion of conceptual decolonization and all works surrounding it, having its philosophical geography from the onset is significant. This will consist of a fleeting sketch of Wiredu's non-professional and professional biography. Like any other scholar, Wiredu was a child of his time. Several factors had enormous influence upon him for which he was able to come with the theme of conceptual decolonization in the way he did. I will particularly break the two dimensions of his biography (that is, the non-professional and professional) into six areas: Akan heritage, formative academic life, colonialism, rationality debate, contemporaries, and personal acumen.

Akan Heritage: Wiredu was a Ghanaian, born in 1931 in Kumasi. He was of the Akan extraction that he fondly identified with. Despite being proselytized and schooled in a largely westernized education system, the Ghanaian star stood tall. One would easily construe, as many do, that having been detached from African experience to pursue his professional career far away from his natives, Wiredu would lose touch with the Akan traditional corpus of knowledge. But reading through his works, it seems this was not the case. For the extent to which his Akanness is depicted in many of his scripts is indeed an intriguing aspect of his biography. Sometimes the finer details of the Akan traditional knowledge exhibited on issues like the consensual form of democracy, the concept of truth in the Akan Language, African Philosophical Tradition: A Case Study of the Akan, An Akan Perspective on Human Rights, and above all the epic Akan debate between him and Gyekye on the Akan Concept of Person, serve to confirm that the kernel of Wiredu's philosophical thought was his traditional Akan view. The rest of the sources helped to trigger and understand better what he inherited from his Akan tradition. Little wonder that he constantly kept advocating for contemporary African philosophers not to disdain their traditional African heritage but employ them as resourceful materials for their philosophizing.

Formative Academic Life: as is the case with every student or scholar that is influenced directly or indirectly by the college environment: professors, syllabus and other resource materials, Wiredu was no exception. This can be drawn from his various education backgrounds, ranging from early formative college experience at the Anglican Boy's school – Adisadel in Cape Coast, to the University of Ghana for Diploma. This would later extend to his formative professional career in the Oxford University for BA in philosophy where he encountered Gilbert Ryle the famous British epistemologist, particularly known for philosophy of mind and critique of Cartesian dualism. Following his graduation in 1960, Wiredu taught briefly at the University

College of North Staffordshire for a year before returning to the University of Ghana. Here it becomes clear that besides other influences this kind of academic formation had on him, that of the Anglophone background of epistemological discourses, particularly the analytic trend can hardly be ignored. It is no exaggeration claiming that conceptual decolonization itself is essentially analytic. This is not by mistake.

Colonialism: the reality of colonialism and all the struggles towards liberating the African from it were too strong realities from which one, like Wiredu or his contemporaries could have hardly remained impervious to. At the University of Ghana, Wiredu spent most of his professional life serving as: lecturer at the university and several other academic institutions both in Africa and America; a member to several academic bodies; and the Vice-Chair of the *Inter-African Council of Philosophy*. At this point in the time of Africa, colonialism and the struggles of liberation were part of the academia. It is therefore no wonder that conceptual decolonization would come out. Seemingly, Wiredu was convinced that the real and fundamental decolonization, hence, freedom has to begin from the mind, as the software of anything liberative.

Rationality Debate: corollary to colonialism was the acrimonious debate on the existence and nature of African philosophy. Sparked by Placid Tempel's publication of the "*La Philosophie Bantue*" (1985) that was later translated into English as *Bantu Philosophy*, the title of the book opened a pandora's box of what had hitherto been silently brewing. It had up till then been a one-sided debate about the western conventional conception that philosophy was unbeknown to the Africans. The title "Bantu Philosophy", notwithstanding the content, alone belied this conventional wisdom by boldly claiming that philosophy was existent among the Bantu in Africa. Thus, having lived at this historical time when this acrimonious debate was raging on, Wiredu as a prolific writer and debater was not spared by it. He was one of its players. This is notwithstanding the fact that seemingly Wiredu did not get consumed by this debate. He rather fairly stared clear of it. Certainly, one cannot rule out that this debate influenced and enriched his philosophical thoughts. It is perhaps on this basis that some writers opine that Wiredu, like Descartes who sought a way out of the quagmire of the previous philosophical discourses through his new system of methodic doubt, found conceptual decolonization as exit strategy to the acrimonious rationality debate.

Contemporaries: consequent to colonialism and the rationality debate, another key factor in academic life of Wiredu that might have had a considerable influence on him was the role played by his contemporaries. Names among others like O. Oruka, P. Hountondji, V.Y. Mudimbe, and D.A Masolo frequently interacted and debated not only in conferences, symposia, and other such like fora, but also in books. Indeed, several Wiredu's scripts attest to this. Like D.A Masolo, some did write the prolegomena to some of his scripts. The aim of bringing the contemporaries here is not for mere historical records. It is to highlight that in their professional interactions, Wiredu's philosophical views might have certainly been directly or indirectly influenced by it. Conceptual decolonization project was no exception to this influence.

Personal acumen: it is said philosophy is more of what is given out than what is received. What is received is done through experience both external and internal. Every human individual is an object of experience. Some of these experiences of course are the same to a particular group of persons. And many definitely have had experiences similar to Wiredu's. However, the amount and quality of what comes out (philosophy) after such experiences (common or peculiar) is subject to personal acumen and industriousness. These are what make one exploit the experiences into fruitful philosophical production. For, one may have the experience and giftedness but fail to industriously turn it into a fruitful end. As Kant would maintain that it is not genius that one should be praised for but industriousness. Wiredu's scripts depict him as a man of intelligence and wisdom well utilized through industriousness. With such a commitment or industriousness and work ethic, it is no surprise that at the end of all the above factors, Wiredu ultimately came up with profound philosophical reflections in his career. Conceptual decolonization is one such a profound reflection.

Conceptual decolonization in African philosophy was therefore born from such a philosophical geography. It renders one to safely hold that finding himself in this context, to Wiredu this became a professional and existential strategy. It was a new philosophical approach advanced as a *conditio sine qua non* for a good African philosophy that any postcolonial contemporary African philosopher needs.

First appearing in 1980 as a research paper presented at the UNESCO conference in Nairobi, the work has come out as Wiredu's brainchild and hallmark. And long before his demise, the Ghanaian black star thought it as the needed key for awakening the postcolonial African philosopher from the slumber (to cite Kant) of prolegomena and schizophrenia. The former (prolegomena), as previously alluded to, highlights the energy and time professional African philosophers had devoted to the acrimonious debate about the existence and nature of African philosophy. It was not the doing of the work. The latter (schizophrenia) highlights the possibility of existence and uncritical use of both African and foreign modes of conceptualization in the minds of African philosophers. Such African philosophers were living in two worlds of conceptual modes. To these categories of postcolonial African philosophers, *Conceptual Decolonization in African Philosophy* was thus a mid-night stunner when their slumber was epic.

Wiredu's Notion of 'Conceptual Decolonization'

Decolonization in current times means many things: political, economic, cultural, technological, educational, tribal, magical, gender, etc. Hence, it is appropriate to examine this concept in the light of Wiredu's thought as found in his *The Need for Conceptual Decolonization in African Philosophy*.[1] This is to help us state clearly what we mean when referring to it in this paper.

In one of his later articles, Wiredu defines conceptual decolonization as "the elimination from our thought modes of conceptualization that came to us through colonization and remain in our thinking owing to inertia rather than to our reflective choices."[2] By 'modes of conceptualization' is meant the categories of thought or conceptual schemes through which realities are conceived and interpreted. Wiredu's earlier scripts, however, as will shortly be seen, employed more the term *conceptual framework*[3] for modes of conceptualization. It highlights the fact that our minds conceive realities according to a thought system within a given history and environment, which in philosophical discourse may be termed philosophical traditions or traditional philosophies. The former (philosophical tradition) refers to the "body of philosophical reflections and works consciously produced by individual philosophers or philosophical schools over a period of time and whose components (or some of their aspects) are internally connected in some way, though not

---

[1] Kwasi Wiredu, "Conceptual Decolonization in African Philosophy", in *Cultural Universals and Particulars: An African Perspective*, Indiana University Press, Indianapolis, 1996, p. 136-144.

[2] Kwasi Wiredu, "Conceptual Decolonization as an Imperative in Contemporary African Philosophy: Some Personal Reflections", in *Dans Rue Descartes 2002/2 (n° 36)*, p. 53-64.

[3] Cf. Kwasi Wiredu, "Conceptual Decolonization in African Philosophy", in *Cultural Universals and Particulars: An African Perspective*, p. 136.

without uniformity."[4] A philosophical tradition in this sense has certain organic relationships between the philosophical ideas constituting it, thereby creating a system. The sources of these ideas or thoughts are known. The latter (traditional philosophy) on its part is a kind of collective, non-scientific world view of a people and usually silent about the individual sources of its components. The silence in question, however, does not deny individuals as the genesis of these collective ideas. Oruka would term the originators of these ideas *sages* with those who go to the level of making "independent, critical assessment to what the people take for granted" as *philosophic sages*.[5] And the latter (that is, the philosophic sages), in turn create philosophic traditions.

Conceptual decolonization, therefore, is a call for the difficult mission of critical reconstruction. Its focus is the elimination of foreign modes of conceptualization superimposed through colonialism in the African minds. This definition, nevertheless, seemingly leaves a lot to be desired. Firstly, it is not explicit whether only the modes of conceptualization are to be eliminated, or the results of the modes of conceptualization (that is, concepts) too. Let us explain this using the example of the concept *person*. Aquinas in conformity with Boethius, as one of the so-called Western classic definitions of *person*, defines *person* as "an individual substance of a rational nature (*individual substantia rationalis naturae*)"[6], under which God, Angels and Humans are connoted. The mode of conceptualization or epistemic status that leads into such a connotation of *person* stems from a metaphysical framework that views reality in three modes:

[4] Godfrey Igwebuike Onah, "Wiredu's Philosophy of Human Nature, in *The Third Way in African Philosophy: Essay in Honor of Kwasi Wiredu*, Olusegun Oladipo (ed.), Ibadan, Nigeria, Hop4e Publications, 2002, pp. 61-81, p. 61.

[5] H. Odera Oruka (Ed.), *Sage Philosophy: Indigenous Thinkers and Modern Debate on African Philosophy*, African Centre for Technology Studies, Nairobi, 1991, p. 34

[6] Tomas Alvira, Luis Clavell, Tomas Malendo, *Metaphysics: Understanding the Science of Being*, Sinag-Tala Publishers, Manila, 2011, p. 123; Cf. Boethius, *De DuabusNaturis et una Persona Christi*, ch.3, in *Migne PL*, 64 col. 1345.

Pure Act (God), Pure Forms (Spirits) and Composed Beings (Hylomorphic existents), so that *person* cuts across the three categories. This would mean there is the epistemic status that entails the metaphysics behind this conception and the concept *person* so that there may be the possibility of three elements for elimination: (i) the mode of conception (the epistemic status or conceptual framework behind such a conception) of *person*, (ii) the concept *person*, and (iii) both (that is, the mode and the concept). But which of the three is to be eliminated or decolonized from the African mind remains rather complex.

To further exacerbate this complexity, there is yet another possibility due to similarities and dissimilarities that may arise in the decolonization of the African mind. Let us take the concept *person* for the Lögbara (that is, my native people), of North-Western and North-Eastern Uganda and the Democratic Republic of Congo, respectively. *Person* (*bha*) among the Lögbara (if I'm not mistaken) is conceived as a communitarian individual of spiritual nature. The paradoxical nature (that is, the communitarian individual) of this definition notwithstanding, two things can be seen in it when juxtaposed to the previously cited Aquinas-Boethius definition. That while on the one hand, some commonalities like 'rationality', 'individuality', and 'spirituality' exist between the two conceptions, on the other hand, there are considerable differences too. For example, though person in the Lögbara definition is an individual, preeminence is accorded to community (communitarian individual), not individuality as is the case with the cited 'classic' Western conception. Similarly, while the Aquinas-Boethius conception connotes Angels and God as *persons*, the Lögbara conception does not explicitly connote the two. In other words, from the western mode of conception, the only connotation of *person* the Lögbara have is the *human person*. This observation is further evidenced by the fact that in the entire Lögbara lexicon, (if am not mistaken), there is no notion for *person* precisely connoting God, Angels, and Human beings. Nonetheless, lately with proselytizing projects, a new word –

adhia has been coined for the three. But clearly it is garbage or philosophical deadwood, to use Wiredu's terms.[7] This is because '*adhia*' in primordial Lögbara syntax connotes 'an unnamed third person' or 'so and so'. To use it for person would be a misnomer to say the least. Take the case of the phrase "One God, three persons" for '*Adro alu, adhia na*" which means "One God, three So and Sos." The garbage in this is too loud and only the natives may realize how preposterous it can get. In the final analysis, the question then remains, what should be eliminated in conceptual decolonization, since there can be some glaring similarities and dissimilarities. Is it: the mode of conceptualization (the epistemic status)?; the result of the mode of conceptualization (the concept)?; both (the mode and the concept)?, or should one only eliminate the dissimilarities/differences, as is the case above in the Lögbara concept of *person*?

Inconspicuous still within the complexity of the above definition of conceptual decolonization is its tacit nature on the African modes of conception or their results. The definition seems to assume the African mode of conceptualization does not need 'decolonization'. What for instance should be done in case the African mode of conceptualization leaves a lot to be desired too? It is not utterly wrong positing that no person of sound mind can deny the fact that some African mentalities clearly reflect questionable modes or conceptual schemes. Tribal mentalities, victimhood mentalities, magical or mythical mentalities, etc. among Africans towards conception of certain realities cannot be entirely desirable. Perhaps these constitute the modes of conception referred to by Wiredu 'unscientific' so that even in his own admission, such mentalities, if not ameliorated, need to be eliminated or 'decolonized' too. Unfortunately, the above definition is silent about the African heritage or mentalities, as far as decolonization is concerned. Therefore, for the subsequent

---

[7] Cf. Kwasi Wiredu, "Conceptual Decolonization in African Philosophy", in *Cultural Universals and Particulars: An African Perspective*, p. 137.

discourse, I choose to use Wiredu's original definition of conceptual decolonization in the 1980 Nairobi paper. I found it quite profounder and more comprehensive, as hereafter explained.

The Nairobi paper posits that the Western colonial agenda in Africa left an indelible mark in the African mind in two complementary ways: negative and positive, both of which constitute the notion of *conceptual decolonization.* Negatively, conceptual decolonization is:

> ...avoiding or reversing through a critical conceptual self-awareness the unexamined assimilation in our thought (that is, in the thought of contemporary African philosophers) of the conceptual frameworks embedded in the foreign philosophical traditions that have had an impact on African life and thought.[8]

The focus here is on decolonizing the mind from foreign modes of conceptualization, that is, whether they are critically examined or not. Positively, conceptual decolonization is the process of "exploiting as much as is judicious the resources of our own indigenous conceptual schemes in our philosophical meditations on even the most technical problems of contemporary philosophy."[9] Certainly, here, Africa's own indigenous tradition is being referred to 'colonialism' only analogously, so that the mind can be 'decolonized' from its undesirable or negative impacts. For it is not a herculean task to know that colonialism by its very nature involves a full or partial control of political power over another group of people to primarily benefit the colonizer. In other words, there's always the element of an external or foreign power as the colonizer so that one's own traditional corpus of knowledge cannot constitute colonialism in any slightest

---

[8] Kwasi Wiredu, "Conceptual Decolonization in African Philosophy", in *Cultural Universals and Particulars: An African Perspective*, Indiana University Press, Indianapolis, 1996, pp. 136-144, p. 136.

[9] *Ibid.*, p. 136.

connotations. It is probably for this reason that Wiredu considers the second type of conceptual decolonization 'positive'.

Accordingly, the original Nairobi notion of conceptual decolonization is a task – a painstaking responsibility on the contemporary African philosopher with twin focuses. It is not unqualified de-Westernization. Decolonization, on the one hand, calls for the elimination of the uncritically examined western conceptions. This is the call by negative conceptual decolonization and is meant to render the African conscious of the extent to which foreign concepts can be relevant or irrelevant. On the other hand, conceptual decolonization equally calls the contemporary African philosopher to focus on the traditional African concepts termed traditional heritage. This is meant to make the African conscious of the extent to which their own indigenous conceptual schemes can be resourceful tools for philosophical works, or how much they are less valuable and hence the need to ameliorate or discard them. In either way, Wiredu's Nairobian conceptual decolonization is a call for a critical self-consciousness of the existence of the two conceptual modes in the contemporary African mind. It is for this compound focus that I find this original Wireduan notion of conceptual decolonization profounder and more comprehensive.

The Domain of Conceptual Decolonization

One question often lingers in the mind of a critical reader of Wiredu's conceptual decolonization project. This question concerns the domain or scope of conceptual decolonization. What is the scope of conceptual decolonization? Differently broken down into three ways, it can be stated thus: is conceptual decolonization limited to *conceptualization* as the name suggests? Or is it limited to only *philosophy* since it arose in philosophical discourse? And/or, if so, is conceptual decolonization only limited to *African philosophy* as spelt by its name (i.e., *The Need for Conceptual Decolonization in African Philosophy*)? Some of the work's critics have already directly or indirectly raised this question. Indirectly, for instance, others have argued that decolonization started at the very onset of the drama of colonization. When many indigenous Africans of various categories resisted this superimposition, they were already in the process of decolonization. Indeed, such a claim may not be entirely dismissed. For even if one were to point that conceptual decolonization is essentially mental or conceptual, they can always point that before any such resistances to colonization, the process first starts in the mind, or at least in the mind of an individual. Hence, decolonization is wide enough to cover anything beyond conceptualization. A further implication of such a claim would not only be about the domain of conceptual decolonization, but the protagonist as well. This is because it would mean, perhaps rightly or wrongly, that to those who posit such a view, decolonization is not a brainchild of Wiredu.

Others fervidly argue that colonialism ended or was something long in the past and so hanging on its ills is simply to play victimhood mentality. The implication of this is that the scope of decolonization was limited to political independence. It is also not uncommon coming across scripts that argue that conceptual decolonization is too confined to the intellectual sphere living far from the social ills afflicting the African of today. The domain of this industry is, accordingly, conceptual. It is confined not only to the intellectual and particularly academic arena, but specifically to the original intentions that were meant to address the ills inflicted on the colonized through foreign modes of thought especially with reference to Africa. Olufemi Taiwo, for instance, avidly advances the view that "the indiscriminate application of 'decolonization' to everything from literature, language and philosophy to sociology, psychology and medicine"[10], completely misses the original point of the decolonization industry. He rather unequivocally asserts that "the decolonization industry, obsessed with exposing slights and cataloguing wrongs, is seriously harming scholarship on and in Africa."[11]

These views, among others, are brought here for expository purposes, that is, to demonstrate the existence of questions surrounding the domain of conceptual decolonization and its critics. Hence, without treating the merits and demerits of each of these views, in this theme I intent to critically examine the question of what the domain of conceptual decolonization is, as envisaged by Wiredu.

Decolonization, to begin with, in Wiredu's conception as per the work herein under examination is primarily conceptual. It precisely calls for elimination of modes of categories (both foreign superimposed by colonialism and traditionally inherited) that have been uncritically entertained in our current African thought systems. Though posited from academic or scholarly standpoint, decolonization in this case is mental, both academic and non-academic.

Secondly, deduced from the above is that decolonization is an all-inclusive project, in terms of the origins of the modes of conceptualization found in the postcolonial African mind. It does not assume "that what comes from Africa is necessarily true, sound, profound et cetera. Much less, of course, should there be an over-valuation of what comes from the West."[12] Clearly, the project of conceptual decolonization is to achieve the supreme

---

[10] Olufemi Taiwo, *Against Decolonization: Taking African Agency Seriously*, Paperback – September 15, 2022. https://www.amazon.com/Against-Decolonization-Ol%C3%BAfemi-T%C3%A1%C3%ADw%C3%B2/dp/1787386929.

[11] *Ibid.*

[12] Conceptual Decolonization as an imperative in contemporary African Philosophy: Some Personal Reflections, No. 4.

importance of philosophical self-identity and self-knowledge[13] through elimination of uncritically entertained African modes of conceptualization and colonial mentality. Wiredu posits this with deep conviction "that any African synthesis for modern living will include indigenous and Western elements, as well, perhaps, as some from the East."[14]

Thirdly, conceptual (mental) decolonization, besides being primarily philosophical, is not confined within the domain of philosophy as a discipline and a way of life. As the former (discipline), philosophy can be speculative (theoretical) and applied (practical). Theoretically, conceptual decolonization enterprise has its domain in the academic and contemplative analysis of the modes and concepts of thought. Such a scope of decolonization is what has come under attack by those who argue that this project (conceptual decolonization) is too domiciliated to intellectualization, thereby distancing itself from many social ills presently afflicting the African society. As the latter (practical industry), conceptual decolonization seeks to critically examine the modes and concepts of our thought not for the main aim of academic and contemplative purposes, but for practical problem-solving skills. Conceptual decolonization, in other words, is an applied and pragmatic philosophical engagement. Africans of today are afflicted with myriads of problems ranging from socio-political and economic domains that cannot rely on speculation. Indeed, while merits must be accorded to the advocates of this school of thought, it would equally be presumptuous to deny the responsibility of speculative decolonizers by replacing it with the practical aspect of decolonization. For it is not the main role of speculative philosophers to draw and implement policies that

---

[13] Cf. Kwasi Wiredu, "Problems in Africa's Self-Definition in the Contemporary World", in *Kwasi Wiredu and Kwame Gyekye, Person and Community: Ghanaian Philosophical Studies*, I (Washington DC: The Council for Research in Values and Philosophy, 1992).

[14] Conceptual Decolonization as an imperative in contemporary African Philosophy: Some Personal Reflections, No. 4.

43

bring social-political and economic changes. Such is properly to the domain of practical or applied disciplines. Nonetheless, a society stands better chance to benefit from a close collaboration between the two strands of professions. It would, for instance, benefit a society if its social scientists like the politicians and political philosophers, or legal philosophers and lawyers, or philosophers of education and education policy makers, etcetera, closely collaborate to bridge the gap between theory and praxis, speculation and pragmatics.

Philosophy as life, is a people's way of living, distinguished from mere academic calisthenics. This properly is the domain of praxis. It is in this sphere that decolonization is to roll from Academic institutions to the day today living. Its objective coincides with that of applied philosophy. It means decolonization is to be found in our: day today language, so that when we use terms *uncritically* because they are being used by foreigners, we need to decolonize; social life, so that when we wear wigs *because* they make us look like Asians, Americans or Europeans, and hence making us better humans, we need to decolonize; political life, so that when our leaders congregate for a summit in foreign nations (be it in Washington, Beijing, Moscow, etc.) after being *summoned*, we must demand of them decolonization; culture, so that when we *uncritically* continue certain traditional practices such as physical circumcision whether for men or women simply because the tradition practices it, we need to decolonize; economic policies, so that when our economic decisions are made and implemented because IMF or the European Union parliament has *voted* or *vetoed* it, we need to decolonize; our education systems, so that when our syllabus is *dictated* by institutions from without Africa, we need to decolonize; our technology, so that when modern textiles are killing our own backcloth industry yet we *do nothing* to promote or protect them, we need to decolonize; our religious life, so that when we consider Non-African traditional practices or proselytizing religious practices *uncritically*, we need to decolonize; business life, so that if I believe that a certain hotel is nice *because* I've seen European or Asian clients there, I must decolonize; eating habits, so that if I consider pizza or ice-creams better *because* Europeans like it, I must decolonize, etc.

Similarly, as previously alluded to, conceptual decolonization in Wiredu's understanding is never domiciled in philosophy alone (whether theoretical or practical). It is to be in all areas of intellectualization or disciplines. Professionals or non-professionals alike.[15] Already long before his demise, he had observed that conceptual decolonization project had spilled over to areas such as literature.[16] Moreover, the notion of conceptual decolonization posited by the Nairobi paper did subsume three spheres of African life that acutely need conceptual decolonization. This is because these spheres were used as tools for colonization during the historical superimposition. They include language, religion and politics. It means conceptual decolonization was already spelt out in the areas of literature (language), religion, and politics right from its inception.

Being the medium through which humans conceive and communicate reality, language has a direct role in colonization of a people's mind. For, it contains "the fundamental concepts of philosophy [which] are the most fundamental categories of human thought".[17] These fundamental concepts reflect specifics of a people's culture, environment, philosophy, religion, politics, economy, technology, education, media, gender, etc. It is for this that language as a colonial tool was able to ease the colonization project in the various spheres of the African life. This, as Wiredu

---

[15] Kwasi Wiredu, "Post-Colonial African Philosophy", 145-153, in *Cultural Universals and Particulars: An African Perspective*, Indiana University Press, 1996, p. 145.

[16] *Conceptual Decolonization as an imperative in contemporary African Philosophy: Some Personal Reflections*, No. 4.

[17] Kwasi Wiredu, "The Need for Conceptual Decolonization is African Philosophy", 146-144, in *Cultural Universals and Particulars: An African Perspective*, Indiana University Press, 1996, p. 136-137.

observes, has been exacerbated by the fact that our African philosophical education has hitherto generally remained in the medium of foreign languages of our erstwhile colonizers: the Anglophone and Francophone respectively employ English and French; Lusophone, Portuguese; Equatorial Guinea, partly Spanish and French. Some of the fundamental concepts found in these languages (but here subsumed in English) include:

> Being, Existence, Thing, Entity, Substance, Accident, Truth, Fact, Mind, Soul, Spirit, Ego, Self, Person, Cause, Freedom, Space, Time, Nothingness, Creation, Religion, Grace, etc.

To drive this point home, Wiredu challenges us the Africans of today to try to think of the above categories in our native languages:

> Try to think them through in your own African language and, on the basis of the results, review the intelligibility of the associated problems or the plausibility of the apparent solutions that have tempted you when you have pondered them in some metropolitan language. These may bring conceptions that have no special involvement with Africa, yet are fully internalized in the African thought system. The result of this is the existence of myriads of idiosyncrasies in the African thought system.[18]

A thoughtful reflection leaves one with lots of them that are either meaningless or make little sense in African conceptual schemes. As a matter of fact, they needlessly carry "other people's garbage"[19]. Interestingly, they have notoriously continued to be part of African scholarly works with no or little efforts to render them intelligible in African thought systems. The list may be expanded beyond the previously nominated.

---

[18] *Ibid.*, p. 137.

[19] *Ibid.*, p. 137.

Of religion as a tool for colonization, Wiredu prudently and vehemently rallied against its decolonization. As is the case with erstwhile languages, he made this call without advocating for repudiation of the proselytizing systems in the continent. His commitment was to seriously investigate many of the underlying concepts employed in conveying the foreign faiths: Christian, Islamic, Hindu, or Judaic. He for instance puts that "the unreasoning profession of any religion, indigenous or foreign, is not a model of intellectual virtue."[20] This is because he strongly holds that "where two incompatible faiths are available through indigenous culture and foreign efforts of proselytism, to go along with the latter for no conscious reason would be the quintessence of supine irrationality. It would, besides, betray a colonized mentality."[21] He critically interrogated concepts, among others, with religious connotations such as *God, ex-nihilo creator, existence*, etc. as earlier noted. Nothing of religion should be left without critical scrutiny including the concept *religion* itself.

A modern Lögbara, for instance, would find this rallying call for critical scrutiny of the concept of *religion* particularly exigent. For, though popularly known to them as '*dini*', a thoughtful reflection will reveal that in the primordial Lögbara syntax this concept was non-existent. It was rather, as Dalfovo would agree, a latter adoption from the Kiswahili notion.[22] But as largely conceived and practiced today, 'religion' or '*dini*'connotes a belief in and worship of God or Supernatural Being. It could be Christian, Islamic, Hindu, Judaic, or any other particular system of faith and worship so that to attribute it to the Lögbara is tantamount to incongruity and reductionism. For, the concept 'religion', if thought in the Lögbara mode of

---

[20] *Ibid.*, p. 142.

[21] *Ibid.*, p. 142.

[22] A.T., Dalfovo, "Religion Among the Logbara. The Triadic Source of Its Meaning", by Nomos Verlagsgesellschatft mbH, in *Anthropos* 96.2001: p. 29-40; https://www.jstor.org/stable/40465451

conceptualization, would connote the belief in the existence of supernatural powers, especially of God, and life lived in accordance to the dictates of this belief that pervades every sphere of human existence. No aspect of life, communally or individually lived, is outside the domain of religion. Religion is life itself. Nothing is outside it and any concept that attempts to signify it turns reductionist. Perhaps such is what Mbiti underscored by his dictum of notoriety of African religion[23]. Okot p'Bitek, as Wiredu notes, puts this better with subtlety:

> For Okot, the absence of a word for "religion" in all African languages means that there is no special compartment that the African calls "religious" that is separate from the day-to-day participation in the life process.[24]

Of politics Wiredu points clear that "Africa has suffered unspeakably from political legacies of colonialism. Unhappily, she continues to suffer from the political tutelage of the West."[25] If taken as the maintenance of political, social, economic, and cultural dominion over people by a foreign power for an extended period (W. Bell, 1991), while language as previously seen plays a vital role in conceptual colonization, politics plays the same role in enforcement and praxis of colonization.

As a tool, in the case of colonization of Africa, politics assumed various facets, both persuasive and violent. Military conquests through coups, proxy wars and enslavement; treaties, and conferences among local and international players characterized the colonial game to partition, with the 1884-85

---

[23] John Mbiti, *Religions and Philosophy*, London: Heinemann, 1969, p. 1.

[24] Kwasi Wiredu, (Ed.), "Okot p'Bitek Critique of Western Scholarship on African Religion", in *A Companion to African Philosophy*, Garlington Road, Oxford, 2006, pp. 34-33, p. 365.

[25] Kwasi Wiredu, "The Need for Conceptual Decolonization is African Philosophy", 146-144, in *Cultural Universals and Particulars: An African Perspective*, p. 143.

Berlin conference being the most iconic, to effectively conquer, subdue and exploit Africa.

Like language and religion, politics has hitherto been used to prolong and enforce colonialism in Africa both directly and indirectly. It would demand a high degree of unsound mind to think otherwise that political colonialism ended with political independence in Africa. After all, politics by its very nature involves the use of power to control, influence and allocate resources. A case in point would be the question of democracy and human rights that have been belligerently presented to Africa. But aside from the political side, lets focus on the more fundamental issue of the two in line with this paper, that is, conceptual decolonization. Wiredu equally argues the incompatibility of the conception of democracy in the current systems of governance. He particularly cites the Majoritarian democracy vs Consensual democracy. The former is "the form of democracy involving more than single party in which, in principle, the party that wins the most parliamentary seats forms the government."[26] The latter is the form of democracy where "government was by the consent, and subject to the control, of the people as expressed through their representatives. It was consensual because, as a rule, that consent was negotiated on the principle of consensus."[27] Modern majoritarian democracy is cheaper and elusive than the traditional African consensual democracy that is more genuine. In consensual democracy "the pursuit of consensus was a deliberate effort to go beyond decision by majority opinion."[28] In Majoritarian democracy, the effort is to achieve majority representation for the purpose of capturing

---

[26] *Ibid.*, p. 144.

[27] Kwasi Wiredu, "Democracy and Consensus: A Plea for a Non-Party Polity", 184-190, in *Cultural Universals and Particulars: An African Perspective*, p. 187.

[28] *Ibid.*, p. 186.

power so that the majoritarian system is, "in principle, based on "consent" without consensus."[29]

Conceptual decolonization has unlimited boundaries. Arising from philosophical tradition, it is proper that conceptualization is the software of every human action. There cannot be any sphere of human existence that lies outside the domain of conceptual decolonization. The fact that it arises from philosophy even makes this more evident. Philosophy's scope covers every reality that is available to the human reason. The only thing outside philosophy's scope is nothing itself, understood as 'absolute nothing'. Odera Oruka puts this subtly that the fact that we are able to talk of PhD in this and that subject underscores the centrality of philosophy, for "almost every subject can be studied to the highest level termed the level of "Doctorate in Philosophy".[30] And Aristotle could not have had this better than underlying that no one should claim to have known anything until they arrive at the level of proper philosophy. Ultimately, conceptual decolonization thus has no limited sphere.

Impact of Conceptual Decolonization

From what one reads of Wiredu's works on conceptual decolonization; it is worth pondering the impact of such a project. This can best be stated in compound terms as: does the conceptual decolonization industry have an impact, and if yes, in what sense?

Philosophy basically concerns a people's worldview about reality. It examines the nature, purpose and meaning of reality. Determination of a people's approaches to decision-making in face of particular problems posed by reality is one of philosophy's

---

[29] *Ibid.*, p. 187.

[30] H. Odera Oruka (ed.), *Sage Philosophy: Indigenous Thinkers and Modern Debate on African Philosophy*, Nairobi, African Centre for Technology Studies (ACTS),1991, p. 5.

main concerns. Accordingly, philosophy has an indirect influence on the development of practical solutions. This influence is what constitutes the impact herein under highlight.

'Impact' commonly connotes consequences or effects of an idea to a society or group of peoples. In this context, impact of conceptual decolonization seeks concerns the effects of Wiredu's decolonization industry whether to Africa or any other peoples. In ordinary usage, impact is majorly limited to visual and corporeal influence or effect externally exerted, and in philosophy this is highly measurable with applied philosophy. Speculative philosophy that deals, among other theoretical aspects, with analysis of concepts like decolonization certainly does leave many expecting to see impact as ordinarily connoted above frustrated.

It would, however, be too simplistic to limit Wiredu's plea for decolonization within the spheres of the three tools of historical superimposition of conceptual categories previously highlighted: language, politics and religion. The call for decolonization is comprehensive. No sphere of African life is excluded from it. Literature, politics, culture, language, economics, education, technology, theology, and the philosophical trajectory itself have all been directly or indirectly impacted.

In philosophy, to begin with, conceptual decolonization has aided the spirit of self-identity, self-confidence and pride among contemporary African philosophers. Besides offering a new philosophical movement as a platform in which an African philosopher deeply engages in philosophy, decolonization has offered the African philosopher a pedestal to voice their legitimate anti-colonial rebuttal. In so doing, the African has gotten to sheave what is authentically African and a true dimension of existential philosophical engagement.

The existential dimension of African philosophy's challenge to Western philosophy in general and Continental philosophy in particular is precisely located in the need to decolonize the mind. As Robert Bernasconi would put (paraphrased), this task is at least as important for the colonized as it is for the colonizer. For the former, decolonizing the mind takes place not only in facing the experience of colonialism, but also in recognizing the pre-colonial, which establishes the destructive importance of so-called ethnophilosophy and sage philosophy, as well as nationalist-ideological tradition.[31] For the latter, decolonizing the colonial mind necessitates an encounter with the colonized, where finally the colonizer (European) has the experience of being seen and judged by those they have denied everything authentic including philosophy and identity through colonialism[32]. The extent to which European philosophy championed colonialism, and more particularly helped to justify it through a philosophy of history that privileged Europe, makes it apparent that such a decolonizing industry is an urgent task for European thought too. Accordingly, African philosophy in general and the conceptual decolonization trend in particular, is already making a unique contribution to the critique of European philosophy.

> If Continental philosophers would open themselves to critique from African philosophy and thereby find that the hegemonic concept of reason had been displaced, and they would be better placed to learn to respect other traditions, including those that are not African.[33]

While continental philosophers, or rather some are still closed up in European philosophy, the contributions (most often

---

[31] Robert Bernasconi, "African Philosophy's Challenge to Continental Philosophy", in *Postcolonial African Philosophy: A Critical Reader*, by Emmanuel Chukwudi Eze (Ed.), Blackwell Publishers, Cambridge, 1997, pp. 183-196.

[32] *Ibid.*, p. 192.

[33] *Ibid.*, p. 192.

critical ones) from non-European philosophies, and particularly African philosophy, would be overwhelming by now. Conceptual decolonization is doubtlessly to say a leading protagonist with great impact in this area.

The above impact of confidence, pride and challenge in the minds of African philosophers has further resulted to explosion of novel forms of philosophical inquiry, not just in Africa, but in other parts of the globe, covering domains such as political, racial and eco-philosophical standpoints. Exciting philosophical themes such as deconstruction of history towards a new critical historiography, de-westernization and decolonization in media studies, decolonization of Bioethics, not only in Africa but have become vibrant scholarly discourses in the entire global south in places such as South America, India, and other parts of the globe have all hard their influences remotely or directly from the decolonization movement. In Africa particularly, it is no wonder that the emergence of scholarly trends such as the *Ubuntu* philosophy, inculturation, family conception of society, etc. all sprung after late nineteen nineties, consequent to the decolonization industry.

Today in the growth of human knowledge, the instrumental role played by Wiredu's decolonization project has witnessed a more inclusive and collaborative approach. Through his emphasis on the significance and pertinence of intellectual pluralism and interdisciplinary exchanges, Wiredu's decolonization industry has aided in creating a culture of openness and dialogue that allows for greater participation and engagement among diverse communities of scholars and thinkers. The first strand of this is within the various philosophical traditions already developed and yet developing in Africa, since the need for decolonization cuts across the domains of African peoples, whether Anglophone, Francophone, etc. Secondly, decolonization, as has become apparent today, is no exclusive feature to Africa. It's a global

IN HONOUR OF KWASI WIREDU

phenomenon that takes different features. It therefore renders cultural openness and dialogue a global phenomenon.

Conceptual decolonization, as well, stands viewed as Wiredu's leeway out of the quagmire of African rationality debate. Having been so bogged down for a considerable period of time on the question about the existence and essence of African philosophy, conceptual decolonization became Wiredu's way out of that entanglement. On this, Joseph I. Omoregbe had the following to say of Wiredu: "Professor Wiredu observes that contemporary African philosophers devote a lot of time on the question of African philosophy. He believes it is necessary at this stage to go beyond talking about African philosophy and get down to actually doing it."[34] This doing of the work got reflected in many of the philosophical essays and themes upon which Wiredu's extensive scripts in African philosophy are based. Key among these include: The Concept of Truth in the Akan Language, The Need for Conceptual Decolonization in African Philosophy, Universalism and Particularism in Religion from an African Perspective, etc. In this way, Wiredu thus paradigmatically shifted the debate in and about African philosophy to the actual doing. It would not be overstatement to maintain that it has revolutionized African philosophy and given it a different trajectory from that which centred on the rationality debate.

In making the paradigmatic shift away from the existence and nature of African philosophy, particularly through Wiredu's stimulating themes, Wiredu initiated robust conceptual dialogues. Conceptual decolonization was a self-pointing project. It did not only highlight the garbage inherent in foreign categories of thought. It as well brought to fore what lay deep yet uncritically entertained in African traditional heritage. Among the Akan

---

[34] J. I. Omoregbe, "African Philosophy: Yesterday and Today", in Emmanuel C. Eze, (ed.), *African Philosophy: An Anthology*, Main Street, Malden Blackwell Publishers, 2006, p. 7.

alone, for instance, the robust dialogue between Wiredu and his fellow Akan compatriot – Gyekye on the Akan anthropology is one a philosophically fascinating development in African philosophy consequent to the decolonization project. And since then, philosophy in Africa has seen this exchange of views among contemporary African philosophers across different conceptual and cognitive relativisms, within and without the various African traditions.

Conclusion

The paper has examined Kwasi Wiredu's theme of conceptual decolonization in the context of its development, notion, domain and impact. This has led to the paper's conclusion that the onset of *conceptual decolonization* ushered in by Wiredu has been one of the greatest phenomena in African scholarship, both in production and praxis. As such, it has tremendously changed the trajectory of African thought in various aspects. In philosophy itself, it for instance moved the rationality debate a notch higher by not only responding to the questions about the essence and content of African philosophy, but to the actuality of doing it. In so doing, it has offered a double-edged challenge for on the one hand, it challenges the cynics of African philosophy to reexamine their beliefs, and on the other hand, it challenges the postcolonial African to move away from the lazy discourse on the existence and nature of African philosophy. The outcome of these challenges has become manifest in the myriad themes existent in African philosophy today.

Besides its concerns and impacts in the African philosophy, conceptual decolonization has impacted intellectual discourse beyond Africa. Today the notion of decolonization ushered in by Wiredu's conceptual decolonization has become commonly used and explored in different scholarly works in the West as well as

East. It thus remains safe to say Wiredu has a name in scholarly production across the globe. He seminally and posthumously remains a shining black star. The honour accorded him in the academia is doubtlessly a little less than actually deserved.

Bibliography

ALVIRA T., CLAVELL L., MALENDO T., *Metaphysics: Understanding the Science of Being*, Sinag-Tala Publishers, Manila, 2011, p. 123; Cf. Boethius, *De DuabusNaturis et una Persona Christi*, ch.3, in *Migne PL*, 64 col. 1345.

BERNASCONI R., "African Philosophy's Challenge to Continental Philosophy", in *Postcolonial African Philosophy: A Critical Reader*, by Emmanuel Chukwudi Eze (Ed.), Blackwell Publishers, Cambridge, 1997.

DALFOVO, A.T., "Religion Among the Logbara. The Triadic Source of Its Meaning", by Nomos Verlagsgesellschatft mbH, in *Anthropos* 96.2001: 29-40; https://www.jstor.org/stable/40465451.

IGWEBUIKE ONAH, G., "Wiredu's Philosophy of Human Nature, in *The Third Way in African Philosophy: Essay in Honor of Kwasi Wiredu*, Olusegun Oladipo (ed.), Ibadan, Nigeria, Hop4e Publications, 2002.

MBITI, J., *Religions and Philosophy*, London: Heinemann, 1969.

ODERA ORUKA, H. (Ed.), *Sage Philosophy: Indigenous Thinkers and Modern Debate on African Philosophy*, African Centre for Technology Studies, Nairobi, 1991.

OMOREGBE, J. I., "African Philosophy: Yesterday and Today", in Emmanuel C. Eze, (ed.), *African Philosophy: An Anthology*, Main Street, Malden Blackwell Publishers, 2006.

TAIWO, O., *Against Decolonization: Taking African Agency Seriously*, Paperback – September 15, 2022. https://www.amazon.com/Against-Decolonization-Ol%C3%BAAfemi-T%C3%A1%C3%ADw%C3%B2 /dp/1787386929.

WIREDU K., *Conceptual Decolonization as an imperative in contemporary African Philosophy: Some Personal Reflections*, Rue Descartes 2002/2 (n° 36).

WIREDU, K., (Ed.), "Okot p'Bitek Critique of Western Scholarship on African Religion", in *A Companion to African Philosophy*, Garlington Road, Oxford, 2006.

WIREDU, K., "Conceptual Decolonization as an Imperative in Contemporary African Philosophy: Some Personal Reflections", in *Dans Rue Descartes 2002/2 (n° 36)*.

WIREDU, K., "Conceptual Decolonization in African Philosophy", in *Cultural Universals and Particulars: An African Perspective*, Indiana University Press, Indianapolis, 1996.

WIREDU, K., "Democracy and Consensus: A Plea for a Non-Party Polity", 184-190, in *Cultural Universals and Particulars: An African Perspective*.

WIREDU, K., "Post-Colonial African Philosophy", 145-153, in *Cultural Universals and Particulars: An African Perspective*, Indiana University Press, 1996.

WIREDU, K., "Problems in Africa's Self-Definition in the Contemporary World", in *Kwasi Wiredu and Kwame Gyekye, Person and Community: Ghanaian Philosophical Studies*, I (Washington DC: The Council for Research in Values and Philosophy, 1992).

African Philosophy and African Education: Implications of Wiredu's Conceptual Decolonization Project on Africa's Educational Policy on Indigenous Languages

Mwenda Godfrey, CMI (Phd. Stud) and Full-time Lecturer at St. Charles Lwanga Major Seminary in Windhoek, Namibia, godfreymwenda111@gmail.com

Abstract

As Heidegger puts it, 'language is the house of being.' Kwasi Wiredu's desiderata for 'growing' African philosophy resonates harmoniously with Heidegger's conception of language as a fundamental tool for 'thinking' and 'articulating' philosophy.[35] This paper critically reflects on the implications of Wiredu's project of conceptual decolonization as a prerequisite for developing sound African philosophy and on contemporary education in Africa, with special focus on indigenous languages. I firstly highlight Wiredu's conceptualization of the nature of African philosophy; its unique sources and concerns (which gives it African identity) and its conceptual links with the Western philosophical thought, by the virtue of which it acquires universal relevance. I secondly consider the role of traditional African languages in the development of African philosophy and its

---

[35] While Heidegger and Wiredu cannot be said to have had similar philosophical projects, their understanding of the relationship between philosophy and language is quite similar. For Heidegger, ontology was the core business of philosophy, and language was the intellectual space in which Being was revealed and articulated. He says, "Language is the house of Being. In its home man dwells. Those who think and those who create with words are the guardians of this home" (Heidegger 1978, 217). For Wiredu, philosophy as critique requires language as the primary vehicle through which concepts are thought through, analysed and expressed.

special concerns with philosophical problematics posed by such phenomena as decolonization, modernity, globalization and neoliberalism.

The paper thirdly considers the nature of contemporary education in Africa. Here, I argue that its aversive attitude towards mother-tongue education, albeit covertly, bears devastating consequences on the development of African philosophy in general and on its project of conceptual decolonization in particular. I consider the future of African philosophy as hanging precariously on the uncritical webs of Africa's contemporary education policy. To escape the impending death of African philosophy, I contend, African philosophers must firstly seek to influence education policy in contemporary Africa, with special advocacy for educational development of indigenous languages. The paper draws the conclusion that, decolonization of today's formal education in Africa is a necessary antecedent to survival and flourishing of contemporary African philosophy and its conceptual decolonization project.

Keywords: Wiredu, African philosophy, conceptual-decolonization, indigenous-languages, education-policy

Wiredu's Desiderata for African Philosophy

The name Kwasi Wiredu is almost irrevocably conjoined with the development of contemporary African philosophy. Wiredu has not only played a crucial role in clarifying problems concerning the nominal definition of African philosophy; his philosophical thought as a whole has also remained seminal to the mapping out of the nature and scope of the discipline.[36] Cognizant

---

[36] I do not suggest, by this statement, that Wiredu's account of what constitutes African philosophy is unproblematic. In fact, Wiredu's entire corpus could be described as an

of the philosophical problematics related to the very phrase 'African philosophy', Wiredu seeks to advance a model of African philosophy that exhibits the very basic ethos of philosophy as love of wisdom; where wisdom signifies the critical character of reason in the pursuit of philosophical truths without prejudice upon the geographical, cultural, racial or historical origins of those truths.

Wiredu's philosophy could rightly be viewed as a 'two-edged conceptual critique' of some facets of colonial and post-colonial perspectives on African philosophy. One cutting-edge of the critique, being directed against the colonialist misuse of philosophy, exposes its undue repudiation of the philosophic value and validity of some pre-colonial publications on account of their African provenance. More tenaciously, this edge provides a biting critique of the colonial Western philosophic hegemony by means of which the project of depriving Africans of all capacity for epistemic engagements was being advanced.[37] The other cutting-edge of the critique is wielded against the tendency, by some African thinkers, to evade their intellectual

---

adversarial defence for possibility and existence of African philosophy, against the colonial project of denial of epistemic or philosophical capability among Africans. For this reason, the conceptual paradigm of African philosophy I proffer in this statement is precisely of the kind; 'Wiredu's conception of African philosophy' (which, essentially speaking, belongs to the universalist school of African philosophy, involving such other African philosophical geniuses as Paulin J. Hountondji, Henry Odera Oruka and Peter Oluwambe Bodunrin).

[37] Referring to J.B Danquah's work, *The Akan Doctrine of God* as an example, published in 1947; long before the independence of Ghana in 1952, Wiredu repeatedly observes that in the years that immediately followed Ghana's independence, the department of philosophy in Ghana 'tended not to develop an impression that there was such a thing as African philosophy' (Wiredu 1998, 2004). Wiredu, rightly maintains that not only did colonialists perceive African cultures as inferior in many important aspects of human life, colonialism also 'included a systematic program of de-Africanization' whereby, even African religions were branded as paganism. In light of such intentional efforts to undermine the value of African cultures, Wiredu sees colonialist personnel, especially in the department of philosophy, as being very unlikely to be willing to consider the philosophical value of such works as that of Danquah (Wiredu 2004).

responsibility; namely, to critically analyse the philosophical legitimacy of the colonialist attempts to annihilate African epistemic fecundity as well as to critically examine the philosophical validity of the very African epistemologies. From such a critique-eyed position, Wiredu lays a foundation for African philosophy, which is adversarial in context but universal in content. It is adversarial in its contextual deconstruction of colonial imperialism; as implied by attempts to counteract, as fallacious, the widespread tendency (among colonialists and their personnel) to undermine or annihilate African epistemic capabilities by interpreting traditional African philosophies via the import of philosophical categories in their Western meaning-signification context. It is, however, universal since it seeks to orient African philosophy towards engagement with fundamental problematics such as the nature of the world, God, human cognition, morality, death and immortality, politics and religion amongst others, as experienced by mankind across the world.

The adversarial pillar of Wiredu's foundation for African philosophy seemingly acquires a more primordial function than that of the universalist pillar. Wiredu views the need for deconstruction of colonial imperialism (as exhibited by its devaluation of African socio-cultural and religious heritage and its disregard and denial of African epistemic capabilities) as more urgent (even though time-bound), if not, a condition for possibility of a justified universalist pillar of African philosophy.[38] By 'adversarial pillar', I refer to Wiredu's conceptual decolonization project of African philosophy, which we may now consider at length.

---

[38] Wiredu states the following, "It is worth emphasizing, besides, that African philosophers in our time cannot live by decolonization alone, but also by direct interrogation of reality...Decolonization even as only one of our preoccupations, is not something that we will be doing forever in African philosophy" (Wiredu 1998, 27-28).

Conceptual decolonization

Wiredu's project of conceptual decolonization could be described as a systematic philosophical procedure to sanitize the intellectual-space, furniture and apparatus for African philosophical practice prior to its proper commencement. Since Wiredu believes that colonialism involved deAfricanization as a systematic program of religious and intellectual deprivation, it is not difficult to recognize the systematic character inherent in the operationalization of his iconic notions of decolonization and Africanization, which run through his entire corpus.

For Wiredu, conceptual decolonization simply refers to the intellectual responsibility of contemporary African thinkers to critically examine the conceptual framework upon which African thought-systems are erected.[39] Wiredu maintains that, orienting African philosophy towards such critique-driven intellectual engagements was necessary and that it would result in two-fold benefit; namely, (i) 'dislodging African Philosophical thinking from all its uncritical assimilation of the Western manners of thought' and (ii) propelling African philosophy beyond folk wisdoms and synthesizing it with the intellectual resources of the modern world (Wiredu 2004,15). It is not self-explanatory, how Wiredu's claim that African philosophy was required to engender the two characteristic marks relates to his project of conceptual decolonization. We would, therefore, need to expound this claim further. To do so, I will return to our analogous description of Wiredu's notion of conceptual decolonization as a 'two-edged philosophical critique.'

Conceptual decolonization as 'doubly critical'

Wiredu's idea of conceptual decolonization is itself a critique of the model of African philosophy popularly known as

---

[39] Wiredu fundamentally conceives of philosophy in general as a critique and accordingly, philosophizing as an exercise in critical examination and re-examination of philosophical positions. See Wiredu 2004.

'ethnophilosophy' and 'traditional African philosophies', much as it remains critical to the colonialist imposition of philosophical categories in their Western contextual meanings. Considering ethnophilosophy and traditional African philosophies as essentially parochial wisdoms of the kind we might call 'customs of culture', Wiredu does not see such African wisdoms as contributing much to the basic concerns of contemporary African philosophy, given its current need to engage with cross-cultural philosophical concerns. As such, traditional African philosophies, for Wiredu, do not engender much beyond the 'narrative' and 'explanatory' character of African anthropologies; thus, strictly speaking, they do not entail the 'critical-examinational', speculative and 'reflective-suggestive' characteristics of philosophy proper (Wiredu 2004).

On account of such limitations, traditional African philosophies are hardly self-critical; they are likely to militantly aver their African-ness as untouchable, without critically examining the philosophical validity and usefulness of the very African conceptual claims. Wiredu is critical of the tendency by some African thinkers, to employ concepts of traditional African philosophies in response to the colonialist denial of African epistemic capabilities without firstly asking the question whether the concepts in question bear homogeneous philosophical significances in both Western-European and African epistemic frameworks. While acknowledging the power of traditional African philosophies to 'reclaim' African epistemic capacities, Wiredu remains apprehensive about their potential to engender a war-like spirit and even racial prejudices against the colonial program in its entirety. Cautioning against the likelihood of traditional African philosophies to result in such volatility (which he terms as 'retrograde inflexibility'), Wiredu sees little, if any, philosophical value for such volatile positions, in relation to the current need for African philosophy to critically engage, participate and contribute to the philosophical discourses concerning modern cross-cultural problems.[40]

It is to be noted carefully, that Wiredu is not at any instance suggesting that traditional African philosophies are not philosophies at all or that they have no philosophical utility at all. On the contrary, Wiredu believes that serious study of African philosophies is a fundamental exercise for proper growth of African philosophy as such; to mean, they enable African philosophy to validly and relevantly respond to its traditional and modern concerns. African philosophy, therefore, must firstly eradicate its undue assimilation of the Western conceptual frameworks and thought systems on the one hand, yet on the other hand, be self-critical with regard to the philosophical validity and relevance of its very own conceptual and thought systems (especially, traditional African philosophies as parochialism vis-à-vis the modern philosophical problems). This is the sense in which Wiredu conceives conceptual decolonization program as 'doubly critical' and as an ideal for African philosophy.

Conceptual decolonization as 'imperative'

Wiredu views commitment to the project of conceptual decolonization of African philosophy as an imperative for contemporary African philosophers, for reasons that are philosophical and inherent in the very notions of decolonization and Africanization, as preconditions for a sound development and defence of a philosophy that is authentically African. First reason on the list is obviously the question concerning colonialist denial of African epistemic capabilities. Wiredu argues that, acceptance of the colonialists' divesture of African epistemic capacities and complete surrender to the colonialist systematic program of deAfricanization would not only be a 'wallowing in colonialized thinking' but also a moment of 'advertising our colonial

---

[40] Acknowledging that some aspects of the colonial program were beneficial to humankind, Wiredu argues that wholesome rejection of everything related to our colonial past would be 'a madness without rhyme or reason' (Wiredu 1998).

mentality' (Wiredu 2004). Such 'wallowing' and 'advertisement of colonial mentality' is, for Wiredu, perhaps the highest expression of 'uncritical' and accordingly, 'unphilosophical mind' on the part of African philosophers. Wiredu, however, acknowledges that, utilization of traditional African philosophies for refuting aforementioned colonialist denial of African epistemic capabilities has not come without posing fundamental philosophical problems. For Wiredu, therefore, it is necessary, in fact obligatory ('intellectual responsibility'), that contemporary African philosophers grapple with the questions in question, if an authentic African philosophy is to stand out. We will attend to a few of such questions.

Consider, for instance, the philosophical problems inherent in refuting the colonialist deAfricanization agenda by 'citing traditional African philosophies as counterexamples' (as ethnophilosophers do). Also consider the problematics inherent in the 'particularistic approach' and the 'domestication approach' which Wiredu himself offers. Besides the 'uncritical' and therefore, 'unphilosophical' character (being 'narrative-explanatory' instead of 'speculative', 'reflective-suggestive') of aforementioned counterexample models, Wiredu also acknowledges that such models are prone to making 'continental-generalizations' and 'postulating unanimity and consensus' (Wiredu 2004). By 'continental-generalization', Wiredu argues that, while certain worldviews (such as the communitarian sociality and ethic) could be common amongst many African societies, ascribing an 'African identity' to them poses a philosophical problem (what he considers as 'continental-generalizations'). Further, counterexample models bear philosophical fallibility especially when they present traditional African philosophies as 'communal philosophies'; they not only risk being termed as parochialism but are also likely to "…postulate unanimity and consensus in philosophical beliefs among traditional peoples for which there is not, and probably can never be sufficient evidence" (Wiredu 2004, 25).

The 'particularistic model' refers to through studies of traditional African philosophies in order to wring out of them that we could consider as purely African concept-formulating principles and thought-systems (without colonial adulteration). Wiredu considers this model as not simply providing counterexamples for the colonialist deAfricanization agenda, but as grasping it by the horns. This model entails critical analysis of traditional African philosophies in relation to the meaning-significances engendered by indigenous use of language (syntax and semantics), which ultimately shows that specific conclusion-claims (often articulated as 'African conception or understanding of' this or that) drawn by some colonialist personnel are philosophically untenable. Wiredu argues that for such analysis to bear philosophical value, it is imperative that the African thinker should ask the critical question, "how is the thesis proffered (by the Westerner) rendered in my vernacular?[41]

The notion of domestication, by which Wiredu refers to the need for African thinkers to integrate certain fundamental domains of philosophy (such as formal logic) within African philosophy for the simple reason that they were not developed in traditional African systems of thought, is mandatory if African philosophy has to be a complete body of philosophy. However, such integration does not call for 'uncritical copying of conclusions made elsewhere'; rather, it demands "…taking up broad intellectual concerns relating to certain subject matters" (Wiredu 2004, 21). From such propositions, is not difficult to see how Wiredu's idea of conceptual decolonization (as deconstruction of the colonialist conceptual superimposition and deAfricanization) interplays with his desiderata for African

---

[41] Wiredu's own analysis of the existential verb 'to be' in the indigenous Akan language, as well as Alexis Kagame's analysis of the same in indigenous Bantu language-groups show that the existential verb 'to be' does not occur outside circumstantial qualifications such as, 'something is there at some place.' This analysis renders Father Tempel's claim that for Africans, 'being is force and force is being' as philosophically misplaced (Wiredu 2004, 24).

philosophy as the call for African philosophers to be 'double-critical' and intellectually responsive towards Africanizing their philosophy in its traditional and modern contexts. This interplay between Wiredian notions of conceptual decolonization (as critical studies of African epistemic foundations) and the problematics of African philosophy in their traditional and modern suits points to a deeper interplay between African philosophy and the indigenous languages in which African conceptual-epistemic systems ought to be generated. We now turn our attention to such considerations.

Traditional African Languages and their Philosophies

For Wiredu, the procedure of generating authentic African philosophies primarily involves 'thinking in one's vernacular.'[42] Although this claim constitutes the most fertile grounds for critiques levelled against Wiredu's project of decolonization of African philosophy, it nonetheless remains consistent with the most profound elements of his entire philosophical thought. Consider, for instance, Wiredu's distinction between the traditional and the modern components of African philosophy. Those concepts and wisdoms that are to be considered as 'Traditional-African' in the narrow sense have to have been

---

[42] Wiredu admits that different thinkers conceive African philosophies in varying manners. Accepting his being classified together with Hountondji as belonging to the 'anti-ethnophilosophy school', he considers his distaste for ethnophilosophy as much less radical than that of Hountondji in as far as he does not take philosophy in the strict sense of a science and insofar as he is sympathetic (to a certain degree) to attributing certain traditional wisdoms to a people. He, however, divorces his conception of African philosophies from the anthropology-like presentation of it (what he terms as 'traditionalist view'), which for him, lacks the critical character of philosophy as such (Wiredu 2004, 4). For this reason, our reference of Wiredu's conception of African philosophies requires the nuanced qualification 'authentic' in order to distinguish it from the 'uncritical' presentations of the traditionalists as Wiredu sees them.

generated in strictly indigenous epistemic and linguistic frameworks. In other words, there is, for Wiredu, a direct relation between genuine traditional conceptual-epistemic systems and indigenous linguistic frameworks.[43] It is only after grasping the genuinely African conceptual-epistemic frameworks that an African philosopher can authentically orient African philosophy towards bearing uniquely African contributions to the contemporary philosophical discourses on modern and cross-cultural problematics.

Wiredu rightly puts it, that the African philosopher has to endeavor to think in the vernacular in order to reconstruct his ancestors' philosophical concepts and thought patterns since they did not leave him with a written heritage of it (Wiredu 2004). Such reconstruction must involve the enormous task of deconstruction of the Western conceptual-epistemic superimposition and deAfricanization of education, religion and philosophy. This is so, for the simple reason that the contemporary African philosopher finds himself or herself in an already colonized epistemic space. For a genuine African philosophy to be generated, the African philosopher cannot but firstly engage in such deconstruction and reconstruction tasks. Wiredu writes,

> Actually, it probably would have been an advantage if contemporary African philosophers had had to begin with a totally clean slate when they began in post-independence time to research into African philosophy. But as it happens, religious and anthropological studies had been made of African world views in departments of religion and anthropology, and these tended to contain elements relevant to African philosophy. Now although these

---

[43] In my reading, Wiredu's claim that 'due reflection' on traditional African conceptual-epistemic systems (as critical analysis of syntax and semantics of African indigenous languages) is necessary for grasping that which is authentically 'African philosophy' is consistent with Hiedeggers phenomenological hermeneutics as a fundamental tool for studies in ontology.

studies were not technically philosophical, they were conducted not only in foreign languages, such as English, French and German, but also in terms of categories of Western metaphysical thought that have become widely received in Western culture (Wiredu 1998, 19).

Wiredu's point here, is that the historical background of African philosophy was marred with conceptual misrepresentations of the African religious and cultural wisdoms. In Wiredu's reading, these misrepresentations not only resulted from the fact that the said wisdoms had been approached in Western categories of thought, they had also been expressed in foreign linguistic frameworks. The fact that such misrepresented wisdoms became the primary sources of African philosophy (for the simple reason that they had been documented and had become widely accepted in the Western culture for their colonialist flavor, whereas the primordial African sages had not bequeathed us with written evidence to prove the colonialist authors wrong), post-independence African philosophers should have firstly engaged themselves in the necessary deconstruction and reconstruction processes.

The question whether African philosophers of the immediate post-independence era had successfully deconstructed the colonialist misrepresentation of Africa, Africans and African traditional wisdoms goes beyond the scope of this paper. However, it is clear that, for Wiredu, such deconstruction task would still have had to be difficult since African thinkers of the immediate post-independence era, like himself, had been educated in colonial languages. For this reason, Wiredu believes that contemporary African thinkers cannot evade the intellectual task of carrying out the said deconstructions and reconstructions. The obvious question that arises is; how exactly could such tasks be carried out in the contemporary time and what would be the benefit of undertaking such tasks? Wiredu sees the answer to these questions as entrenched in the power of thinking and expressing philosophy in African indigenous languages.

Oral tradition has remained a profound means of transmitting, reconstructing and imbibing African traditional wisdoms. Much as most Africans who went through formal education have been educated in the colonial Western languages (so-called 'modern' languages), exposure to such languages does not rob Africans of their capacity to express themselves in their indigenous dialects. For this reason, Wiredu would think, ancestral conceptual-epistemic heritage is still accessible in its original form. This is so because its primordial genres such as riddles, sayings, proverbs, mythical stories, songs and dances remain fairly uncorrupted by the presence of colonial languages. Wiredu is convinced that, what has changed about traditional African philosophies is not their content per se, but the conceptual interpretation and representation of them. For Wiredu, therefore, the use of African vernaculars is a powerful tool for the task of deconstructing colonialist misrepresentation of the traditional African philosophies and for reconstruction of their seemingly dormant capacities. This claim is proved right by the numerous examples of particularistic studies such as: *The Akan concept of truth*; *The Yoruba conception of a person*; *The Chewa notion of afterlife, God, spirit and morality* and many others (Wiredu 2004, 23). For Wiredu, such works, whether they exhibit philosophical critique or not, acquire authenticity as traditional African wisdoms by their capacity to faithfully represent the said wisdoms in their original meaning-significances. Faithfulness to this originality of meanings, concepts and thought-formation processes remains, for Wiredu, the golden egg, out of which authentic African philosophy hatches and successfully deals with traditional and modern philosophical problems. It is however questionable, whether contemporary Africans have remained faithful to this ideal.

Modernity, Globalization and the African Identity

'Modernity' and 'globalization' are blanket terms. While they have become part of our everyday conversation as concepts referring to world-wide social-political and cultural-economic paradigms of human interaction and development, they are never neutral terms in the world of scholarship.[44] In light of the concerns for this paper, I will refer to these terms from the more general perspective; namely, advancement in social-political and cultural-economic structures of the contemporary world.

In relation to Africa, modernity and globalization could be viewed from two fronts; namely, the Western front and the African front. By Western front, I refer to the European views of Africa's development in cultural, political and economic spheres. By African front, on the other hand, I refer to Africans' own aspirations for development in aforementioned aspects. By this distinction, I do not suggest that all Europeans throughout history have held uniform views on Africa's development. By the same token, I do not insinuate that Africa as a whole has presented homogenous aspirations for development over the centuries. However, this dualistic consideration of the notions of modernity and globalization brings to light certain power-relations, which

---

[44] The view of the world as a 'global village' is widespread in our day, thanks to the ever-widening advancement in information technology and transport infrastructure. Such a view has generated conventional use of the concepts, 'modernity' and 'globalization' as if they were mutually inclusive or even interchangeable. However, contemporary scholarship has shown that these terms could also imply mutual exclusivity, especially when interpreted in light of contemporary dynamics of politics, economics, ethics and religion as practiced across the world. While some scholars have viewed globalization as a channel for positive development of humankind, others have regarded it as a strategy by first-world countries (so-called 'modern' and 'developed') to exploit the second-world and third-world countries. With regard to Africa alone, consider, for instance, some proponents of global-politics, economics and citizenship (Kemal and Conroy 2018; minkov et al. 2021) against some opponents of global-politics and global-economics (Lere 2014; Moore 2001; Matunhu 2011; Nwobodo 2021). Scholars in this debate have attempted to distinguish between the proponents and opponents of globalization by the use of terms such as 'pro-globalizers' and 'anti-globalizers' (Lere 2014).

when critically examined, help us discover far-reaching implications of such terms regarding the general wellbeing of Africa and her peoples' conceptual-epistemic heritage (what I consider as 'African identity').

Let us describe the Western front. The first European entry into Africa happened in the 15th century when Portuguese missionaries, sailors and traders arrived in the Congo. As the missionaries were engaged in converting Africans from their traditional religious worship to Christianity, some sailors aimed at discovering new link-routes between Europe and Africa while others sought evidence for or against already documented claims about Africa and Africans in world studies. The traders on their part, thanks to the accomplishments by the missionaries and sailors, quickly transited from trading in spices and sugar into the infamous trans-Atlantic slave-trade. A closer look into the nature of these early European-African interactions reveals superimposition and subordination power-relations whereby the Europeans acquire almost absolute control of the Africans. From such relations, it is not difficult to recognize the devaluating and dehumanizing attitudes of the Europeans towards Africa and Africans. From this European attitude, arose derogatory description of Africa as 'the dark continent', 'where there is nothing' and 'lions' jungle' among others. With such descriptions of the land, as from the 1880s, many European countries hastened to conquer and occupy Africa, in what was called 'scramble for Africa', characterized by seizure of fertile agricultural lands and complete take-over of the social-political structures, which resulted in forced labour, detention and murder of those Africans who rebelled against the European powers. This phenomenon, later called 'colonization' seemed to have acquired legitimacy in the European social-political and cultural systems, justification being that, colonization was nothing but an attempt by Europe, to civilize, educate and Christianize the primitive Africa.[45]

Now we describe the African front. By the end of the 1970's, when most African countries had regained self-rule from the European colonial powers, there had been a complete overhaul of the African identity. Traditional African religions and their practices, political and judicial systems, medical practices, as well as cultural structures had taken a complete turn-around, if not an absolute surrender to the European paradigms.[46] Such deep magnitudes of transformation of the traditional African systems also came with worrying, if not saddening attitudes of Africans towards their traditional past. To a large extent, the categories 'traditional' and 'indigenous', having been understood by many

---

[45] For descriptions regarding the European infiltration into Africa, I depend on Robin Hallet's analysis. See Hallet 1995.

[46] For instance, politically, traditional kings were now replaced by paramount chiefs, political power was nationalized, creating such offices as; district and provincial officers, prime minister and president. Council of elders were replaced by judicial magistrates, judges and chief justices as the Juridical systems now embraced the European structure and its categories. Traditional religions had now been declared 'pagan' while practices akin to them were now seen as satanic; new categories of God, worship and belief had now taken precedence over the traditional African ones. Socially, Africans were now embracing typically European manners of dressing, eating and even talking; embracing such European life-styles, added to the ability to speak in the colonial languages such as English, Portuguese, French, German and Dutch was now viewed as being civilized (a category through which traditional life-styles and languages were viewed as primitive). Traditional education, which was fundamentally oral, had now been termed as 'informal' and was replaced by the 'formal education' with schools, colleges and universities taking the European structures and the medium of instruction being dictated by the language of the colonizing European power. There was now full embrace of the monetary trade, replacing the traditional barter-trade; new categories such as weighing of goods in kilograms, banking, loaning and the use of time categories such as years, months, weeks, days and hours for calculating salaries, wages and interests for services traded came to be the hallmarks of post-independence African economic practices. These are just but a few examples to show the magnitude by which traditional African social-cultural, political, economic and religious systems had undergone European-transformation, with special focus on the attitude of the African people themselves; namely, their willingness to embrace the European systems and the categories by means of which those systems were being operationalized.

Africans in tandem with the European description of anything African as, 'primitive', 'wild', 'backward' and 'uncivilized', saw the advent of Africans' dissipation of their own past and its traditional products. Many Africans had not only turned away from their social-cultural, political, religious and economic practices because they had now been passed by time (after the establishment of Westernized systems), they also despised the traditional structures, the wisdoms and categories from which they originated as well as the indigenous ways of expressing them. This was not only a form of 'self-hate' but also a kind of 'self-rejection' which later fueled the phenomena of apartheid and racism against Africans, now referred to as 'blacks' or 'Negros' in the negative sense.

To our day, debates on modernity and globalization have majorly revolved around the category of development (in relation to the social-cultural and political-economic systems), where the meaning-signification of the term 'development', more often than not, depends on the front from which one's perspective and self-identification arises. Assessment of African politics, sociality, cultural-economic and religious structures has often been guided by the Western categories and standards of measuring development. Such assessments often dismiss the value and role of the so-called 'primitive cultures' and 'traditional wisdoms and techniques' in effecting development because they view them as retrogressive. Sadly, definition, development and assessment of African philosophy has often suffered the same fate; the question whether there is such a thing as African philosophy being a typical example.[47]

While Wiredu's expression that, wholesome rejection of all products of the European colonial program (by extension,

---

[47] Tendency to understand and interpret African philosophy from the European perspectives of the meaning and contents of philosophy has often laden the question whether there is such a thing as African philosophy with the baggage of colonialism, colour prejudice and racial-discrimination (Chimakonam and Chemhuru 2021).

European standards for development and philosophy) would be a form of 'madness', his description of wholesome assimilation of the Western conceptual systems as 'wallowing in colonial mentality' affords us a scheme against which to assess contemporary Africans' conceptions, attitudes and strategies for development vis-à-vis modernity and Globalization. Examples of contemporary areas of consideration in carrying out such assessment would include (but not limited to): family setups, naming, rites of passage, religious worship, ethics, economics, politics and philosophy. Education systems, policies and practices play a decisive role in shaping these areas of life. In light of this paper's concerns, we now turn to the consideration of African education in relation to the Wiredu's argument for the value and role of indigenous languages in decolonizing African philosophy.

Contemporary Education in Africa and its Ultimate Goals

Currently, Africa has 54 countries, each of which bears unique historical, geographical, social-cultural and political-economic backgrounds, which present varying sets of experiences, challenges and prospects. Accordingly, there is not a uniform system of Education in Africa today. That notwithstanding, it is generally true that, education system in a specific African country today largely reflects the structure of education found in the European power which colonized it.[48]

Classical definition of Education as "the deliberate, systematic and sustained effort to transmit, provoke or acquire knowledge, values, attitudes, skills or sensibilities as well as learning that results from the effort" (Cremin 1976, ii) largely

---

[48] The phenomenon of European influence on education in Africa is experienced even in Ethiopia and Liberia (the two African countries that were never colonized); they follow education systems that largely reflect the Western systems of education.

constitutes the formal guidelines for today's educational policies, aims and practices. From a critical examination of this definition, it is clear that the category 'education' appeals to the formal and systematic procedures of imparting and acquiring knowledge, skills and attitudes in tandem with pre-established theories and goals. Many scholars have rejected this perspective of education on account of its instrumentalism (Kozol 1985; Noddings 2007; Meyers 2023), whereby education is often conflated with the schooling trajectory towards pre-designed academic content and professional careers. Other scholars have argued for reason-centered education (where learners are expected to critically search for reasons for believing in certain contents) other than for content-centered education (Scheffler 1960), while others argue for integration of informal education with the formal one (Mahruf 2019; Du Bois-Reymond 2003). These critiques already point to the fact that contemporary educational practices are largely one-sided; they tend to be more scientific, formal and school-based and often override the role of the informal, traditional-home-based and non-scientific practices and methods of imparting and acquiring knowledge.

With the contemporary notion of development being closely tied with ideals of modernization and globalization as argued above, the scientific-capture of contemporary systems of education is intractable. This phenomenon contains far-reaching implications on the fate of traditional African frameworks of imparting and acquiring knowledge. To explore these implications, we will consider education in relation to categories such as science, technology, language and communication.

Firstly, education is a principle vehicle of development. Research, discoveries and appropriation of inherited knowledge lead to advancement of life in general and of specific areas of study in particular. This held constant, with the contemporary conception of development in the categories of modernization and globalization, science and scientific technology seem to take over most domains of the formal education. Most African countries find themselves giving undue priority to scientific technology; as if it was the only means of achieving development. In the process, the value of traditional African technologies in effecting development is not only downplayed but also foreclosed due to the conception of such traditional technologies as 'outdated' if not 'primitive.' Consider, for instance, Kenya's conception of its newly launched Competency-Based Curriculum (CBC) as a 'flagship of the Kenya Vision 2030' program (KICD 2016). A critical look at the ideals of Kenya vision 2030 agenda (the attempt to make Kenya a middle-income and industrializing economy by the year 2030) already suggests that development through science-technology and industrialization constitute the primary motivation for the recent curriculum reforms in Kenya. Such an ideal of development clearly creates the opportunity, not only for the hard sciences and scientific-industrial technologies to take precedence over the human sciences, but also for education in general to pay little concern, if not, to totally neglect the value of traditional technologies on account of their largely non-scientific and non-formal structures.

The natural sciences, industrial sciences, medical sciences and engineering sciences as taught in today's primary, secondary and tertiary education institutions in Africa majorly use categories and formulae that are fundamentally European in origin and expression; they are difficult to articulate in the so-called traditional African languages. This not only makes it appear as if there has never been an African origination of anything scientific, but also creates a tendency to think that for any discovery to be acknowledged as genuinely scientific, it must be expressed in the Western categories of science and language. Such tendencies in educational beliefs and practices have led to unhealthy perspectives on the value and role of indigenous languages (especially those of the African origin) for development in general and scientific, industrial and technological development in particular.

The place of indigenous languages in contemporary African Education

Having highlighted the largely Westernized approaches to the very concept 'education', its aims and practices and having explicated the historical origins of school-based instruction in the Colonial-West, it follows almost necessarily, that the medium of instruction had to be Western in origin.[49] While having the Western-colonial languages as media of instruction in Africa would be justified, at least in the years of the primordial establishment of the formal education, maintaining the status quo to our day is completely awkward.

Appropriation of pedagogical methods, skills and attitudes ought to have been the priority of educators in the post-independence period. Such appropriation would have included the tasks such as, translation of the subjects and contents of formal education into the indigenous linguistic structures, categories and expressions. However, research has shown that all sub-Saharan African countries exclusively use former colonial languages as the media of instruction at least for secondary and tertiary education (Rajesh 2017). While former French and Portuguese colonies use the colonial languages right from primary school education through to secondary and tertiary levels, former British colonies partially use mother-tongue as medium of instruction in the initial years before switching to English as from upper primary education (Albaugh 2014). In Kenya, for instance, the

---

[49] Most pre-colonial, colonial and post-independence African schools had European missionaries as founders, teachers, principals and managers. Owing to the Western origins of the educators, subject matters and pedagogical techniques, coupled with the Westerners' devaluation of Africans and their social-cultural settings, it was not only difficult for the educators to use local dialects in teaching; those very languages were generally viewed as 'primitive' and therefore unfit for use as media of instruction. Local educators, having been products of the pre-colonial missionary schools or the colonial ones, were themselves employees of the colonial government; even post-independence tutors, as observes Wiredu, were themselves using the colonial languages for instruction (Wiredu 2004).

practice of mother-tongue education and instruction in mother-tongue as it had originally been prescribed (Ministry of Education, Government of Kenya 1976) had ceased until 2012 when it was reasserted (Moe and MoHEST 2012). As of today, not only has the utilization of mother-tongue as medium of instruction in lower levels of leaning been faced with skepticism and hostility, but the very attempt also to have mother-tongues as subjects to be taught at school has often been viewed (even by parents) as being of little value (Mberia 2016). In the case of Kenya, for instance, while the policy to use mother-tongue as medium of instruction in early development years and the direction to teach mother-tongue in primary schools remains in place, the ministry of education, however, does not demand strict adherence to that policy in primary schools. In practice therefore, mother-tongue education remains optional. This clearly shows that the place of indigenous languages in educational policies and practices across the better part of Africa has remained foreclosed since the colonial era to our day.

The obvious outcomes of such educational foreclosure of the role of indigenous languages range from hindering the development of the very languages to limiting the conceptual and cognitional capacities of the learners (Rajesh 2017; Mandillah 2019; Kretzer and Oluoch 2022). Critics of mother-tongue education and the use of mother-tongues as media of instruction often claim that, with globalization and neoliberal economics, learners need high levels of proficiency in 'modern' languages such as English, French and German for efficiency in international communication and eligibility for international job-market. However, many scholars have rightly observed that multilingualism in African education would be a balanced strategy for promoting development of indigenous languages while at the same time enabling African learners to be competent for international communication and global job-market. Most scholars holding this view also rightly observe that intellectual independence is intertwined with preservation of culture, for which indigenous languages play an essential role (Kioko et al 2008; Mazrui 1997). This argument not only involves a direct bearing to Wiredu's concerns but also points to the basic concerns of this paper; namely, investigations into the value and the role of indigenous languages in the development of legitimate African philosophy.

The Future of African Philosophy

This kind of argument can be detected in Okoni Akiba's reasoning. As Wiredu rightly sees it, the relevance of African philosophy today lies in its capacity to use traditional African wisdoms in order to respond to traditional and modern problems. The traditional component of African philosophy could include reflections on philosophical problems that arise from African culturally based ethics and morality, logic, metaphysics and epistemology. Such problems would include (though not limited to); women suppression (polygamy, under-age cum forced marriage, wife-inheritance and women circumcision), tribal intolerance, multifarious identities of God, religion and religious beliefs, conflicting conceptions of beauty, death and immortality and questions surrounding witchcraft, divination and fortune telling. The modern component of African philosophy on the other hand, would include critical reflection on issues emerging from modern ideologies, policies and practices of governance and politics, economics, education and religion among others. There is a thin line between the two components since none of the aforementioned areas of reflection could be termed either as exclusively traditional or exclusively modern, except with regard to specific contexts. Therefore, these components must be viewed as two sides of the same coin.

Contemporary African philosophy has much to attend to. Consider for instance, the questions we have alluded to in our discussions concerning modernization and globalization.

However, the question whether the philosophical outcomes of our engagement in philosophy (as African philosophers claiming to be doing 'African philosophy') could be termed as authentic African philosophy still remains. While some philosophers have dismissed the value for such a question [claiming that we simply need to engage ourselves in philosophy for its own sake (preference for issue-based philosophy without regard for identifying philosophy as African, Western or Asian)], they fail to recognize the centrality of decolonization as an integral part of the concerns of philosophy. Such an argument amounts to a giving in to the colonialist denial of African epistemic capacities and a betrayal of African intellectual capabilities and the philosophical responsibilities akin to them.

With the resurgence of undeniably colonial tendencies, being felt in the political, economic and social-cultural relations between Africa, Europe and Asia today, African thinkers cannot overlook the potential of the decolonization project in responding to this phenomenon. For decolonization project to be a feasible response to traditional and modern philosophical concerns regarding Africa, Africans and their social-political and cultural-economic aspects of life, African thinkers, critically using African categories of thought must put themselves to task. Such is the task which Wiredu rightly considers as African philosophy proper.

Since African philosophy involves the use of indigenous wisdoms for reflecting on traditional and modern problematics, contemporary attitudes towards indigenous languages is a matter of life and death with regards to its development and authenticity. We have explicated, however, the fact that contemporary African educational policies, aims and practices have paid little attention, if not completely neglected or despised commitment towards development of indigenous languages. Accordingly, such an attitude spells devastating consequences on the fate of African philosophy and its ability to deal with traditional and modern problems facing Africa and beyond. Philosophy's primary task is to provide essential foundation for all human disciplines. This task has always been carried out by way of questioning; philosophers ask essential questions by pointing out those fundamental elements of reality which may have been taken for granted or left at stake. The question philosophers must now ask is; what is the fate of Africa's authentic development in general and of African philosophy in particular, if development of African indigenous languages continue to be ignored, if not, suppressed?

Conclusion

This paper has provided an analysis of Wiredu's notion of conceptual decolonization in relation to his convictions regarding of the fundamental nature, sources and concerns of African philosophy. Precisely, it has outlined the 'double-critical' and 'imperative' character of conceptual decolonization, not only as means for re-claiming African epistemic capabilities but also as intellectual responsibility for African thinkers to develop a robust African philosophy.

Paying attention to Wiredu's concerns with in-depth studies of traditional African philosophies as sources of African philosophy, this paper has further analyzed Wiredu's claim that proficiency in indigenous languages is critical for authentic development of African philosophy. It has therefore demonstrated that, for Wiredu, there is a direct relation between traditional African epistemic formations and indigenous linguistic frameworks. Arguing that introduction of formal education and instruction in colonial languages (so-called 'modern languages') does not warrant dissipation of informal education and instruction in indigenous languages, this paper views Wiredu's notion of conceptual decolonization as a biting critique of African educators and education policy-makers insofar as they foreclose the place of indigenous languages in effecting development.

The paper, therefore draws the conclusion that, decolonization of contemporary African education is a necessary antecedent to authentic development of African philosophy. The paper recommends, therefore, that African philosophers should endeavor to influence contemporary African education policy, aims and practices, towards educational development of African indigenous languages.

Bibliography

ALBAUGH, E. A. 2014. *State-Building and Multilingual Education in Africa*. Cambridge: Cambridge University Press.

CREMIN, L. 1977. *The Education of the Educating Professions*. Washington D.C: The American Association of Colleges for Teachers Education.

CHIMAKONAM J. O., CHEMHURU M. 2021. "Eight Practical Issues in Contemporary African Philosophy." In *Essays on Contemporary Issues in African Philosophy*, edited by CHIMAKONAM J.O, ETIEYIBO E. and ODIMEGWU I., 1-26. Springer, Cham. https://doi.org/10.1007/978-3-030-70436-0_1.

DU BOIS-REYMOND. 2003. *Study on the links between formal and non-formal education*. Strasbourg: Council of Europe, Directorate of Youth and Sport.

GOVERNMENT OF THE REPUBLIC OF KENYA. 2007. *Kenya Vision 2030*. Nairobi: Government Press.

KEMAL, D. and CONROY, C. 2018. "Global politics for a globalized economy." Accessed on January 14, 2023. www.brooling.edu.

KENYA INSTITUTE OF CURRICULUM DEVELOPMENT (KICD). 2016. *Report on Needs Assessment for School Curriculum in Kenya*. Accessed on January 13, 2023. www.kicd.ac.ke/news/presentation-on-competency-based-curriculum-activities

KOZOL, J. 1985. *Illiterate America*. New York: Doubleday & Company Inc.

HALLET, R. 1995. "The European Approach to the interior of Africa in the Eighteenth Century." *The Journal of African History* 4 (2): 191-206. https://doi.org/10.1017/S0021853700004023.

HEIDEGGER, M. 1978. "The way to language." In *Basic Writings*, edited by D.F. Krell, 393-426. London: Routledge.

KIOKO, A. N., MUTIGA, J & MUTHWII, M. J. (2008). *Language and Education in Africa: Answering the Questions.* Nairobi: UNESCO.

KRETZER, M and OLUOCH-SULEH, E. 2022. "(Hidden) potentials for African languages in curriculum reforms: examples from Kenya and South Africa." *SN Social Sciences* 2 (154). https://doi.org/10.1007/s43545-022-00440-6.

LERE, I. 2014. "Globalization and Development. The impact on Africa: A Political Economic Approach." *OIDA International Journal of Sustainable Development* 7 (9): 153-162. https:/ssrn.com/abstract=25 60140

MAHRUF, S. and HOWES, A. 2019. "The relevance of formal and non-formal primary education in relation to health, well-being and environmental awareness: Bangladeshi pupils' perspectives in the rural contexts." *International Journal of Qualitative Studies no Health and Well-being* 13 (1). https://doi.org/10.1080/17482631.2018.1554022.

MANDILLAH. L. 2019. "Kenya Curriculum Reforms and Mother Tongue Education: Issues, Challenges and Implementation Strategies." *Education As Change* 23. https://doi/10.25159/1947-9417/3379.

MATUNHU, J. A. 2011. "A critique of modernization and dependency theories in Africa: Critical assessment." *African Journal of History and Culture* 3 (5): 65-72. https://academicjournals.org/article/article 1381858116_Matunhu.pdf.

MAZRUI, A. 1997. "The World Bank, the language question and the future of African education." *Race and Class* 38 (3): 35-48. https://doi.org/10.1177/030639689703800303.

MBERIA, Wa Kithaka. 2016. "Mother tongues as media of instruction: The case of Kenya." *The University of Nairobi Journal of Language and Linguistics* 5: 46-59. http://erepository.uonbi.ac.ke/handle/11295/96015.

MEYERS, M. 1993. "An Argument against educating young children." *Education* 113 (3): 485512. Accessed on January 11, 2023. https://go.gale.com/ps/i.do?p=AONE&id=GALE%7CA14125481&v =2.1&it=r&sid=googleScholar&asid=25bda208&userGroupName=an on%7Eddac764c&aty=open-web-entry.

MINKOV, M., KAASA, A. and WELZEL, C. 2021. "Economic Development and Modernization in Africa Homogenize National Cultures." *Journal of Cross-Cultural Psychology* 52 (8). https://doi.org/10.1177/00220221211035495.

MINISTRY OF EDUCATION, GOVERNMENT OF KENYA. 1976. "The Report of the National Committee on Education Objectives and Policies of 1976." Accessed on January 13, 2023. http://academia-ke.org/library/download/re port-of-the-national-committee-on-educational-objetives-and-policies-the-gachathi-report-1976/?wpdmdl=8385&refresh=604a3clfacc441615477791.

MINISTRY OF EDUCATION AND MINISTRY OF HIGHER EDUCATION, SCIENCE AND TECHNOLOGY. Republic of Kenya. 2012. "Sessional Paper no. 14 of 2012 on Reforming Education and Training Sectors in Kenya." Accessed on January 13, 2023. http://academia-ke.org/library/download/ me-and-mhest-sessional-paper-no-14-of-2012-on-reforming-education-and-training-in-kenya/?wpdmdl=7351&reflesh=604a52le0c2971615483422.

MOORE, D. 2001. "Neoliberal Globalisation and the Triple Crisis of 'Modernisation' in Africa: Zimbabwe, the Democratic Republic of the Congo and South Africa." *Third World Quarterly* 22 (6): 909-929. https://www.tandfonline.com/doi/abs/10.1080/01436590120099713.

NWOBODO E. E. Ratzinger. 2021. "Africa and the Challenges of Modernity." *Nnadiebube Journal of Philosophy* 5 (1). www.nnadiebube.org

NODDINGS, Nel. 2007. "Curriculum for the 21st century." *Educational Studies in Japan* (2): 75-81. https://doi/10.7571/esjkyoiku.2.75

OLUOCH, E. 2019. *Implications of Mother Tongue as a Medium of Instruction: in Public Primary Schools in Kisumu Town East Constituency, Kenya.* Nairobi: Lap Lambert Academic Publishing.

RAJESH, R. 2017. "Medium of instruction policies and efficacy of education systems in sub-Saharan Africa." *United Nations Educational, Scientific and Cultural Organization (Global Education Monitoring*

Report). Accessed on January 13, 2023. https://unesdoc.unesco.org/ark:/48223/pf0000259578.

SCHEFFLER, I. 1960. *The Language of Education*. Springfield, Illinois: Charles C. Thomas press.

Conceptual Decolonization of the African: In Search of a New Mentality for African Development

Nelson Shang, PhD., Senior Lecturer of Philosophy at The University of Bamenda, Cameroon, and at the Catholic University of Cameroon (CATUC), nelsonshang@gmail.com

Abstract

How can we explain the fact that in the 21st century a multitude of Africans still live in abject poverty whereas the continent is very rich in natural and human resources? Drawing inspiration from Kwasi Wiredu's views on conceptual decolonization, my argument in this paper is that there are four 'mentalities' (colonial mentality, tribal mentality, the mentality of laziness and the mentality of sorcery/magic) that we need to eliminate if we are to regain our African identity and to develop. The next step is to fill our minds with knowledge, scientific knowledge that flows from indigenous African experiences. Thus, our educational systems should focus more on training African students how to think (not what to think) about African realities, critical thinking and problem-solving skills. Education that blends theory and practice is the vehicle of development. Looking back at the Monrovia Declaration and the Lagos Plan of Action on the question of development in Africa, this paper argues that an African science revolution is not just urgent but a *conditione sine qua non* for an African development in this era of globalization.

Key Words: Wiredu, Conceptual Decolonization, Development, Colonial mentality, Education, science, Technology

Introduction

History tells us that Africa is the cradle of civilization and that human beings originated in Africa.[50] Archaeologists and palaeontologists have scientifically confirmed that "the first humans migrated from Africa to populate other regions of the world."[51] In searching for "the genes that make us human", Graeme Finlay declares emphatically, "we are all Africans."[52] It is a matter of historical record that for many years before European civilization, Africans had been extracting minerals from the depths of their continent and used them to produce numerous things. Artisans fabricated iron tools and weapons, architects built tall stone structures, and merchants sold gold that not only adorned African bodies but also circulated in Western and Oriental markets.[53] What this means is that Africa has never really been isolated from the rest of the world. Through commerce Africa was actively involved the main current of global interaction and trade. James Delehanty rightly observes that Roman coins and artifacts from the second and third centuries of the Common Era have been unearth in lands south of the Sahara, evidence that Africa's great desert was traversed occasionally in early days.[54]

In Medieval times, Africa was not deemed particularly backward, primitive or frightful. Paintings from this time show Africans simply as another shade of human beings and writings

---

[50] Yosef Ben-Jochannan, *Black Man of the Nile*, (New York: Alkebu-Lan Books, 1970), p. 55-57.

[51] GROSZ-NGANTE M., HANSON, J. H. & O'MEARA, P., (eds.), "Introduction", *Africa,* 4th Edition, (Bloomington: Indiana University Press, 2014), p. 4.

[52] Graeme Finlay, "The Emergence of Human Distinctiveness: The Genetic Story", in Malcolm Jeeves (ed), *Rethinking Human Nature",* (Michigan: William B. Eerdmans Publisning Company, 2011), p. 108.

[53] GROSZ-NGANTE M., HANSON, J. H. & O'MEARA, P., (eds.), "Introduction" in Africa, p. 1-2.

[54] J. Delehanty, "Africa: A Geographic Frame", in GROSZ-NGANTE M., HANSON, J. H. & O'MEARA, P, (eds.), *Africa*, p. 11.

CONCEPTUAL DECOLONIZATION OF THE AFRICAN

from this time have no racist or anti-African expression. The reason for this is offered by Delehanty from the perspective of living standards both in Europe and Africa. There wasn't any much difference:

> On both continents nearly everyone lived off the land, most in agriculture. Diet was unvaried. Hunger was common. Life span was short. Almost no one on either continent was well educated. Why should Europeans have considered Africans, five hundred years ago, to be in any manner inferior? There was no material reason for Europeans to stigmatize Africa and Africans in particular at this time, and generally they did not.[55]

The above era of equality and fairness described by Delehanty, however, came to an end after the Renaissance with the emergence of modern science in Europe. The scientific revolution led to a certain Euro-centricism and by the 16th and 17th centuries (and beyond), one finds in writings and paintings, European descriptions of Africans as poor, uneducated, technologically unsophisticated, underdeveloped and non-Christian:

> If we are white, they are black; if we are good, they are bad; if we are Christian, they must be immoral; if we are sophisticated, they must be primitive; if we are enterprising, they must be lazy; if we are cerebral, they must be physical; if we are moral, they must be licentious; if we are orderly, they must be chaotic; if we are a people capable of self-governance, they must need our help.[56]

What did the scientific revolution do to the European mind? Why did Africa and Africans suddenly become the antithesis of everything that made Europe great? The answer is that the emergence of modern science led to a change in living standards and this did not happen in Africa. To make matters worse for the

---

[55] J. Delehanty, p. 12-13.
[56] J. Delehanty, "Africa: A Geographic Frame", in *Africa*, p. 14.

African, Europeans 'invented' the trans-Atlantic slave-trade which drained Africa of its human resources. Those transported in slavery to Europe and the New World were strong and vibrant Africans. To justify this inhuman act, Europeans described Africans in derogatory terms – beasts, savages, primitives, pre-logical etc. As the era of slavery and slave-trade was coming to a close, then came the era of colonialism from 1884. By the 1960's when African countries were declaring independence here and there, neo-colonialism came in. Colonialism and neo-colonialism drained and continue to drain Africa of her natural and human resources. There is a whole debate as to whether the colonial era was transformative for Africa.[57]

It is clear that the above external factors have contributed and are still contributing to underdevelopment in Africa but the question now is: what have we as Africans done to redress the situation? What can we do to better ourselves? We are all conscious (and there is ample literature on it) that conflicts, endemic corruption, poverty, bad governance, climate and other factors have been advanced as reasons why Africa is still developing. Before discussing what Africans should do so as to develop the continent, let us first of all examine the concept of development.

Development

Development, taken generally, denotes either a process or a state associated with such concepts as material well-being, progress, social justice, economic growth, personal blossoming or even ecological equilibrium.[58] It is from this perspective that when a country lacks infrastructures such as roads, hospitals,

---

[57] Akare Aden J. & J. H. Hanson, "Legacies of the Past: Themes in Africa History", in *Africa*, p. 32.

[58] Gilbert Rist, *The History of Development from Western Origins to Global Faith,* (3rd Ed.,), Zed Books, London and New York 2008, p. 8.

schools, electricity etc, it is said to be underdeveloped. Sub-Saharan Africa is said to be the least developed because it continues to have relatively low levels of industrialization and urbanization and instead subsists on narrow economic bases, overly dependent on primary commodities and foreign aid. Livelihoods and life expectancy in Africa are low as well as literacy rates and access to health and education.[59] From a political dimension, African countries are still underdeveloped given that "governance institutions are week, as evidenced by the fragility of democracies emerging after three decades of authoritarianism, heavily politicized bureaucracies and judiciaries, and weak policy environments that frequently respond more to patronage networks than to competitive ideas and interests."[60] The negative effects of this bad politics are felt in the economic sphere. African economies have grown and are still growing slowly since the early years of independence in the late 1950s and 1960s compared to those of other nations, especially in Asia, that came into independence at the same time.

If we look at the concept of development only from the economic or political dimension, then we shall leave out other very important aspects of development. Walter Rodney in his celebrated *How Europe Underdeveloped Africa* defined development as "increased skill and capacity, greater freedom, creativity, self-discipline and material well-being."[61] Rodney does not limit development only to the economic sphere. Development is more integral taking into consideration the condition of the human person as a whole.

Thus, we cannot limit development only to the multiplication and accumulation of wealth. Real development is

---

[59] Raymond Muhula and Stephen N. Ndegwa, "Development in Africa, Tempered Hope" in *Africa*, p. 275.

[60] Muhula and Ndegwa, p. 275.

[61] Walter Rodney, *How Europe Underdeveloped Africa,* (Washington: Howard University Press, 1982), p. 9.

integral and takes into account the moral, intellectual, physical and spiritual dimensions of the human being. This, for Njoku, is called human development which focuses on the "factors that affect the growth and development of the human person in their internal and external dynamics."[62] Thus, while economic development is good and must be pursued, it is not the only form of development that Africa and Africans need. We need to pay particular attention to our intellectual development: our mindset, our knowledge, our world-view etc. If we have natural resources without the knowledge of their usefulness, without the technical know-how, without the ability to tap these natural resources then we are doomed. Those who have the knowledge will come and make us of them for their own interests making us feel that they are helping us. We also need a true history of the African people and heritage, we must know where we are coming from, where we are now and why, and where we could be and what we need to do to get there. The German philosopher, Hegel (and he may not be good thinker to quote at this point given his racist views about Africans) holds that the development of human history is characterized by the idea of increasing self-consciousness on the part of human beings.

Many scholars agree that human development remains the most important aspect of development. There is, therefore, the urgency to resolve the "tension between the need to have more and the aspiration to be more fully human. There is a need to retain the distinction between being and having."[63] Yet human personal development requires that we "sit up, cogitate, reflect on our situation and experience, and thereby raise our consciousness and get prepared and set to forge ahead in spite of odds and

---

[62] Francis O. C. Njoku, *Development and African Philosophy, A Theoretical Reconstruction of African Sociopolitical Economy,* (New York: University, Inc., 2004), p. 6.

[63] N. OGUGA, *Towards a Grand Development Paradigm for Africa: A Philosophical Perspective,* p. 80.

romance development."[64] This would naturally lead to the need for a "total reconstruction of our society; in short, both re-examination and re-evaluation of values, choices, life options and structural transformations."[65] Hence, the dignity and well-being of the human being must be at the center of all development. Man must therefore be end or finality of all development as Njoh Mouelle says (*l'homme doit etre la finalite de tout developpement*).[66] A developed society is one that produces enlightened human beings, free creators capable of using material possessions as a means to an end not an ends. Human Persons should be able to say no in some circumstances and to stand for freedom and dignity.[67] Education plays an important role in this developmental process.

Education as a Vehicle for Development

Education is central in promoting development in Africa. Olivier Reboul presents the celebrated words of Helvitus thus: "L'education peut tout"[68], that is, education can do everything. Through education, Africans can acquire the knowledge and maturity which will enable them to promote development in their various countries. Let us keep in mind the etymological meaning of the word education. Education comes from *educare* which means to support and nurture the growth of, and *educere* which means to draw out or to cause to come out. Education from this perspective is a process whereby desirable physical, intellectual, moral and spiritual qualities are instilled into a child. Education is the act of developing knowledge, skill and character in a child.

---

[64] *Ibid.*, p. 81.

[65] *Ibid.*, p. 81.

[66] Ebenezer Njoh Mouelle, *Developper La Richese Humaine,* (Yaounde: Cle, 1988), p. 5.

[67] *Ibid.*, p. 195.

[68] Olivier Reboul, *La Philosophie De L'Education,* 9e, Collection *Que Sais-Je?,* (Paris: Presse Universitaire de France, 2001), p. 21.

It is the act of bringing up, rearing, guiding or directing a child. What one takes from this etymological definition is that the principal goal of education in its imparting and instructing students is holistic with the aim of forming integral human beings capable of distinguishing right from wrong.

Students then must be trained to think for themselves. The capacity to think for oneself is a much needed good if we are to develop. This is because as *as we think, we live* and as such, the more we improve our thoughts, the more we improve our lives. Hector Amezquita holds that "a root cause of major human problems is the fact so many of us learned *what* to think instead of *how* to think."[69] His explanation is fascinating:

> Knowing *how* to think involves conscious awareness of truth, learning new ways of thinking and making the decision to be very careful of what we think. Knowing *how* to think liberates us to use our total freedom of conscious choice. Instead of being dominated by unwanted thoughts that arise in the absence of something better, the mind can easily trained to think only what we allow it to think.[70]

What this means basically is that we should exercise our ability or what Amezquita calls 'freedom' to choose our thoughts. Our everyday experience shows that every time we want to stop thinking about something we do not like, we cannot easily change that thought. Why is that? Because our educational system did not train us early on to be used to exercising our unlimited freedom of choice to determine our thoughts. We simply learned to think automatically, spontaneously. Education should rather train us to start selecting our thoughts and managing them. Why is it necessary to do that? Simply because "everything we do is preceded by a thought. Our thoughts are the producers of our

---

[69] Hector Amezquita, *Thought, The Greatest Power of All*, (Marina Del Rey: Devorss Publications, 1997), XVII.

[70] *Ibid.*

present and the builders of our future. If we want to be producers, directors and stars of the film called *Living on Planet Earth*, we must learn *how* to think."[71]

The above quotation puts us within the confines of our discussion on development. Education should enliven us with ideas so we could determine the course of our actions. Education is "about self-development and empowerment."[72] Education should therefore "create human beings, real human beings who are creative."[73] Creativity speaks of novelty, innovation, technology and hence, development. If education is the "art of the utilization of knowledge"[74], then it is imperative that we put in good quality thoughts in to our minds so as to yield quality results. The computer jargon "garbage in – garbage out is very relevant here. "If we put in good quality thoughts into our minds, we get good quality lives. On the other hand, if we think upon what is Universal Good, we put in our lives, love, health, abundance, wisdom and joy."[75]

Any educational system that really seeks development must beware of what Whitehead calls inert ideas or dead knowledge: "In training a child to activity of thought, above all things we must beware of what I call "inert ideas" that is to say, ideas that are merely received into the mind without being utilized or thrown into fresh combinations.... Education with inert ideas is not only useless, it is above all things harmful."[76] A student who studies a

[71] *Ibid.*

[72] Martha Roth, *Aims of Education Address*, (Chicago: The University of Chicago, 2012), p. 7.

[73] Gerald Bennaars, *Ethics, Education and Development*, (Nairobi: East African Educational Publishers, 1993), p. 52.

[74] Alfred North Whitehead, *The Aims of Education and Other Essays*, (New York: The Free Press, 1967), p. 10.

[75] Hector Amezquita, *Thought, The Greatest Power of All*, (Marina Del Rey: Devorss Publications, 1997), XVII.

[76] Alfred North Whitehead, *The Aims of Education and Other Essays*, p. 2.

variety of subjects and does not properly understand them, does not see any relationship among these subjects and cannot apply the knowledge from these subjects into their practical day to day activities is acquiring inert ideas or dead knowledge. Education for development is not only aimed at producing literate people but also those who can be useful and fruitful in their society by putting knowledge into good use. We need people full of true knowledge, cultural values and practical skills. In this light Whitehead says:

> A merely well-informed man is the most useless bore on God's earth. What we should aim at producing is men who possess both culture and expert knowledge in some special direction. Their expert knowledge will give them the ground to start from and their culture will lead them as deep as philosophy and as high as art. We have to remember that the valuable intellectual development is self-development.[77]

Teachers therefore have the duty to impart knowledge in a way that encourages the students to turn inert knowledge into active, vibrant and engaged tools.[78] Teachers stand in a unique position with a unique mission to impart knowledge not just to preserve received wisdom. Teachers must test, distil, generate, recombine and reconceive knowledge. They must transmit this knowledge to prepared and receptive students, who will in their turn challenge, refine, refute and generate yet more knowledge. Teachers and students must therefore collaborate in cultivating a body of knowledge actively and deliberately.[79] Education can do everything. A good and integral education will lead us to development.

---

[77] *Ibid.*, p.10.

[78] Roth, p. 3.

[79] Franz G. Riffert, *A. N. Whitehead on Learning and Education*, (Newcastle: Cambridge Scholars Press, 2005), p. 71.

The principal problem that arises at this stage is that in Africa, we have many intellectuals. The level of illiteracy is reducing everyday as more and more people are being educated. The question then is, why is Africa still lacking behind when it comes to development? If the thrust of this paper is that education will bring us out of misery into development, and Africans are educated, then what is the problem?

What Kind of Knowledge Is Needed for Development?

Every society functions on the basis of what its inhabitants know. Our knowledge has a variety of sources, values and functions. But not all forms of knowledge are necessary for development. For instance, development will not be a reality if we possess and cherish knowledge that comes through popular opinions, gossips, "forwarded as received" texts on Whatsapp and other social media platforms etc. while the social media is a blessing to us in several forms, vis, communication, education, advertisement, entertainment, etc, its negative effects too abound such that our African youths are losing their potential to work for development by being distracted with social media platforms like tiktok, influencers, posting unhelpful videos on Whatsapp, twitter, instegram, etc. Indeed, we live in a culture of mass distractions. Yet, these social media platforms could be used to advertise new inventions and educational videos that could help inspire others to engage in science and technology, art and culture. Africa is home to multiple renewable energy sources. Videos on how to tap and use these renewable sources of energy for home and industrial use would be far better than videos showing dance moves, stupidity in the name of fun, sexual promiscuity, etc. African youths should take advantage of the social media for the promotion of useful practical knowledge necessary for development.

In the same light knowledge that is esoteric and initiative cannot lead to development because it is discriminatory knowledge, the privilege of a few. We are meant to live and share our existence with others and so the esoteric knowledge does not help that much. Truth has the character of being universal. Also, we cannot develop if our knowledge is based solely on our personal lived experience, this form of knowledge is very much subjective and relative.

For us to properly develop, we need rational knowledge, knowledge that flows from the construction of human reason, particularly theoretical and practical reason. This is where modern science and technology come in. As I argue below, this is only possible if we have an educational system that confers a new mentality in our students. A mentality is capable of generating what I call an African based scientific revolution. Thus, our states/politicians need to live up to the promises and resolutions they took more than thirty years ago at the Monrovia Declaration of 1979 and especially the "Lagos Plan of Action for the Economic Development of Africa, 1980 – 2000." Heads of various African states we recognised "the need to take urgent action to provide the political support necessary for the success of the measures to achieve the goals of rapid self-reliance and self-sustaining development and economic growth" of their various nations. They then resolved, among other things, to "put science and technology in the service of development by reinforcing the autonomous capacity of our countries in this field" and to "develop indigenous entrepreneurship, technical manpower and technological abilities to enable our peoples to assume greater responsibility for the achievement of our individual and collective development goals."[80] Where are we on this? It is necessary that our political leaders put in place appropriate funds to promote science-driven educational research that would usher in rapid

---

[80] Anonymous, "Lagos Plan of Action for the Economic Development of Africa, 1980 – 2000", Reprinted by the OAU, Addis Ababa, 1980.

development on the continent. Thus, a knowledge-based development model would marshal in an African-based scientific revolution vital for the development of the continent.

Conceptual Decolonization Confers a New Mentality Necessary for Development

Thinkers like Kwasi Wiredu, Albert Memmi, Franz Fanon, George James and others have argued that the fundamental problem of the post-colonial African is the colonial mentality that we inherited from the colonizer. This mentality is depicted in our dependence on the colonial masters in several areas of our livelihood as individuals, states and as a continent. George James, for instance, in his *Stolen Legacy,* proposes as a solution what he calls the Philosophy of Redemption: a psychological process, involving a change in belief or mentality to be followed by a corresponding change in behavior. To him, it signifies a mental emancipation or reformation, in which the black people will be liberated from the chain of traditional falsehood, which for centuries has incarcerated them in the prison of inferiority complex and world humiliation and insult. This emancipation or redemption has two functions. Which are general and specific. In his general sense, emancipation transcends the limitations and boundaries of race, and therefore includes the whole world, Black and White people, since we are all victims of the same chain and traditional falsehood, that has incarcerated the modern world. It becomes specific (emancipation or redemption) when it refers to the freedom of the Black from such conditions.[81]

For Kwasi Wiredu, conceptual decolonization which is, an authentic redefinition of one's identity as an African, hinges on aspects such as, guarding against uncritical assimilation of

---

[81] George James, S*tolen Legacy. Greek Philosophy is Stolen Egyptian Philosophy*, (The journal of pan African studies 2009 eBook), p. 112.

western conceptual schemes, and formulating conceptual schemes in African languages is a way out from conceptual colonization. The main agents of this conceptual colonization of the African, for Wiredu, are language, politics, and religion. In the first place, Wiredu argues that our philosophical education has generally been in the medium of foreign languages and this, to him, is the most fundamental, subtle, pervasive and intractable circumstance of mental colonization.[82] The languages of our colonial masters such as English, French, Spanish, and German, later developed even after their departure to national languages and were then used primarily in schools for instruction and generally for communication. This has contributed greatly to our mental colonization, such that the way we think, talk, and act are all western. So, for K. Wiredu, as a remedy we have to learn our African languages in such a way that we can be able to think and formulate concepts, first of all, in our native languages before transposing into any of the foreign languages[83]. When we must have succeeded in doing this, we shall boast of having been conceptually decolonized especially linguistically; but what about religious decolonization from the west.

Secondly, with the coming of European missionaries, Wiredu contends, all African religious practices were considered either as idolatry or paganism. Thus, the western missionaries created a conducive environment that permitted them to effectively do away with African religious values[84]. After this, they went on to reconstruct the African minds in line with western religious values and beliefs. But for K. Wiredu Africans have to make an auto reference, and adopt, those positive African religious values which their forefathers upheld. Akan, for instance, he says, has a real traditional believe about the Supreme

---

[82] *Ibid.*, p. 112.

[83] Kwasi Wiredu, *Cultural Universals Particulars,* (Bloomington: Indian University Press, 1996, p. 142.

[84] *Ibid.*, p. 142.

Being; no one teaches even a child about the Supreme Being[85]. His existence is so obvious to everyone. Thus, an Akan simply needs to know that there are reasons enough to justify whatever metaphysical claim there is for a Supreme Being as that brought by the West, then, he freely adopts[86]. But in fact, a non-critical Akan would simply attribute his knowledge of a Supreme Being, to a certain colonial mentality, (the conceptual condition to accept everything as right because it is western) and not bother to question any concept about the religious beliefs and practices that are foreign to him[87].

Finally, Wiredu maintains, that Africa has suffered unspeakably from the political legacies of colonialism[88], and continues to suffer either directly or indirectly from the political tutelage of the West, due to a series of causes masterminded by them[89]. But in fact, he thinks that after years of subjection to untold severities of one party dictatorship, it cannot be the will of the Africans to continue suffering under such unfamiliar form of government[90]. In Africa, he insists, there is now visible enthusiasm among many intellectuals and politicians, in favour of multi-party democracy. Many African political pundits mistake democracy for multi-party politics[91]. Unfortunately, such a political doctrinal framework seems antithetical to the underlying traditional statecraft of Africa. Thus, an applauded effort, for K. Wiredu, is rather that of those African leaders who suggested a one-party system for their states[92]. This in a way is greatly linked to the African traditional systems of governance;

---

[85] *Ibid.*, p. 141-142.
[86] *Ibid.*, p. 141.
[87] *Ibid.*, p. 141.
[88] *Ibid.*, p. 143.
[89] *Ibid.*, p. 143.
[90] *Ibid.*, p. 143.
[91] *Ibid.*, p. 143.
[92] *Ibid.*, p. 143.

notwithstanding, this linkage for K. Wiredu, was spurious and disingenuous, though they strived to harmonize the contemporary practice of politics and the real African traditional forms of government[93]. In our contemporary quest for democracy, K. Wiredu exhorts, we have to look at the early African communities[94]. From the traditional African philosophy of government, he reiterates, there existed varied forms of governments, but always a certain unity of approach at any rate, "that unity consisted in the insistence on consensus as the basis of political decision-making."[95] Such consensus is what K. Wiredu calls democratic consensus.

There is, thus, a need for a new mentality, aided by an African based scientific revolution that would take into consideration our African realities. Only a proper education focused on critical thinking and problem-based-learning can user in this African-based scientific revolution. The scientific revolution, in the West, brought in a new cosmology[96], a distinct state of mind[97], a new view of the world. All of these were made possible thanks to the revival of learning in Western Europe after the Dark Ages. Albert Einstein rightly maintains that the survival of the human race depends very much on the development of a new way of thinking. Though his focus is on world peace, what he says is important for our present consideration. For him:

> We need an essentially new way of thinking if mankind is to survive. Men must radically change their attitudes toward each other and their views of the future. Force must no longer be an instrument of politics .... Today, we

---

[93] *Ibid.*, p. 143.

[94] *Ibid.*, p. 143.

[95] *Ibid.*, p. 143.

[96] Alfred North Whitehead, *Science and the Modern World*, (New York: The New American Library of World literature, inc., 1926).

[97] William E. Hocking, "The Struggle for Power and Peace", online at http://www.harvardsquarelibrary.org/IsGodNecessary/The-Struggle-for-Power-and-Peace.php, (page consulted on the 23rd of January 2022).

do not have much time left; it is up to our generation to succeed in thinking differently. If we fail, the days of civilized humanity are numbered.[98]

Drawing from the above, it must be said that the survival of Africa and Africans depends greatly on a new way of thinking. A new mindset is indispensable for the development of Africa. The American process philosopher Alfred North Whitehead is convinced that the "mentality of an epoch springs from the view of the world which is, in fact, dominant in the educated sections of the community in question."[99] This explains why Whitehead considers philosophy as having an important role to play in shaping this mentality:

> Philosophy, in one, of its functions, is the critic of cosmologies. It is its function to harmonize, refashion, and justify divergent intuitions as to the nature of things. It has to insist on the scrutiny of the ultimate ideas, and on the retention of the whole of the evidence in shaping our cosmological scheme. Its business is to render explicit, and so far as may be efficient, a process which otherwise is unconsciously performed without rational tests.[100]

Whitehead looks at modern science as a state of mind, a mentality or a mode of thought that rapidly spread throughout Europe. For him, the beginnings of the scientific movements were confined to a minority among the intellectual elite. However, the quiet growth of science has practically recoloured our mentality so that modes of thought which, in former times, were exceptional are now broadly spread throughout the educated world. This mentality, it must be noted, is transferable from country to country, from race to race, wherever there is a rational society[101].

---

[98] Albert Einstein, quoted by David P. Barash & Charles P. Webel, *Peace and Conflict Studies,* 3rd Edition, (California Sage Publications, 2014), p. 3.

[99] Alfred North Whitehead, *Science and the Modern World,* VIII.

[100] *Ibid.*

[101] *Ibid.,* p. 2.

What characterizes modern science, then, for Whitehead, is "its universality." It is clear that modern science was born in Europe but its home is the whole world. Yet Whitehead maintains that "the new mentality is even more important than the new science and the new technology." The reason for this is simply that this new mentality has, in the words of Whitehead, "altered the metaphysical presuppositions and the imaginative contents of our minds; so that now the old stimuli provoke a new response."[102]

If we go by Thierry Zomahoun's argument that "Africa is becoming a generator of knowledge, innovation, creativity and technology, rather than being simply an adapter of trends produced elsewhere in the world"[103] then it is incumbent on our politicians and educational institutions to provide conditions for this new mindset to flourish so as to facilitate development. Zomahoun is of the opinion that if we have a creative, skilled and educated young African population combined with the implementation of science and evidence-based pan-African and national public policies and investments then we can be assured of a large-scale social transformation and improved well-being[104]. It is therefore the urgent that

> African governments must first take concrete, specific actions to produce and disseminate knowledge around the continent. Deliberate strategies should be centred on three main challenges: (1) How to improve countries' regulatory frameworks to enable knowledge-led societies, most specifically in the two policy areas of industry and science; (2) How to foster the relevant skills and capacity for a scientific and creative culture to take root in Africa;

---

[102] *Ibid.*, p. 2.

[103] Thierry Zomahoun, "It's Time to Foster Africa's Science Revolution" in *OECD Observer*, www.oecdobserver.org | It's time to foster Africa's science revolution, March 2020, p. 2. (Page consulted on 21st of March 2023).

[104] *Ibid.*, p. 3.

CONCEPTUAL DECOLONIZATION OF THE AFRICAN

and (3) How to design efficient partnerships and structured financing to build the first two pillars.[105]

But how shall all these be achieved if our continent continues to swelter in conflicts and wars, corruption and money laundering, laziness and the placement of mediocre people in high places on the basis of nepotism, family connections and tribalism?

Conclusion

There are four mentalities that we must eliminate if we want to develop: the colonial mentality, the psychological legacy of the colonial era that is still present in our continent today – a form of direct or indirect dependence on the colonial masters. This is most prominently visible in Francophone Africa in the monetary, political, linguistic and military spheres. Then there is the mentality of laziness that must be eliminated. While students in other parts of the world are very much animated by the spirit of competition and excellence, by an incessant creative advancement into novelty, ours are very often comfortable with mediocrity, simply fine with validating courses, graduating with no skills that can enable them be entrepreneurial. The easiest things for our students to do seem to be posting videos on tiktok and other social media platforms; the new soft power that seems to suck the life of creativity out of our African youths. Next, we need to eliminate the mentality of tribalism, discriminating and favouring people on the basis of tribe and not merit. We need to enlarge our margins and go for merit. And finally, the mentality of socery and magic needs to be eliminated. We cannot develop with such a mindset.

There is, thus, a need for a new mentality, aided by an African based scientific revolution that would take into consideration our African realities. Only a proper education

---

[105] *Ibid.*, p. 3.

focused on critical thinking and problem-based-learning can user in this African-based scientific revolution. The scientific revolution, in the West, brought in a new cosmology, a distinct state of mind, a new view of the world. Thus, we must move from understanding and valuing human beings for who they are to being creative and able to use our available resources to transform our societies.

Bibliography

AKARE, A. J. & HANSON, J. H., "Legacies of the Past: Themes in Africa History", in *Africa*, GROSZ-NGATE M., HANSEN, J.H. & O'MEARA P., (eds.), 4th Edition, Bloomington: Indiana University Press, 2014.

AMEZQUITA, H., *Thought, The Greatest Power of All*, Marina Del Rey: Devorss Publications, 1997.

ANONYMOUS, "Lagos Plan of Action for the Economic Development of Africa, 1980 – 2000", Reprinted by the OAU, Addis Ababa, 1980.

BENNAARS, G., *Ethics, Education and Development*, Nairobi: East African Educational Publishers, 1993.

DELEHANTY, J., "Africa: A Geographic Frame", in *Africa*, Grosz-Ngate M., J.H. Hanson &P O'meara, (eds.), 4th Edition, Bloomington: Indiana University Press, 2014.

EINSTEIN, A., quoted by David P. Barash & Charles P. Webel, *Peace and Conflict Studies*, 3rd Edition, (California Sage Publications, 2014).

FINLAY, G., "The Emergence of Human Distinctiveness: The Genetic Story", in Malcolm Jeeves (ed), *Rethinking Human Nature"*, Michigan: William B. Eerdmans Publisning Company, 2011.

GROSZ-NGATE M., HANSEN, J.H. & O'MEARA P., (eds.), "Introduction", *Africa*, 4th Edition, Bloomington: Indiana University Press, 2014.

HOCKING, W. E., "The Struggle for Power and Peace", online at http://www.harvardsquarelibrary.org/IsGodNecessary/The-Struggle-for-Power-and-Peace.php, (page consulted on the 23rd of January 2022).

JAMES, G., S*tolen Legacy. Greek Philosophy is Stolen Egyptian Philosophy*, (The journal of pan African studies 2009 eBook), 112.

MUHULA, R. & NDEGWA S. N., "Development in Africa, Tempered Hope" in *Africa*, GROSZ-NGATE M., HANSEN, J.H. & O'MEARA P., (eds.), 4th Edition, Bloomington: Indiana University Press, 2014.

NJOKU, F. O. C., *Development and African Philosophy, A Theoretical Reconstruction of African Sociopolitical Economy*, New York: University, Inc., 2004.

NJOH, M. E., *Developper La Richese Humaine,* Yaounde: Cle, 1988.

REBOUL, O., *La Philosophie De L'Education*, 9e, Collection *Que Sais-Je ?*, Paris: Presse Universitaire de France, 2001.

RIFFERT, F. G., *A. N. Whitehead on Learning and Education*, (Newcastle: Cambridge Scholars Press, 2005.

RIST, G., *The History of Development From Western Origins to Global Faith*, (3rd Ed.,), Zed Books, London and New York 2008.

RODNEY, W., *How Europe Underdeveloped Africa*, Washington: Howard University Press, 1982.

ROTH, M., *Aims of Education Address*, Chicago: The University of Chicago, 2012.

WIREDU K., *Cultural Universals Particulars*, (Bloomington: Indian University Press, 1996).

WHITEHEAD, A. N., *The Aims of Education and Other Essays*, New York: The Free Press, 1967.

WHITEHEAD, A. N., *Science and the Modern World*, New York: The New American Library of World literature, inc., 1926).

YOSEF, B. J., *Black Man of the Nile*, New York: Alkebu-Lan Books, 1970.

ZOMAHOUN, T., "It's Time to Foster Africa's Science Revolution" in *OECD Observer*, www.oecdobserver.org | It's time to foster Africa's science revolution, March 2020, 2. (Page consulted on 21st of March 2023).

Wiredu's Idea of Conceptual Decolonization and the Decolonization of Epistemic Inquiry in Africa

Prof. Anselm Kole JIMOH, PhD., SS. Peter and Paul Catholic Major Seminary Bodija, Ibadan. jimohanselm@gmail.com.

Abstract

The aim of this paper is to employ the idea of conceptual decolonization to advance the argument for the need to decolonize epistemic inquiry in Africa. I argue that the conduct of epistemic inquiry following the dominant Western procedural methods and paradigms of evaluation is not entirely beneficial to knowledge practice in Africa. Even though knowledge is conceptually universal, the ways by which we arrive at our knowledge of reality is contextual because of the sociocultural factors and other relations that are incontrovertible components of epistemic inquiries. Therefore, any epistemic inquiry that does not take into account these components as part of its procedural method and/or thought process would not only be counterproductive to the cognitive goal of inquiry but also antithetical to our understanding of reality. Hence, the need for the decolonization of epistemic inquiry in Africa. To engage in the latter requires that we re-examine knowledge formation in Africa to divest it of undue Western (colonial) epistemologies, while we are careful at the same time, not to allow disagreeable aspects of traditional tribal cultures dictate modern African thought process. Wiredu's idea of conceptual decolonization provides reasonable grounds for this. In this paper, I adopt the qualitative method of analysis to: (i) critically analyze Wiredu's idea of conceptual decolonization, (ii) theorize epistemic decolonization in Africa, and (iii) argue that for genuine decolonization of epistemic enquiry in Africa, we must decolonize the African mind by decolonizing our curriculum of studies in Africa. The paper concludes by insisting that Wiredu's idea of conceptual decolonization is a call to reclaim the intellectual heritage of Africa that the single or monolithic and therefore, partial narrative of Western epistemologies have stifled over the centuries.

Keywords: Conceptual decolonization, Epistemic decolonization, Epistemic inquiry in Africa, Knowledge, Western epistemologies.

Introduction

Kwasi Wiredu's conceptual decolonization is an attempt to reclaim the intellectual heritage of Africa. Wiredu calls on African scholars to divest African thought of the foreign elements that have asphyxiated it, and deprived the African intellectual landscape of authentic African philosophy that is true to the lived experiences of Africans. His focus was on the uncritical use of foreign categories of thought in African inquiry because of the historical adversity of colonialism. Against this trend, Wiredu insists on eliminating from African philosophical thinking those undue influences from our colonial past that would not allow us produce a good African philosophy. His conceptual decolonization complements the project of epistemic decolonization, which seeks to dismantle the colonial matrix of power that have marginalized and subjugated epistemic practices of ex-colonized populations. The hegemonic tendency of Western epistemic practices fails to recognize that the conceptual universality of knowledge does not imply that all epistemic practices, regardless of its sociocultural contexts, must operate with the same methodology and paradigms of evaluation. For this reason, epistemic inquiry in Africa is boxed into employing the

procedural methods and paradigms of evaluation of Western
epistemologies if it must gain legitimacy. This is
counterproductive to the search for truth, just as it is antithetical
to an authentic African understanding of reality. To reverse this
situation, there is need for the epistemic decolonization of inquiry
in Africa. In this paper, I argue that Wiredu's conceptual
decolonization provides reasonable grounds for the project of
epistemic decolonization. To articulate my argument, I explicate
the ideas of conceptual decolonization and epistemic
decolonization. Thereafter, I examine why and how we can
engage in the epistemic decolonization of inquiry in Africa. Here,
I propose the decolonization of our curriculum of studies in
Africa, using the undergraduate curriculum of Philosophy in
Nigeria as a specific case. The proposal is hinged on the belief
that decolonizing our curriculum would contribute to
decolonizing our minds. My conclusion is that Wiredu's
conceptual decolonization provides the reasonable grounds and
direction for our project of decolonizing epistemic inquiry in
Africa.

Wiredu's Idea of Conceptual Decolonization

According to Kwasi Wiredu, conceptual decolonization is a
precondition for good African philosophy. By a good African
philosophy, he means a philosophy that is true and faithful to the
African culture and thought system, yet able to engage useful
insights from modern resources of knowledge and reflection
(Wiredu 2002, 54). Wiredu rightly claims that colonialism
occasioned conceptual entanglements in the thoughts of
contemporary Africans because of the intermixing of Western and
African intellectual categories. Colonialism was pursued with
some degree of violence that subjugated the cultures of the
colonized, even though it aspired towards modernity. The
colonizers considered the colonized inferior, as such, they
imposed their cultures and practices on the colonized, thereby,

subjecting the colonized populations to mental and psychological predicament, which has left them with a colonial mentality – the feeling of being culturally inferior to the colonizers. Contemporary African philosophy and intellectual life continues to suffer from the afflictions of this mentality, because it left indelible scars on the psyches of many Africans. Consequently, Africans have the tendency to overvalue what comes from the West for the simple reason that it comes from the West.

To undo the conceptual entanglements warranted by colonialism, Wiredu argues that we must condemn and eliminate colonial mentality in all its ramifications. For this project, he proposed the engagement of conceptual decolonization, which will enable us to establish the appropriate grounds to construct a philosophy that suits our present existence as Africans, through a rational reconstruction of African philosophical heritage. It will also enable us to understand the real visages of our philosophic inheritance. Conceptual decolonization would require that African philosophers engage in two complementary activities. The first one would be to avoid or reverse "the unexamined assimilation … of the conceptual frameworks embedded in the foreign philosophical traditions that have had an impact on African life and thought." And the second one is for us to judiciously exploit "the resources of our own indigenous conceptual schemes in our philosophical meditations on even the most technical problems of contemporary philosophy" (Wiredu 1995, 22).

The first requirement which is negative, is a necessary precondition for the second which is positive. It implies the elimination of the modes of conceptualization imposed on African thought through colonialism, which, because of our inaction against it, remains with us (Wiredu 2002, 56). Even though we consider it a negative requirement, it is the converse of the second requirement, which is positive. But as Wiredu explains, it has to come first because the idea of decolonizing itself is necessitated by our historical exigencies as Africans; namely, the imposition of foreign categories of thought on our thought systems. Therefore, if we are to effectively accomplish the positive requirement of conceptual decolonization, we must undo that which has subjugated and almost obliterated our indigenous modes of knowing. Wiredu identified language, religion and politics as the avenues by which colonialism superimposed foreign cultures and categories on African thought. I am going to dwell on the language avenue in this work, not because I disagree with religion and politics as avenues of superimposition of foreign categories and culture on African thought, neither do I consider them unimportant, but because I find the language avenue more germane to the cause of this paper.

Language was the fundamental means through which foreign culture and categories were imposed on African thought. According to Wiredu (2002, 56),

African philosophy, both in gestation and dissemination, is done mostly in Western languages. Languages (in their natural groupings) carry their own kinds of philosophical suggestiveness, which foreign as well as native speakers are apt to take for granted. If by virtue of a colonial history, you are trained right from the beginning in a foreign language and initiated thereby into the professing of philosophy, then certain basic ways of thought that seem natural to native speakers might become natural to you too.

Since it provides the tools for our thinking process, language inescapably determines our conceptual schemes and greatly influences the configuration of thought. Then as the principal means of communication it is a veritable avenue of transferring the content of thought from one interlocutor to another. To engage a foreign language in one's thought process, alienates the person from her own indigenous conceptual modes of knowing. Considering how fundamental language is in conveying conceptual schemes, if we must accomplish the project of decolonizing our conceptual framework, we must reverse our language of thought. In other words, we must disengage with Western languages and engage our indigenous languages in doing African philosophy. To this end, Wiredu provides a long list of philosophical concepts like: Reality, Being, Existence, Belief, Knowledge, Space, Time, Nothingness, etc., which he claims to be just part of the bunch of concepts that we can begin to think through in our vernacular as a recipe for decolonization. According to him, if we think about philosophical concepts in foreign languages, like English for instance, we would be thinking in English about these concepts. By this he meant, we would inadvertently be mentally de-Africanizing these concepts (Wiredu 1995, 23-24).

Wiredu acknowledges that it is not by any means easy to extricate ourselves from the foreign conceptual framework that colonialism has burdened us with. Because of the trajectory of our colonial past, we are mostly trained in the foreign languages of the colonizers, and having been introduced to philosophizing in their categories it has become natural to us to do philosophy in categories foreign to our native languages. There is a genuine possibility that we are not even "aware of the likely neo-colonial aspects of [our] conceptual framework" (Wiredu 2002, 56). This is certainly a concern because it is a great impediment to conceptual decolonization as we cannot begin to undo what we have not realized to be antithetical to a proper African philosophy. Our forebears in African philosophy were victims of this, when they provided accounts of African thought materials as perceived through their Western conceptual lenses.

Regardless of the above, Wiredu (2002, 57) believes that "the influence of language on philosophical thinking is not irreversibly deterministic, [since] it is possible for philosophers, if need be, to resist the suggestiveness of even their own languages or to become reflectively aware of it." The point here is that human beings are not imprisoned by language, they can operate within or above a language. This is what makes philosophical conversations possible between people of different cultures. When people from different cultures constantly interact, they become familiar with their different languages and philosophies. Therefore, if we are able to eliminate the error of racial superiority associated with colonialism, there can be a mutual interaction of ideas, which will bring us closer to the very motivation for conceptual decolonization. That is, to undo "the superimposition of Western intellectual categories on African cultural elements" (Wiredu 2002, 58).

The central point of Wiredu's conceptual decolonization is, therefore, to develop the right frame of mind to be authentically African in our understanding and interpretation of reality. Given that intellectual insights and/or error are not particular to any culture, conceptual decolonization does not advocate the repudiation of all foreign sources, because some of them can be intellectually edifying. It does not assume that everything African is true, profound and sound, neither does it permit overvaluation of everything Western. In this wise, I consider conceptual decolonization a plausible grounding to advance the necessity for epistemic decolonization of knowledge inquiry in Africa, which is what this paper seeks to do. But first, we need to theorize, for proper conceptualization, the notion of epistemic decolonization.

What is Epistemic Decolonization?

The core mandate of epistemic decolonization is to think outside the box of Western epistemic superiority, and thereof, affirm the legitimacy of African knowledge systems. Thus, as a project in African philosophy, with specific reference to epistemology, it seeks to dismantle the coloniality of knowledge. By the coloniality of knowledge, I refer to "the enduring legacy of colonialism in the global domain of knowledge" (Jimoh 2022, 423). Specifically, I refer to the state of affairs wherein, Western knowledge systems (which I will henceforth refer to as Western epistemologies), perpetuate the legacies of colonialism that subjugate ex-colonized populations, based on the false assumption that Western epistemologies possess the patrimony of truth and genuine knowledge. Coloniality of knowledge is derived from the theories of coloniality, power and ego-politics in intellectual inquiry within institutions of learning (Poloma & Szelēnyi 2019, 637). It is a form of "epistemic arrogance" in which alternative forms of knowledge, that is, non-Western epistemologies, are subalternated because they differ in thought and methodologies from the dominant Western epistemologies. The epistemic arrogance of Western epistemologies is grounded on the misconceived idea that Western methodologies and paradigms of evaluation are the most adequate, and the *only* means to access truth.

We should not collapse coloniality into colonialism, as they do not express the same phenomenon. Colonialism refers to the historical experience of political and administrative domination suffered by Africa and some other third world countries from the Western world. Although, it has since disappeared and most nations of the world are now politically and territorially independent, however, it left behind a suppressing influence on the cultures and epistemic practices of the ex-colonized that has developed into a profound and comprehensive structure of global power. This is what coloniality describes; the western domination established on the inferiorization of places, persons, knowledges and subjectivities. Thus, coloniality is an analytic concept that elucidates the power structure that evolved from colonialism, and has outlived colonialism through its continuing impact on culture, labor interpersonal relations, and knowledge practices. The distinction between colonialism and coloniality may be clearer if we conceive colonialism as a historical experience that is constitutive of coloniality, which means coloniality is not reducible to colonialism.

Ex-colonial authorities imposed their cultures and epistemic practices on their former colonies because they believed, even though wrongly, that they were superior. They dismissed indigenous cultures and knowledge practices as superstitious, uncritical and illogical. Thus, they assigned knowledge to their own Western systems of knowledge, and by doing so, indigenous cultures and modes of knowing were suppressed (Ndlovu-Gatsheni 2013). According to Eduardo Restrepo (2018, 3), the coloniality of knowledge hierarchizes knowledge into the authentic, and therefore, relevant, and the inauthentic, and therefore, irrelevant knowledge. The latter is inferiorized as ignorance or superstitions and silenced to the point of extinction. Based on these, the coloniality of knowledge does not explore the possibility of employing the methodologies and principles of knowledge systems considered inferior and irrelevant. Thus, the latter is maligned and not allowed to flourish. This is the predicament of African indigenous knowledge systems occasioned by the coloniality of knowledge. Epistemic decolonization in Africa is aimed at undoing this predicament by delinking with hegemonic Western epistemologies that discount non-Western epistemologies.

To address the epistemic wrongs of colonialism, epistemic decolonization investigates non-Western epistemologies, like traditional African modes of knowing, that were formerly colonized, with the intention to reconstruct them and establish their legitimacy (Dreyer 2017). To this end, epistemic decolonization challenges the dominance of Western epistemology, and advocates instead, a multicultural or polycentric epistemology that would allow intercultural communication and the exchange of experiences in epistemic inquiry. Epistemic decolonization interrogates these latent Eurocentric elements of colonialism in the dominant forms of knowledge in view of reconstructing the subjugated and silenced African knowledge systems. What this would require is a disinfection of our academic activities of the colonizing elements that have corrupting influence on truth which is the cognitive goal of epistemic inquiries.

Lerato Posholi (2020) identified two approaches to epistemic decolonization; the radical and the moderate approaches. The radical approach is the view that ex-colonized populations should fundamentally delink with Western epistemologies and engage reality from the point of view of their lived experiences. Considering the idea of epistemic privilege, advocates of this approach, like, Boaventura de Sousa Santos (2016) and Briana Toole (2019), argue that from their standpoint as marginalized and subjugated populations, ex-colonized people can engage the reality of their being in ways that Western scholars cannot, or may ignore. Even though this sounds plausible, its suggestiveness to completely reject Western epistemologies does not accord with the cause of multicultural epistemology. Instead, it would de-essentialize Western epistemology, only to essentialize non-Western epistemologies, at which point, non-Western epistemologies would become guilty of the hegemonic crime of Western epistemologies.

Walter Mignolo's (2003) argument provides a mitigation to the proposal of the radical approach. According to him, epistemic decolonization should be considered as a demand that we conduct inquiry outside or beyond the Western paradigms of evaluation, and not a complete rejection of Western epistemologies. The implication here, as Arturo Escobar (2004), points out is that epistemic decolonization is about the rejection of the elements in Western epistemologies that essentialize its evaluative paradigms as the *only* framework for authentic inquiry. A typical example of such essentializing elements of Western epistemologies is the dualistic ontological conception of reality that situates everything between idealism and materialism, or between rationalism and empiricism. The idea that whatever is outside these conceptions, like the communalistic idea of African ontology that grounds

African epistemologies is uncritical, is a reflection of the hegemonic tendency that is reminisce of colonialism.

The position of Mignolo introduces us to the moderate approach to epistemic decolonization. The view that despite the entanglements of Western epistemologies with the colonial tendencies towards domination, we cannot completely discard the ideas of Western epistemologies. According to Rajeev Bhargava (2013, 416), "we can neither ignore Western ideas nor fully show how they can be rescued from the pernicious effects of their own imperial imprint," because the reality of modern Africa, is that Africans have so internalized Western thought, that it would be impossible for us to think outside of its framework. Also, we cannot dismiss the fact that Western thought systems provide us with conceptual tools that can, in some ways, be useful in our engagement with reality and to comprehending the world (Posholi 2020, 6). Therefore, the moderate approach is that we should "critically engage Eurocentric thought within the context of our marginalized past – our cultures and forms of knowledge that colonialism subjugated" (Jimoh[b] 2022, 86). In this way, even though we engage the useful conceptual tools of Western epistemologies, we would be careful not to blindly accept the conclusions they lead us to. We must subject the motivations and goals that undergird their conclusions to critical interrogation to determine if they are edifying to African thought. Therefore, although we may engage the categories of Western epistemologies in African epistemic practices, we must scrutinize the categories and reconstruct them in the context of our lived experiences as ex-colonized people who have suffered marginalization and cultural subjugation.

I find the moderate approach to epistemic decolonization more plausible and realistic than the radical approach, and so I support and advocate moderate epistemic decolonization. We cannot undo the fact of history, namely, that we are a people whose contact with foreign cultures has diluted and altered our perception. To claim that this is not the case is pretentious and a denial of our present reality, just as it is unrealistic, to assume that we can totally disengage from them. It seems to me that the radical approach to epistemic decolonization has not taken into account how unrealistic it is to fundamentally disengage with Western conceptual thoughts. To the contrary, the moderate approach is open to the trajectory of our marginalized and subjugated past and open to new ways of perceiving reality, in so far, these new ways do not disregard, or distort our cultural values, beliefs and ways of understanding reality. Given the understanding of epistemic decolonization that I have presented, my concern now is, how do we proceed with the project of decolonizing epistemic inquiry in Africa. I would assume that a response to this would keep in view why, in the first place, we need to decolonize our epistemic inquiry.

Decolonizing Epistemic Inquiry in Africa

I want to address one of the issues I raised above, namely, why we need to decolonize epistemic inquiry in Africa. But let me make a few comments about epistemic enquiry and its subject matter, the concept of knowledge. Epistemic inquiry is about issues related to human knowledge; the sources, limits, transmission and validation or justification of knowledge. Although, knowledge is a universal concept that designates human understanding of the truths of reality (at least, in its general sense), however, how we derive these truths and validate their truthness, vary between sociocultural environments. In other words, even though what knowledge means does not depend on sociocultural, and/or other factors, its derivation and what counts as knowledge does. Because, the way people arrive at what they consider to be constitutive of knowledge depends on social, cultural and environmental factors and relations that inform their understanding and interpretation of reality. My emphasis is that there is no single or universal procedural method, and/or

paradigms of evaluation for knowledge. Therefore, no single
epistemic culture or form of knowledge can be correctly referred
to as *the only*, authentic form of epistemic inquiry, as the
dominant Western epistemologies purport to be.

Let me elucidate further the basis for this argument. Human
beings have a natural proclivity to interpret things according to
their backgrounds; namely, their historical antecedents (lived
experiences), cultural contexts, conceptual schemes and
worldviews. It is unrealistic to separate the knowledge of a people
from these contexts. Does this suggest that knowledge is
invariably relative, in the sense that the meaning of knowledge is
contextual? I do not think so. Whatever way we define
knowledge, either as justified true belief, as it is in Western
conception (although this definition has been highly contestable
in Western epistemology), or as a holistic and integrative
understanding of phenomena, as I conceive it from the African
epistemological perspective, knowledge connotes the same thing.
Namely, that the individual who claims to know is in possession
of the facts of the state of affairs that she claims to know.
Nonetheless, that the meaning of knowledge is not contextual, as
I tried to explicate above, the fact as I see it, is that the knower's
determination of what constitutes the facts of the state of affairs
she claims to know, is always dependent on factors that are
incontrovertible components of the knower's claim. Therefore,
whereas knowledge is not relative, the underlying presuppositions
of knowledge are relational to the history, culture and social
relations of people. And these contexts are not universal, they are
different from place to place. I have argued in a previous paper
that,

Lived experiences constitute ideation, cognition, and
consciousness, [therefore], how people make sense of the world
in which they live is based on their sociocultural contexts. An
individual's social environment constitutes the source of her
thinking because her thought is influenced by her experiences and

her community. This implies that human knowledge is situated; it is knowledge from a certain socially and culturally grounded position. Such sociocultural grounds are a given in society, and they exist prior to an individual's experience and representation of reality. They provide order, and shape the individual's cognitive experience, regardless of the sociocultural situatedness. They provide the individual with a natural way of interpreting reality (Jimoh[c] 2022, 2).

The point that I am establishing here is that there are fundamental differences between peoples' narratives about reality based on how their lived experiences allow them to conceive it. It does not seem to me that we can plausibly doubt or refute that our lived experiences implicate our epistemic inquiries, and these experiences cannot be replaced with the experiences of other people. Therefore, it is counterproductive to the quest for truth as the cognitive goal of inquiry, as well as antithetical to our knowledge of reality, when we do not take factors that are inalienable in epistemic inquiry into account.

Epistemic inquiry in Africa (which I prefer to describe as African communitarian epistemology (ACE), in order to underscore the communalism of African ontology on which it is established), recognizes, and takes into account, how sociocultural factors and other relations determine the formation of knowledge. Thus, epistemic inquiry in Africa considers knowledge as a derivative of the interaction between the agent and the object of cognition. Africans approach the world as a mind-independent reality which they come to know through the mind's association with the objects in the world. The latter impose themselves on the mind through the windows of the senses, and the mind assimilates them, conceptualizes, and interprets them based on the experiences, culture and environment of the agent (Jimoh and Jemibor 2020, 16-17). The African does not consider herself a separate entity from the world; she understands her being to be interconnected in a mutual relationship with others, the visible and invisible, the human and the spirit. Hence, Molefi Asante (2000) avers, and I agree with him, that there is an underlying sense of commonality that informs the African approach to the universe, the environment, society and the divine, it is indicative of the African idea of the unitiveness of existence. Whereas this notion of communality is reasonable to the African, it does not appeal to the linearity of the Western notion of reality that is characterized by an empiricism that depends solely on the operation of the senses. Consequently, unlike the communality of African thought wherein, all aspects of reality are interconnecting, and one aspect makes meaning only in relation to the other aspects of reality, the Western notion of reality is absorbed in the fixed and rigorous distinction between the rational and the empirical.

The foregoing is to establish that there is a fundamental difference between the Western and African conception of reality that are intrinsic to the procedural methods and evaluative paradigms employed in their epistemic inquiries. Western epistemic conceptions consider environmental, social and cultural relations antithetical to knowledge, but African epistemic conceptions consider these factors intrinsically linked to knowledge because they determine how we formulate and establish the validity of the truths of our beliefs. If we consider the diversity of the sociocultural backgrounds of human beings, the inescapable conclusion would be that it is not reasonable to essentialize a particular epistemic system as a universal paradigm of knowledge. If we do, as it is assumed with Western epistemologies, other forms of knowledge like African epistemic inquiry would always be disparaged as lacking the logicality and criticality for rational inquiry. Therefore, to objectify and superimpose Western epistemic conceptions as a one-for-all model is not only unjustified, it is not justifiable. It subjugates and destroys other forms of knowledge and their conceptual schemes, a situation that has been described as epistemicide, the killing of other, non-dominant forms or systems of knowledge (see Hall and Tandon 2017; Bennett 2007).

Epistemicide is an epistemic violence that consist in bullying non-dominant knowledge systems to follow the methodology of the dominant Western system of knowledge. Epistemicide closes the door on African epistemic inquiry and suffocates the epistemological and cultural heritage of Africa, but it validates Western epistemologies and its hegemonic role as the determiner of what counts as knowledge and what does not count as knowledge. It is an epistemic injustice that inferiorizes and subjugates African epistemic inquiry. To redress this epistemic injustice, we must purge African epistemic inquiry of those Western modes of conceptualization that are not beneficial to its flourishing, that is, the hegemonic elements of Western modes of thought that we have uncritically assimilated into our thought system. This is what Wiredu's conceptual decolonization and the project of decolonizing African epistemic inquiry is about.

Conceptual Decolonization and the Decolonization of Epistemic Inquiry in Africa

At this point, I turn to the question of how to decolonize epistemic inquiry in Africa. It seems to me that if we must engage in a genuine epistemic decolonization, we must first decolonize the mind of Africans. To do this, I propose the decolonization of our curriculum of studies in African institutions. Wiredu's conceptual decolonization correctly identified a historically peculiar situation that holds true, even till date, the fact that we are "brought up [intellectually] in Western-style educational institutions" (Wiredu 2002, 55). He further elucidates the implication of this by noting that our sources of learning are Western, and we conduct our philosophical researches and report our findings in Western languages. I want to emphatically add to what he has said that even the content of our educational curriculum is overladen with Western ideas. Let us take for consideration here, the curriculum for first degree in philosophy, as we have it in Nigeria.

In almost all the universities in Nigeria, out of over 40 philosophy courses only 6 courses (sometimes, less), are on African Philosophy and thought. This is true of the University of Ibadan, Federal University, Lafia, Ambrose Alli University, Ekpoma, University of Calabar, Nnamdi Azikiwe University, Awka, and University of Nigeria, Nsukka. Courses in the History of Philosophy are usually divided into four, viz. Ancient Philosophy, Medieval Philosophy, Early Modern Philosophy, Recent Modern Philosophy. The focus in these courses are on Western philosophies and philosophers. The same is applicable in the following courses: Introduction to Philosophy, Analytic Philosophy, Metaphysics, Philosophy of Value, and even Social and Political Philosophy. These are courses with significant African thought content but the course descriptions do not reflect these African content. A curious twist in Ancient Philosophy arises when we begin to consider why it is often dated to the Greek civilization, citing philosophers like; the Milesian thinkers, Socrates, Plato, Aristotle, the Sophists, Empedocles, Zeno, etc. What has happened to the ancient Egyptian civilization and their mystery schools where some of these notable names in Western philosophy have studied? Why are the thoughts of Ptahhotep, Imhotep, Akhenatem, ignored? Why do we attribute the popular ancient Egyptian precept from the Temple of Luxor, 'man know thyself' to Socrates? In the same vein, we study the thoughts of Descartes, Hume, Kant, Hegel, Heidegger, Husserl, Wittgenstein, Russell, Kuhn, Habermas, Gadamer, Rorty, Bradley, Gettier, Goldman, Sosa, Greco, Zagzebski, etc., But we neglect the thoughts of Tempels, Masolo, Mudimbe, Sogolo, Wiredu, Oruka, Oluwole, Makinde, Oladipo, Ogundowole, Asuzu, Iroegbu, etc. When, and if the latter set of philosophers are studied, their thoughts are considered as commentaries and criticized using Western ideas, methodologies and paradigms. Perhaps, we may argue that at graduate levels of study, where one makes a choice of the particular area of specialization, the African thought is studied in more depth by those who choose to major in the area. I disagree with this thinking on the grounds that the first degree is the foundation level where students need to be introduced to African thought. It is the formation stage of their inquiry and whatever they learn at this point goes a long way to expose their minds to the elements of colonialism that continue to linger in our systems of inquiry.

I think it is reasonable to consider that the content and style of an individual's education is fundamental to the kind of beliefs she holds, which invariably informs her attitude to life. Education as a process of transmitting the epistemic goods of knowledge and understanding, magnifies the individual's ability to reason and make judgements. In other words, it programs our thinking process and orientates our minds along particular directions. This implies that education is pivotal to the formation of our thought and the contents of our beliefs. Therefore, I consider it significant in the project of epistemic decolonization, because, if we are going to eliminate the uncritical assimilation of Western hegemonic ideas in African thought, we need a reorientation of mind. That is, we must recognize the fact that the Western ideas that are hegemonic are not beneficial to genuine inquiry authentic to the African world, that they do not provide reliable grounds for an authentic African conception of reality. In so far as we continue to believe that authentic epistemic inquiry can only be achieved following the methodology and paradigms of the West, we would continue to suffocate African thoughts and sustain epistemicide.

I do not consider an intellectual landscape, like our departments of philosophy in universities in Nigeria, that are saturated with courses whose primary contents are Western, a conducive intellectual environment for producing authentic African thought. That is why I argue that to decolonize epistemic inquiry in Africa, we need to begin by decolonizing our curriculum of studies which in turn would contribute to the decolonization of the minds of our potential intellectuals. Decolonizing our curriculum of studies implies that we should Africanize what we teach in our universities by making the contribution of African scholars, especially those who have attempted to divest their works of Western ideas, paradigms and methodology of analysis, the substantial part of our academic content. I do not assume that decolonizing our curriculum necessarily implies that we should completely remove anything Western in our curriculum. Recall that neither Wiredu's conceptual decolonization nor the moderate approach to epistemic decolonization that I advance in this work agree with a complete severance from whatever is Western. Recall also that decolonization of inquiry does not simply mean to de-Westernize.

I want to draw on the idea of humanizing pedagogy (see Oelofsen 2015, 144), to further my argument for the need to decolonize our curriculum. Humanizing pedagogy talks about a process of education that reinforces in the learner the dignity of her identity irrespective of the fascination of foreign ideas. It takes into consideration pedagogical practices that are aligned with, and validate the culture, language and lived experiences of the learner. The goal is to eliminate any ideas of inferiority, while also advancing the values of equity and social justice in the learner. I think if we Africanize our curriculum it would serve the purpose of humanizing pedagogy and contribute greatly to the decolonization of the mind, and therefore, the decolonization of epistemic inquiry in Africa.

Wiredu's conceptual decolonization and the moderate approach to epistemic decolonization share the same idea, which positions the former as a veritable framework in the project of decolonizing epistemic inquiry in Africa. Wiredu did not merely draw from extant decolonial literature, he explicates how the entanglements of concepts from Western and African culture can be a disservice to genuine African conceptualization of reality by emphasizing the influence of linguistic schemes as conveyor of thought. Thus, he argues that we should critically reflect on the concepts the foreign languages of the colonizers have enforced on us in our own African languages. A thorough review of their intelligibility in relation to the African context and culture would expose their plausibility, if they are plausible, or the problems associated with them (Wiredu 1995, 23). He carried out this experiment himself with the Cartesian concept of certainty in the Western epistemological debate on skepticism. He analyzed the conflation in the Western categories of "certainty" and "infallibility," as they relate to the discourse on skepticism. As he explains, this is a situation that would not arise in his African Akan linguistic schemes, where to say "I am certain" means that "I know very clearly." Or, to claim that something is certain generally translates as "it is indeed so." Neither "I know very clearly" nor "it is indeed so" can be easily equated with "it is infallible" in Akan linguistic schemes. The implication of this analysis, as Mary Carman (2016, 238) correctly expresses, is that, "a conflation between two terms that drives a contemporary English-language debate about skepticism is not likely to arise if the debate were taking place in Akan." Wiredu's explication of how Western conceptual categories can negatively influence African conception of phenomena establishes the theoretical grounds for the need to decolonize the conceptual categories employed in epistemic inquiry in Africa.

Conclusion

It goes without saying that the task of decolonization can be frustrating especially in the context of modernity that purports a global civilization. According to Sanya Osha (1999, 157), "[d]ecolonization ... is a painful ordeal because it necessitates the destruction of certain conceptual attitudes that inform our worldviews... it usually entails an arduous attempt at the retrieval of a more or less fragmented historical heritage." Even though I share Osha's sentiments about the complexities and difficulties associated with decolonization, I strongly believe that it is, nonetheless, the right thing to do, if a previously subjugated epistemic culture must take its rightful place and be duly recognized, in global epistemic practice. We cannot deny that ex-colonized people were excluded from dominant knowledge practices on the grounds that they lack the rational ability to aspire towards knowledge at its highest level. To put it simply, that they lack the analytic, logical and critical resources for genuine knowledge. This is a refusal by the colonizers to acknowledge the rationality of colonized people. Given that rationality is basic and inherent to the human person, to deny one's rationality is to deny her humanity. The aim of epistemic decolonization is to assert that ex-colonized people are not just rational, but also, have the capacity to fully exercise their rationality. In this way, it serves the complementary purpose of restoring their humanity as victims of a marginalized and subjugated group (see Matolino 2020, 3). The dominance of Western epistemic practices in our intellectual endeavors as Africans has stifled our intellectual heritage. Wiredu's conceptual decolonization is a genuine call on African scholars to reclaim this stifled intellectual heritage, just as it provides a direction for the epistemic decolonization of inquiry in Africa.

Bibliography

ASANTE, M. K. 2000. *The Egyptian philosophers: Ancient African voices from Imhotep to Akhenaten.* African American Images.

BENNETT, K. 2007. "Epistemicide! The Tale of a Predatory Discourse." *The translator*, 13, no. 2 (November): 151-169. https://dx.doi.org/10.1080/13556509.2007.10799236.

BHARGAVA, R. 2013. "Overcoming the Epistemic Injustice of Colonialism." *Global Policy*, 4, no. 4 (November): 413-417. https://doi.org/10.1111/1758-5899.12093.

CARMAN. M. 2016. "A Defence of Wiredu's Project of Conceptual Decolonization." *South African Journal of Philosophy*, 35, no. 2: 235-248. https://doi.org/10.1080/02580136.2016.1176349.

DREYER, J. S. 2017. "Practical Theology and the Call for Decolonization of Higher Education in South Africa: Reflections and Proposals." *HTS Theological Studies*, 73, no.4 (November): 1-7. https://www.doi/10.4102/hts.v73i4.4805.

ESCOBAR, A. 2004. "Beyond the Third World: Imperial Globality, Global Coloniality and Anti-Globalization Social Movements." *Third world quarterly*, 25, no. 1 (February): 207-230. https://doi.org/10.1080/0143659042000185417.

HALL, B. L. & TANDON R. 2017. "Decolonization of Knowledge, Epistemicide, Participatory Research and Higher Education." *Research for All*, 1 no. 1 (July): 6-19. https://doi.org/10.18546/RFA.01.1.02.

JIMOH, A. K. 2022. "Coloniality of Knowledge, Epistemicide, and the Imperative of Decolonization of African Epistemology." In *Truth in the Waters of Wisdom: Relevance of Old and New Fountains of Knowledge for our Time*, edited by F. Adedara and P. Akunne, 422-446. Ibadan: Kraft Books Limited.

JIMOH, A. K. 2022. "Decoloniality, Epistemological Decolonization and African Knowledge Practices." *Bodija Journal*, 12 (November): 77-96.

JIMOH, A. K., MOSES M. A. A. and PEACE O. J. 2022. "The Epistemology of African Sociological Knowledge Practices." In *The Oxford Handbook of Sociology of Africa*, edited by R. Sooryamoorthy and Nene Ernest Khalema. C2.S1- C2.S6. Oxford: Oxford Academic Online. https://doi.org/10.1093/oxfordhb/9780197608494.013.2.

JIMOH, A. K., 2018. "Reconstructing a Fractured Indigenous Knowledge System."*Synthesis Philosophica*, 33, no. 1 (2018): 5-22.

JIMOH, A. K., and PEACE O. J. 2020. "Knowledge Derivation in Thomistic and African Communitarian Epistemologies." *WAJOPS: West African Journal of PhilosophicalStudies*, 20 (November): 1-26.

MATOLINO, B. 2020. "Whither Epistemic Decolonization." *Philosophical Papers*, 49, no. 2: 1-19. https://doi.org/10.1080/05 568641.2020.1779605.

MIGNOLO, W. D. 2003. "Philosophy and the Colonial Difference." In *Latin American Philosophy: Currents, Issues, Debates*, edited by E. Mendieta, 80-86. Bloomington, IN: Indiana University Press.

NDLOVU-GATSHENI, S. J. 2013. *Empire, Global Coloniality and African Subjectivity*. Oxford:Berghahn Books.

OELPFSEN, R. 2015. "Decolonization of the African Mind and Intellectual Landscape." *Phronimon*, 16, no. 2 (January): 130-146.

OSHO, S. 1999. "Kwasi Wiredu and the Problem of Conceptual Decolonization." *Quest*, 13, no. 1-2: 157-164.

OLIVIER, B. 2019. "Decolonization, Identity, Neo-Colonialism and Power." *Pronimon*, 20, no. 1 (March): 1-18. https://doi.org/10.25159/2413-3086/3065.

POLOMA, A. W. and SZELÉNYI, K. 2019. "Colonilaity of Knowledge, Hybridization, and Indigenous Survival: Exploring Transnational Higher Education Development in Africa from the 1920s to the 1960s." *Compare: A Journal of Comparative and International Education*, 49, no. 4: 635-653. https://doi.org/10.1080/ 03057925.2018.1445962.

POSHOLI, L. "Epistemic Decolonization as Overcoming the Hermeneutical Injustice of Eurocentrism." *Philosophical Papers* 49 (2). 2020, 279304. https://doi.org/10.1080/05568641. 2020.1779604.

RESTREPO, E. 2018. "Coloniality of Power." In *The International Encyclopedia of Anthropology*, edited by Hilary Callan. John Wily & Sons Ltd. http://www.ram-wan.net. PDF.

SANTOS, Boaventura de Sousa. 2016. *Epistemologies of the South: Justice against Epistemicide*. Abingdon: Routledge.

SANTOS, Boaventura de Sousa. 2013. Reflections: Interview with Aram Ziai. *Development and Change*, 44, no. 3: 727-738.

TOOLE, Briana. 2019. "From Standpoint Epistemology to Epistemic Oppression." *Hypatia: A Journal of Feminist Philosophy*, 34, no. 3 (September): 598-618. https://doi.org/10.1111/hypa.12496.

WA THIONG'O, N. 1986. *Decolonizing the Mind: The Politics of Language in African Literature.*Nairobi: Heinemann.

WIREDU, K. 2002. "Conceptual Decolonization as an Imperative in Contemporary African Philosophy: Some Personal Refections." *Rue Descartes* 36 (June): 53-64.

WIREDU, K. 1995. *Conceptual Decolonizations in African Philosophy: 4 Essays.* Selected and Introduced by Olusegun Oladipo. Ibadan: Hope Publications.

Kwasi Wiredu, Jürgen Habermas and Alasdair Macintyre: Universals and Moral Relativism

Dr. John Mundua, AJ, Full-Time Lecturer Apostles of Jesus Institute of Philosophy and Theology, Nairobi – Kenya; Part-time Lecturer Tangaza Institute of Philosophy, Nairobi – Kenya; and Part-time Lecturer Consolata Institute of Philosophy, Nairobi – Kenya; johnmundua@gmail.com

Abstract

The Ghanaian philosopher Kwasi Wiredu argues that, in every culture there are cognitive and ethical standards that constitute what he terms as cultural universals. He arrives at the concept of cultural universals by engaging in a philosophical analysis of human communication and action. He finds out that the good and actions directed to achieving it are determined and universalised by human biology and articulated in human communication. Wiredu therefore concludes that the basis of cultural universals (ethical universals for that matter) is the common basic biology of humans as members of the same species, such that, his conclusion is a thesis of a kind of ethical naturalism. Another philosopher who examines human communication in an attempt to derive "ethical universals" is the German Philosopher Jürgen Habermas, who establishes the theory of communicative action. Like Wiredu, Habermas engages in the analysis of human communication and finds out that, the basic unit of linguistic meaning (speech act) is intersubjective in character and offers the potential grounding of consensus agreement about what is good. Thus, the good in Habermas' theory is determined by discourse that yields a consensual agreement. Meanwhile, the Scottish philosopher Alasdair Macintyre proposes a theory of tradition-constituted-ethical rationality as he strongly argues like Wiredu, for a derivation of the concept of the good from human biology. Therefore, like Wiredu, MacIntyre advances a form of ethical naturalism. However, the understanding of biology in MacIntyre is different from that in Wiredu. The former understands human biology in the Aristotelian teleological sense (Metaphysical biology) while the latter understands human biology apparently in the modern sense. This study is a commentary on the concepts of; the good, ethical universals and discourse in the three philosophers, and the problem of moral relativism.

Key words: Cultural universals, ethical naturalism, linguistic turn, Metaphysical-biology, moral relativism.

Introduction

In this paper we will examine the thoughts of Wiredu, Habermas and MacIntyre, with a particular attention on the articulation of ethical enquiry in each of these thinkers. In conclusion, we will analyse the differences in their various theories of ethical enquiry and examine them against moral relativism. The paper will unfold in four parts. In the first part, we will analyse Kwasi Wiredu's philosophical reasoning on the biological foundation of universal norms, his ethical naturalism and the ethical principle of sympathetic impartiality. In the second part we will turn to Habermas' theory of communicative action and discourse ethics. In the third part, we shall review MacIntyre's tradition-constitutive and tradition-constituting ethical enquiry. Next, we will turn to his ethical naturalism by critical and comparative analysis of social and metaphysical teleology. We will then examine the concept of human action in MacIntyre and its community foundation and orientation. We shall end the third part by analysing the functional understanding of the human moral agency in the naturalist ethics in MacIntyre. The fourth part of the paper is a discussion on moral relativism;

its nature and implication in moral reasoning, and an examination one after another, of the ethical theories in Wiredu, Habermas and MacIntyre against moral relativism.

Kwasi Wiredu[106]

One the theses in Kwasi Wideru's thought is the affirmation of what he calls cultural universals, through which human communication is possible. The nature and meaning of cultural universals is presupposed by the very fact of the possibility of human communication[107]. To explain the claim of the existence of cultural universals, Wiredu engages in a philosophical analysis of human communication. He defines human communication as "the transference of a thought content from one person or group of persons to another."[108] This definition brings out two aspects which he critically examines in the pursuit of explaining the concept of cultural universals. The first, is the *thought content,* and the second is, the medium of transfer/carrier of the thought content. The second, is a semantic unit (proposition-in a particular language) that is capable of being evaluated. The transfer takes place between two points. From, the persons who has thought content, to the receiver of the thought content. The delivered thought content has intelligibility that invites evaluation for falsity or truthfulness from the side of the receiver. From the above explanation, are deduced the fundamental presuppositions,

---

[106] Kwasi Wiredu is a Ghanaian, considered one of the greatest pillars in African philosophy. After elementary education in his native country, he attended Oxford University and studied under the renowned British philosopher of mind Gilbert Ryle. The studies under Ryle significantly influenced his mature philosophical writings in that, he exhibits thoroughly the tenets of analytic philosophy (see, The Palgrave Handbook of African Philosophy, 61).

[107] Kwasi Wiredu, *Cultural Universals and Particulars: An African Perspective* (Bloomington and Indianapolis: Indiana University Press, 1996), p. 13.

[108] Kwasi Wiredu, *Cultural Universals and Particulars: An African Perspective* (Bloomington and Indianapolis: Indiana University Press, 1996), p. 13.

which are the essential conditions of communication. They are the presuppositions of; shared meaning, objectivity of concepts and conceptual constructs, without which communication is not possible[109]. For example, two people can only interact when there is a shared meaning of the content of what they talk about. The thought content is a product of conceptualisation, while the carrier of the thought content is semantic articulation. The first pertains to the cognitive realm, while the second to the linguistic realm. Thus, in Wiredu's analysis, communication is both cognitive and linguistic.

The cognitive dimension of communication is the result of conceptualisation. According to Wiredu, concept formation is the refinement of the capacity of humans to react to the environment, which is characteristic of all living things[110]. The basic response to the environment by living things, is the instinctual drive for equilibrium and self-preservation. This basic level of response is found in the lower animals, but perfected in humans. The humans go beyond the instinctual drive in their response to environment by means of; reflective perception, abstraction, deduction, and induction[111]. Reflective perception refers to the awareness applied to objects and situations encountered by humans due to their consciousness. Wiredu implicitly thereby underlines the nature of humans that differentiates them from other living things, namely, consciousness.

Biological Foundations of Universal Norms

The intelligibility of thought content between two parties in communication implies that, they are able to evaluate it. Wiredu

---

[109] Kwasi Wiredu, *Cultural Universals and Particulars: An African Perspective* (Bloomington and Indianapolis: Indiana University Press, 1996), p. 14.

[110] Kwasi Wiredu, *Cultural Universals and Particulars: An African Perspective* (Bloomington and Indianapolis: Indiana University Press, 1996), p. 22.

[111] Kwasi Wiredu, *Cultural Universals and Particulars: An African Perspective* (Bloomington and Indianapolis: Indiana University Press, 1996), p. 23.

then establishes the standards by which the thought content is evaluated. Such standards should be known and acceptable to both parties. Otherwise, they are the necessary condition for intersubjective communication that make interaction with others possible[112]. Wiredu asserts that the source of the standards, which he refers to as common norms of thought cannot be in things that account for diversity in humans, such as, history, culture or ideology, but rather in something that accounts of human commonality. The human commonality for Wiredu is the basic human biology. For this claim, Wiredu's thought can be categorised as naturalist. It argues that not only human experience but also the universal norms for human action are accounted for on the basis of human biology[113]. Therefore human biology is the basis of the universal norms of knowledge and morality in Wiredu. He argues that epistemological and moral universality in humans is founded on human biology, not just in the sense of the human bodily constitution but more in the sense of how human corporeality mediates moral values as standards of regulation in living with others. Thus, for Wiredu human corporeality is relational. He holds that certain logical and moral standards are common to all humans in all cultures just by the virtue of their human *qua* human being[114]. It can be deduced from his thought that both truth and the moral law are not acquired a prior from a transcendent source[115]. Instead, they emerge from the human capacity to draw conclusion for experience.

In his epistemological naturalism, Wiredu apparently holds a theory that is contrary to what is technically referred to as the

---

[112] Kwasi Wiredu, *Cultural Universals and Particulars: An African Perspective* (Bloomington and Indianapolis: Indiana University Press, 1996).

[113] Adeshma Afolayam and Toyin Falola, eds. *The Palgrave Handbook of African Philosophy* (USA: Palgrave Macmillan, 2017), p. 65.

[114] Barry Hallen, *A Short History of African Philosophy* (Indiana: Indiana University Press, 2002), p. 25.

[115] Adeshma Afolayam and Toyin Falola, eds. *The Palgrave Handbook of African Philosophy*, p. 66.

objectivist's theory of truth, which presents truth as an independent property of a timeless and transcendent fact that humans must strive to acquire[116]. In Wiredu's theory, truth is something discovered, known, and defended by a human being from some perspective and in a specific time[117]. Thus, truth can be described as opinion. What Wiredu strive to underline through these assertions is that truth is a fact qualified from human perception and rational enquiry, rather than something given from a transcendental reference source. However, he defends himself against the relativist tag. According to him, to say that truth emanates from human agency based on human biology does not imply that, the knowledge of truth can degenerate into subjectivism and relativism. Otherwise, describing truth as opinion is not meant to be in a narrow and subjective sense. In Wiredu opinion means a firm thought and he describes it as a 'considered opinion'. The notion of considered opinion means that such opinion must be entertained from some wider point of view and guaranteed because it emanates from an intersubjective context and grounded on some commonly shared standards of rational enquiry[118]. It is the intersubjective character of considered opinion that Wiredu uses to defend his thought against the accusation of sliding into subjectivism and relativism.

Ethical Naturalism

What has been discussed in the preceding part constitutes what can be referred to as Wiredu's epistemological naturalism. We can now turn to look at his ethical naturalism i.e. how he derives the moral standards from human biology. Before delving into Wiredu's moral theory, it is paramount to understand the relationship between epistemology and morality. Epistemology

---

[116] Barry Hallen, *A short History of African Philosophy*, p. 23.

[117] Barry Hallen, *A short History of African Philosophy*.

[118] Barry Hallen, *A short History of African Philosophy*, p. 23.

involves the description of the content of our awareness of the truth. However, morality requires that we describe such awareness with honesty. Another relationship between the two is that epistemology presents to us the truth, while morality requires us to choose the good and act in pursuit of the good according to the truth. One can therefore relate Wiredu's theories of naturalistic epistemology and morality. Any moral theory must answer the question; how ought one act such that his action can be judged as morally justifiable? The answer to this question can be established in the moral theory that Wiredu advances. His moral theory is based on what humans are as members of the species *homo sapiens*. This is a radical shift from traditional moral theory that is derived from, for example, commands of supernatural sources, utility, deontology etc.[119]

In his moral theory, Wiredu takes human biology as those which accounts for human experience and moral laws. He distinguishes between two distinct sets of moral rules that regulate human conduct. The first set of moral rules is what he refers to as strict moral rules. They are characteristically objective and immutable. The second set is broad moral rules, which are contingent and mutable. Strict moral rules and broad moral rules are equated to Wiredu's cultural universal and particulars respectively. Strict moral rules are the moral statements that ought to be true in all human cultures because they embody transcendental moral truth, meanwhile broad moral rules are contextual and culture bound[120]. The next question to be asked is; how does Wiredu then derive moral theory from human common basic biology?

---

[119] Adeshma Afolayam and Toyin Falola, eds., *The Palgrave Handbook of African Philosophy*, p. 68.

[120] Motsamai Molefe, *An African Philosophy of Personhood, Morality and Politics* (Switzerland: Palgrave Macmillan, 2019), p. 99.

Principle of Sympathetic Impartiality

In Wiredu's ethical naturalism, the moral principle arises from human behaviour. He argues that humans have interests, some of which are common and others are conflicting. For coexistence to be possible, they need to reconcile the conflicting interests. Such reconciliation is the ethical priority to harmonise individual interest with the interest of others. The tendency to reconciliation is what Wiredu formulates into a principle that he refers to as the principle of sympathetic impartiality. This moral principle is based on basic, natural and universal human attribute of sympathy for their own species, stated as "it is always good to act in such a way as to avoid doing things, that have effects on others that one would not welcome if one would be in the situation of those in an otherwise identical re-enactment of the action"[121]. The statement of the moral principle of sympathetic Impartiality is similar to the Christian golden rule "do to others what you would expect them to do unto you". It is also similar to Kantian categorical imperative.

Whereas in Kant, the categorical imperative is a law already written in the nature of humans and comes into play in the operation of reason and will, in Wiredu's principle of sympathetic impartiality, morality is understood as a function in the relational nature of the human *qua* human being as a species. If Wiredu views morality as function in the relational realm of human life, then context, and especially cultural context is important in the principle of sympathetic partiality. This is not the case in Kant. For Kant, social context plays a role only in providing the conditions in which the sense of moral duty is natured. In Wiredu, the social condition of humans is the casual context of the moral awareness of sympathetic impartiality[122].

---

[121] Kwesi Wiredu, *Cultural Universals and Particulars*, p. 41.

[122] Adeshma Afolayam and Toyin Falola, eds., *The Palgrave Handbook of African Philosophy*, p. 68.

Jürgen Habermas[123]

Habermas ushers in a new paradigm of discourse of truth in the history of western metaphysics, popularly referred to as the linguistic turn. It is constituted by his thesis that, language is the historical and cultural embodiment of the human mind and therefore, a correct method of analysis of mental activity begins with the analysis of the linguistic expression as opposed to beginning with immediate analysis of the intentional phenomena as in the consciousness paradigm held by traditional metaphysics. Habermas shifts the cidatel of rationality from propositional to the illocutionary component, such that the attachment of the validity conditions of truth claims to the propositional component is loosened[124]. In order to understand Habermas' argument, let us consider the question of the possibility of objective knowledge and truth in the linguistic medium of reasoning. There are two possible positions in this regard. First, is what can be termed as objectivist position. It posits truth as an independent reality towards which different interpretations and articulation in languages finally converge. The second, is the relativistic position, which holds that every possible description only mirrors a particular construction of reality that inheres grammatically in a language. The relativist position intends to assert that truth does not stand independently outside the linguistic expression of a particular language community. In these two positions, the starting point is either reality or language.

The limitation of the first position is that, the gap between language and the truth that is posited independently outside language, renders problematic to defend the position. Language is limited by the context that it sets for its use. To arrive at truth,

---

[123] Jürgen Habermas is a German philosopher and social theorist, who is a key protagonist of the Frankfurt school, and famously known for his theory of discourse ethics.

[124] Jürgen Habermas, *Postmetaphysical Thinking*, William M. Hohengarten, trans. (Massachusetts: Massachusetts Institute of Technology Press, 1992), p. 75.

a particular language has therefore to break off from the confinement of context. Otherwise, a trans-contextual leap to truth would be an absurdity. Yet, on the other side, if we begin from reality (truth), it is still problematic to defend the position. Otherwise, truth has an imposing quality of unity (cannot be divided into perspectives of individual languages). It is transcendental i.e., transcends the linguistically created contexts. According to Habermas, we should find a position that lies between language and reality as a starting point. The starting point according to him should be the formal analysis of language that is not restricted to semantics but extended to its pragmatic dimension[125]. This process leads us to formal pragmatics of language, which are the presuppositions that guide linguistic exchanges between speakers and hearers of any language in every day conversation. It means that linguistic utterances are used in everyday communication as claims of validity, thanks the role of formal pragmatics of every language[126].

Habermas refers to the formal pragmatics as the universal pragmatics. They are universal in the sense in which they apply to every speaker of a particular language. The universal pragmatics are therefore understood as the general presuppositions of communication in a particular language. Their role is to identify and reconstruct universal conditions in communication in a particular language, of possible mutual understanding (*verständigung*)[127].

The universal pragmatics therefore render communication to be an activity that is oriented towards mutual understanding. Understanding brings about an agreement (*einverstandnis*) which

---

[125] Jürgen Habermas, *On the Pragmatics of Communication*, Maeve Cooke, ed. (Massachusetts: MIT Press, 1998), p. 2.

[126] Jürgen Habermas, *On the Pragmatics of Communication*, Maeve Cooke, ed. (Massachusetts: MIT Press, 1998), p. 3.

[127] Jürgen Habermas, *On the Pragmatics of Communication*, Maeve Cooke, ed. (Massachusetts: MIT Press, 1998), p. 23.

terminates in the intersubjective mutuality or reciprocal comprehension, shared knowledge, mutual accord among the speaker and the hearer[128]. Without such reciprocal comprehension, communication would not be possible in the first place. Thus, communication is an action that presupposes an idea of undistorted inter-subjectivity, which is expressed in mutual comprehension and understanding between subjects in communication[129]. Communication works by a kind of pressure that drives the participants to understanding by reaching agreement. In it there is an irresistible pressure to cooperate which the participants cannot escape[130]. The analysis of universal pragmatics therefore reveal that communication is constituted by consensual speech acts and the claims to right and wrong are implicit in communication. The speech act as an action takes place against a background of mutually recognised values, norms, rules and conventions[131]. This leads us to interrogate ethical rationality in Habermas.

Communicative rationality

Habermas takes a position regarding truth, expressed by the theory of communicative rationality, which according to him is neither relativistic nor upholding the idealizing concept of truth. The theory of communicative rationality describes human rationality as an outcome of successful communication, in which the speech acts of the participants are consensually coordinated, and the agreement reached is evaluated in terms of the

---

[128] Jürgen Habermas, *On the Pragmatics of Communication*, Maeve Cooke, ed. (Massachusetts: MIT Press, 1998), p. 21.

[129] Jürgen Habersmas, *Religion and Rationality: Essays on Reason, God and Modernity*, Edwardo Mendieta, edit. (London: Polity Press, 2002), p. 82.

[130] Judith Butler, Jürgen Habermas, Charles Taylor and Cornel West, *The Power of Religion in the Public Sphere*, Edwardo Mendieta and Jonathan Vanantwerpen, edits. (New York: Columbia University Press, 2011), p. 115.

[131] Thomas McCarthy, *The Critical Theory of Jürgen Habermas* (Massachusetts: MIT Press, 1978), p. 325.

intersubjective recognition of validity claims[132]. According to this theory, the potentials of certain kinds of reason is inherent in communication itself and therefore, reason is concerned with the clarification of norms and procedures by which agreement can be reached. The participants in communication are in consensual agreement, and they make validity claims to; truth, rightness, and truthfulness[133]. It therefore holds a view of reason as public opinion. The elements that constitute communicative rationality are; first, discussion, which refers to the process by which speakers of a language engage in argumentation with the aim of reaching a consensus. Consensus is regarded as the objective-correct outcome of the discussion, namely, the truth. Second, inter-subjectivity. By its nature, communicative rationality is oriented towards consensus building, and therefore inter-subjectivity is a necessary condition for validity. Third, speech-act. It is the validity-claim that a sentence uttered in a particular language context raises, which attracts appraisal and anticipates the unconstrained discussion needed to resolve that status of claim. Fourth, consensus. Its refers to the accomplishment of the communicative reasoning. Communicative reasoning is dialogical and a multilateral thinking that ends in a consensus that has the status of truth.

We can clarify further what communicative action is by distinguishing it with what Habermas refers to as strategic action in communication. According to Habermas, strategic action seeks to influence the behaviour of the listener (others) by means of threat of sanction or the prospects of gratification in order to cause the inter-subjective interaction to flow in the direction desired by the speaker (actor)[134]. Whereas, in communicative action the

---

[132] Jürgen Habermas, *Moral Consciousness and Communicative Action* (Massachusetts: MIT Press, 1990), p. 58.

[133] Jürgen Habermas, *Moral Consciousness and Communicative Action* (Massachusetts: MIT Press, 1990).

[134] Jürgen Habermas, *Moral Consciousness and Communicative Action* (Massachusetts: MIT Press, 1990).

speaker seeks to motivate the listener (or others) rationally by using the illocutionary bonding effect (*bindungseffekt*) that the speech act offers. In other words, the actor persuades the others to reason with him in order to reach a consensus. In that way, communicative action also serves for the transmission of culturally stored knowledge. Cultural tradition is replicated through communicative action oriented towards consensual understanding[135].

Discourse Ethics

Habermas subscribes to a moral rationality that is based on his theory of communicative reasoning, called discourse ethics. Some second sources about Habermas thought refer to it as communicative ethics. It is an ethical rationality that is grounded on the fundamental norms of communicative action, and therefore it is consensual in character[136]. Habermas' discourse on consensual ethics has Kantian influence. Just like Kant, he considers the respect of autonomous moral agent at the centre of moral reasoning. However, the difference between Kant and Habermas lies in the fact that, for the former the respect for autonomous moral agent is considered in subjectivist sense, whereas for the later, it is considered in dialogical sense. Thus, comparatively in Habermas is found a revision of Kantian ethical rationality where there is a shift of the frame of reference from the solitary reflecting moral consciousness to the community of dialoguing subjects[137]. Practical moral reasoning in Habermas discourse ethics is dialogical, involving the community of moral agents within the same context engaging in discussion to determine the good and what actions are considered to be good action, through consensus. The role of discourse is to deliver

---

[135] Jürgen Habermas, *The Theory of Communicative Action: A Critique of Functionalist Reason*, Vol. 2., Thomas McCarthy, trans. (Boston: Beacon Press, 1981), p. 63.

[136] Thomas McCarthy, *The Critical Theory of Jürgen Habermas*, p. 325.

[137] Thomas McCarthy, *The Critical Theory of Jürgen Habermas*, p. 326.

consensus about which interests are generalizable. The individual desires, needs and interests are not excluded, otherwise consensus is sought precisely to accommodate them[138]. Once a consensus is reached about a moral judgement, consensus is sought it is then considered on all those who take part in the discourse. In other words, a moral norm is considered valid when its foreseeable consequences and effect of its observance for the interest and value of each individual member is jointly accepted by all in the discourse, without force.

Therefore, the principle of universalization of moral judgement in Habermas discourse ethics is the consensus agreement. To arrive at consensus that is to treated valid, Habermas' theory lays down three conditions as follows; first, there must a discourse. Second, there must be a moral statement of the semantics of unconditional norm on which discourse takes place, which binds all those who subscribe to it once a consensus is reached. Third, there must be an articulation of the pragmatics of discourse. Thus, the principle of universalization of morality is not the requirement that moral norms must take the form of unconditionally universal 'ought' statements[139]. Valid moral norms arrived at by consensus become foundation of egalitarian community of autonomous agents. In such an egalitarian structure, the moral judgement of an individual agents counts reasonable if it is a product of participating in discourse with all those affected. In this way, the validity of moral judgement does not simply mean that one seeks the input of others in forming a moral conscious, but the agent solicits the consensus of other agents in the moral discourse[140].

Generally, Habermas' discourse ethics is a form of critique of the 'monological' presupposition of the Kantian ethics. In

[138] Thomas McCarthy, *The Critical Theory of Jürgen Habermas*, p. 327.

[139] Jürgen Habermas, *Moral Consciousness and Communicative Action*, p. 64.

[140] Jürgen Habermas, *Moral Consciousness and Communicative Action*.

Habermas' ethics, rationality and universality of maxims of action are not decided by solitary reflecting moral consciousness. They are instead ascertained through dialogue in unrestricted and unconstrained intersubjective discourse. Thus, in Kantian ethics, what each can will without contradiction becomes a general law, whereas in Habermas' discourse ethics, what all can will in agreement becomes the universal norm. According Habermas, a rational will is not something that can be certified and secured privately as in Kantianism, but it rather something inextricably bound to communication process in which it emerges as a common will that is both 'discovered' and 'formed'[141].

Alasdair MacIntyre[142]

Tradition-constitutive and tradition-constituting ethical enquiry

MacIntyre stands out for his sharp critique of modern ethical enquiry and his proposal of tradition-based ethical enquiry as an alternative. He argues that moral concepts (including the concept of the good), principles and practices can only be understood by learning from their historical and social context[143]. By history and social context, MacIntyre refers to more or less the same thii.e., the social sphere in which ethical concepts are not only formulated but also their meanings and interpretations are embedded. In the MacIntyrean thought, ethical concepts and principles are constitutive of forms of life in such a way that, understanding them is part and parcel of understanding the society in which they are embedded and vice versa. It is in a social context that ethical enquiry and contestation regarding practical reasoning

---

[141] Thomas McCarthy, *The Critical Theory of Jürgen Habermas*, p. 326.

[142] Alasdair MacIntyre is an American-Scottish contemporary Aristotelian-Thomistic philosopher famously known for his sharp critique against modernity.

[143] Alasdair MacIntyre, *A Short History of Ethics*, p. 1-2.

are advanced, modified, abandoned and replaced. There is no other way to engage in formulation, elaboration, rational justification and criticism of accounts of ethical reasoning if not from a particular ethical tradition through conversation, cooperation and conflict among members who share the same tradition[144]. Therefore, MacIntyre characterises as illusory the thinking which sustains the thesis that, ethical concepts are fixed, universal, transcended and non-discursive in such a way to imply that their meaning can be interrogated outside a historical context[145].

Ethical reasoning in its entirety is community framed and for that reason, it is a form of social agreement, which gives form to ethical authority that prescribes what is good and evil[146]. Thus, ethical reasoning is not merely a mental process in accordance with the basic rules of logic, but includes the justification of ascription by the individual to the self, others and the community framed system to which the individual ascribes belief. The self of the individual is therefore an important component in ethical inquiry according to MacIntyre. However, it is not the isolated self in the modern Cartesian sense but the one inserted in history and consequently acquires a personal history. In MacIntyre's thought, the personal history is only intelligible to the self in its being part of the larger history of the community. Thus, personal history constitutes a critical component of ethical enquiry, yet personal history is itself comprehensible if and only if it remains part of the history (socio-cultural context) of the community to which the individual belongs.

Since ethical enquiry is history and tradition bound, we can talk of plurality of ethical rationalities that come to be determined by peculiarity of history and tradition. In MacIntyre's thought, a

---

[144] MacIntyre, *Which Justice, Whose Rationality?*, p. 350.

[145] MacIntyre, *Epistemological Crisis*, p. 5.

[146] MacIntyre, *Secularization and Moral Change* (London: Oxford University Press, 1967), p. 37.

person who stands outside all traditions cannot engage at all in any ethical enquiry since such a person will lack the resources for the enquiry to begin with in the first place. Thus, the thesis of a neutral locus without any tradition for ethical reasoning is an illusion. Human relationship in the community is therefore an essential component of ethical reasoning in MacIntyre's theory of moral enquiry. Though there can be differences due to particularity and peculiarity of social-historical contexts, professional moral philosophers and non- philosophers ask the same existential questions about the nature and significance of human life and what is good for it[147]. What varies is the context in which such questions are raised, the attempts to give answers to them and the acceptance and rejection of the proposed answers to them.

Social and Metaphysical Human teleology

In MacIntyre's characteristically Aristotelian ethical enquiry, the point of departure is the question; What is the purpose of human life? In other words, what is the purpose of 'being' human? It is in the answer to the question that the concept of the good and any ethical principle is derived. According to MacIntyre, the question can be intelligibly asked and answered only in the context of a moral tradition embedded in the community. Its answer can as well be pursued only within a complex social order where human being occupy roles and functions in various ways. For example, one cannot intelligibly ask whether X is a good father, judge, lawyer, etc. unless one first knows what fathers, judges and lawyers are supposed be and do and what kind of society is a good one. But then, in order to understand what a good person living in a good society is, we should first understand what it means to be human. This implies the understanding of the ultimate meaning of human life. For

---

[147] MacIntyre, *Three Rival Versions of Moral Enquiry*, p. 127.

MacIntyre, we can have a coherent ethical discourse only if we understand what it means to be a human being. We can then correctly proceed to ask the question What does it mean to be a good person and to be a good action to engage in? only after having understood the fundamental meaning of 'being' human. Thus, his theory of ethical reasoning progresses from a social to a deeper and more fundamental metaphysical teleology.

In the first part, he expounds a theory of ethical reasoning that is essentially social. He develops a theory that emphasizes the communal dimension as necessary for the intelligibility of human action in an ethical rationality. However, in that theory, a coherent ethical discourse ultimately requires the understanding of the meaning of what it means to be human. Then we can proceed to pursue what is means to be a good person and what actions can be characterized as good. His argument is that a good person or action is defined in relation to the understanding of what it essentially means to be a human being. It also entails the understanding of the concept of the good as the end of human action and human life at large. The good understood as the end of human action ultimately entail the good as the end of 'being' human. But the concept of the good and the resources for discerning it can only be acquired in the community. Therefore, MacIntyre's theory of the end as the good is first sociological. It is first about the good desired by an agent as a member of the community, which enshrines a tradition of ethical enquiry in which the agent shares. The good is defined and rendered intelligible by that ethical tradition enshrined in the community. Thus, the good is understood in the first sense as a cultural universal of a particular community to which the agent belongs. In should be noted that "MacIntyre assumes that one tradition can indeed show itself to be superior to others, but because of the incommensurability of their criteria, different traditions cannot communicate seriously with each other or even learn from each other"[148]. Second, the end as the good is metaphysical and it is derived from the functional understanding of human nature. It emerges from the fundamental question 'What does it mean to be human?' The end as the good is grounded on the metaphysical understanding of the nature of the human 'being'.

The Community and Human Action

One of the themes in MacIntyre's ethical enquiry is that of human action, which he describes as an interplay between human desire and the *end* (good) towards which the desire is directed[149]. Against the psychoanalytic theory and the theory of mid-twentieth century social sciences, MacIntyre argues in defence of Aristotelian-Thomistic thesis that human action is *end* oriented[150]. He rejects the Freudian "causation and effect" mechanistic model of human behaviour as a correct explanation of human action. He equally rejects the Hobbesian, Hume's and Kantian views about human action, which portray the will as a kind of efficient and necessary cause of human action. He argues that the anthropological foundation of both mechanistic and deterministic theories of human action is the Cartesian dualism that he refutes in the first place[151]. MacIntyre's theory of human action is instead based on the conception of human nature that integrates the body and soul in an immediate substantial unity. So, the good as the

---

[148] Jürgen Habermas, *The Liberating Power of Symbols: Philosophical Essays*, Peter Dew, trans. (Massachusetts: MIT Press, 2001), p. 34.

[149] MacIntyre, *Ethics in the Conflicts of Modernity*, p. 1.

[150] MacIntyre understands human action as freely chosen by the agent in order to accomplish goals that the agent pursues. Whereas human behaviour as understood by the mid-twentieth century determinist social scientists is an outward activity of the subject that is said to be caused entirely by environmental influences that are beyond the control of the subject.

[151] The Cartesian dualism conceives human nature as separate entities of body and soul. Thus, on one side, human action is interpreted as mere effect on physiological and neurological causes in the body. On the other side, human action is interpreted as consciousness that sets in motion human movements (*See*, MacIntyre, *"Antecedents of Action"*, 193).

end of human action is explained in relation to that nature as a substantial unity. The point underscored in MacIntyre's theory of human action is that, the interpretation of the reason for human action cannot be merely mechanical but rather teleological since it is end oriented. The end cannot be understood separately from the role of belief and knowledge of the agent. More so, it is the community of which the agent is a part that offers and characterizes in its own terms the resources for the explanation of the agent's beliefs. Therefore, it is through social relationships and participation in tradition embedded practices that moral agents come to form beliefs and understand the end for which they act.

MacIntyre's position is that the human agent understands the end (good) desired through shared rational deliberation and action of members of the community embedded in the ethical tradition of the said community of which the agent is a part. In the same way, excellence in judgement about the good and action are developed through participation in the life of the community[152]. MacIntyre's theory of human action is also narrative. It means human action is intelligible in so far as it is considered as part of a whole story that is embodied in the life of the agent, just like a single plot in a play can only be intelligible in reference to the whole play[153]. A single human action is intelligible only in virtue of its relatedness to the sequence of actions of which the action in question is a part, and in relatedness of that sequence to the web of different other sequences that constitute different transactions of the agent. Thus, for an action to be intelligible, it should be considered in relation to the agent's antecedent states and relationships to others in the community[154].

---

[152] MacIntyre, *Dependent Rational Animals*, chapter 8.

[153] MacIntyre, "Can One Be Unintelligible to Oneself?"

[154] To say that human action is intelligible only if considered in a narrative form is to say that it constitutes not only a chronicle without an ascribed end, but that it simultaneously constitutes the plot of the narrative and the occasion which exhibits

The narrative understanding of human action entails ascribing the end as that which constitutes the best reason for the agent to execute the action in a situation in such a way that, others are capable of appraising it as that which constitutes the best reason for acting. In other words, the intelligibility of human action in MacIntyre's narrative theory entails accountability of the moral agent for their actions to other members of the community. Human action is intelligible only in relatedness to other actions of the agent, which are in turn collectively intelligible in cross sectional intersections with actions of other moral agents in the community of a shared moral tradition. The concept of human action in MacIntyre has therefore an essential social dimension and implies human interpersonal relationships as necessary parameter in its interpretation.

Functional understanding of the human 'being'

The question 'What is does it mean to be human?' is all about the *telos* of the nature that is characterised as human. It entails the concept of human *qua* human good. The good of the human nature that is not bound by any historical and social context. In reasoning with the first principle, the nature of the human being is found to be related to its end. It is only because human beings have an end towards which they are directed by reason of their specific nature, that we come to understand the moral concepts such as the good and virtues[155]. MacIntyre's argument is influenced and justified by St. Thomas Aquinas, who elaborates a teleology of human nature by explaining the *finnis* or the *telos* in relation to the proper nature of the human agent. Aquinas argues that, the good is understood as the end or goal that moves the agent and directs their actions towards itself. The good has the ratio of a *finis* proper to the agent's substantial form or

---

the moral and intellectual character of the agent. The occasion exhibited forms part of the entire history of the life of the agent embedded in a tradition of rationality.

[155] MacIntyre, *After Virtue*, XI.

nature. Therefore, the human good can only be understood as an end towards which humans tend by the reason of their nature *qua* humans.

The Thomistic argument is that, each species of being has its own good proper to its specific nature. Thus, the human agent acts for the good understood as the goal by the virtue of their human nature. The human nature is distinguished from other animal natures by its additional capacity to evaluate the end (the good)[156]. There is an inherent capacity in the good to move and direct the human agent towards itself, thanks to its intrinsic relation to the nature of the being of the agent. There is also a corresponding capacity of interpretation of the good as desirable on the part of the agent. The relationship between the capacity of the good to move and direct the agent towards itself and the corresponding capacity that arises from the human nature of the agent to recognise and interpret the good as desirable, is the foundation of the Thomistic thesis on the concept of the human good. Concurring with Aquinas' argument, MacIntyre then points out the human good to be the Aristotelian *eudaimonia.* Consequently, the moral good and truth in MacIntyre comes to be re-elaborated and understood in reference to that which is good for humans *qua* humans but understood within a community of a tradition of ethical rationality. The human *qua* human good understood as the *telos* of human nature implied in MacIntyre is human flourishing.

Moral Relativism

Moral relativism refers to moral rationality in which there are no absolute or objective standard norms that hold for all men at all times. What is wrong and right are determined by different standards that are relative such that they do not objectively exist.

---

[156] MacIntyre, *After Virtue*, XI, p. 23.

Since there is no objective right and wrong in moral relativistic rationality, we can make sense of radically different moral values, beliefs and practices contemporaneously. What is emphasised is not their universal binding moral force but just the recognition of their differences[157]. Thus, moral relativism is opposed to the traditional understanding of morality as resting on objective foundation. In moral relativism, the truth claims of morality are subjective and there is no such a thing as moral commitment to foundational and objective moral truth. The commitment to objective moral truth is replaced by commitment to what Ratzinger terms as the priority of tolerance and co-existence[158]. The epistemic foundation of relativism in general is claim that there are no neutral criteria and standards of rationality that are independent of personal and social context. Such an epistemic foundation claims that knowledge of reality is therefore from a particular perspective. We can find such epistemic tradition already in the ancient philosophy e.g. in Protagoras, who maintained that man is the measure of all things and therefore anything "is to me as it appears to me and is to you as it appears to you"[159]. Protagoras' epistemic thesis leads to individual relativism in regard to the moral truth which Nietzsche and Jean-Paul Sartre in his existentialist phase championed in contemporary philosophy[160]. In Nietzsche and Sartre, moral right and wrong depend upon the individual and accordingly, the scope of morality is individual.

In the epistemic foundation of relativism, truth is reduced to belief and no sense is given to any idea of truth apart from what

[157] John Haldane, "Ethics, Religion and Relativism" in *The Review of Metaphysics*, Vol 6, 1 (Sep. 2006), p. 134.

[158] Joseph Ratzinger, *Without Roots: The West, Relativism, Christianity, Islam* (New York: Basic Books, 2007), p. 128

[159] Roger Trigg, "Religion and the Threat of Relativism" in *Religious Studies*, Vol. 19, 03 (September 1983), p. 297

[160] Hazel Barnes, trans. *Sartre's Being and Nothingness* (New York: Philosophical Library, 1956), p. 626-27.

people believe. Given that truth depends on the fact of belief, one does not believe something because it is true, rather that thing is true because one believes in it. Thus, moral truth is simply a subjective position which depends on the individual's judgement[161]. Moral truth depends on the fact of belief. In an enlarged sense, relativism reduces truth to the believe and judgement of communities or groups of people. At the level of groups of persons or community, the standards by which moral claims are qualified are not substantial but rather formal. In other words, moral claims are not substantive universals that are culturally invariant but rather cultural universal that are culturally variant. Moral claims are not transcendental but rather contingent claims about morality. The ground for moral relativism at its extreme can decline from subjective belief to subjective feeling and taste, such that the question about moral good and evil becomes at par with matters of preference and taste[162]. An example is the twentieth century emotivism which holds that, all evaluative judgements are nothing but mere expressions of preference of attitude or feelings in so far as they are moral or evaluative in character[163].

Wiredu, Habermas and MacIntyre and Moral relativism

A synoptic review of the moral enquiry in Wiredu, Habermas and MacIntyre leads to identifying three major areas on which discussion can be based. The three elements are; the possibility of intersubjective moral enquiry, universalization of moral enquiry and inter-cultural moral enquiry. Concerning the first element, Wiredu, Habermas and MacIntyre all explain moral rationality as an intersubjective activity and responsibility. That means, it is the subjects in community that are bound together by

---

[161] Roger Trigg, "Religion and the Threat of Relativism", p. 297.

[162] Roger Trigg, "Religion and the Threat of Relativism".

[163] Alasdair MacIntyre, *After Virtue*, p. 11-12.

common interests and contextual destiny that engage in moral reasoning for a common good. This challenges what MacIntyre calls the enlightenment project of justifying morality in which the principles for justifying morality are set to come from pure reason that is abstracted from any embodiment of history and social-cultural contexts. The enlightenment project assigned to the human subject a universally sweeping capacity for rational moral discourse that makes reference to timeless principles, with appeal to reason, that is completely independent of human contextual parameters such as tradition, kinship, culture etc. For example, Kant's categorical imperative is generated subjectively then universalized. It is a rational monologue. In Wiredu, Habermas and MacIntyre, the moral principles enshrined in the Kantian categorical imperatives should be arrived at through intersubjective rationality. The universal element for the possibility of intersubjective moral enquiry is explicitly stated in Wiredu as cultural universals, and in Habermas as universal pragmatics. Meanwhile, it is implicit in MacIntyre.

The second element is the principle of universalization of morality. Even if the moral enquiry in the three thinkers is socio-cultural and context bound, they try to offer a universalization principle for the normative aspect of their theories to apply to all humans. For example, it is rather clear that the principle of universalization of morality in Habermas is the consensus arrived at in moral discourse. In Habermas' discourse ethics, the emphasis is not on the moral content of the discourse but rather on the process of arriving at consensus. Thus, it is not the universalization of the moral content that would be expressed in moral principles and laws, but rather the consensual agreement that should be binding to all. In Wiredu, the principle of universalization is found human biology. He singles out a disposition in the human species, namely, the universal disposition of sympathy towards a member of the human species. However, Wiredu's ethical naturalism to get a principle of universalization of ethics is stronger than Habermas' consensus principle. Whereas, in MacIntyre, the principle of universalization of ethics is the human-*qua*-human telos (flourishing). The standard, that is used to judge an action to be good or bad is, if such actions would enhance the human-*qua*-human *flourishing* i.e. irrespective of culture, race, social-context etc. The concept of human good used as moral standard, and understood in the MacIntyrean assertion is transcendental to all human cultures, since its definition is not culture bound.

The third element is inter-cultural (inter-contextual) moral enquiry. A question arises; given the principles of intersubjective moral enquiry and universalization in Wiredu, Habermas and MacIntyre, is it possible to secure moral objectivity from the three thinkers? In Habermas, it is apparently clear that discourse ethics leads to moral relativism, first and foremost because it does not put premium on the moral content of the discourse but rather on the process. So, what is morally good or evil is not defined by content but by consensual agreement of the participants in the discourse. So, what is ethically normative binds only those who define it so by a consensual agreement. We find a very sharp critique of Habermas' discourse ethics in Ratzinger who aptly argues that truth is discovered in the order of reality and not merely constructed through debate or deliberation, and contents that there exists a truth that is antecedent to any political activity of establishing truth, which actually makes such activity possible[164]. Therefore, consensus as the principle of universalization in Habermas cannot be applied between two groups engaged in two different discourses. In other words, it inevitably leads to moral relativism. Moreover, the discourse ethics in Habermas leads to instrumentalization of moral rationality, reducing it into a technical function for prioritising

---

[164] Joseph Ratzinger, *Without Root*, p. 128.

tolerance and co-existence without commitment to objective moral truth[165].

Wiredu's ethical theory as well cannot secure moral objectivity. A challenge to his theory is that, the human disposition to sympathy which he uses to universalize moral rationality, can be actualized or destroyed by training in a culture. Thus, moral education in sympathy is culture bound. Much as he seeks to set an objective base for the determination of morality in human biology, the failure to anchor it in metaphysics leaves culture to be the defining authority of biological element identified to universalize morality, namely, sympathy towards members of the human species. This leads to ethical relativism than objectivity. Likewise, the tradition bound ethical rationality in MacIntyre leads to incommensurability of moral reasoning. Thus, the consensual ethics in Habermas, ethical naturalism in Wiredu, and tradition constitutive moral enquiry in MacIntyre can all be indicted for moral ethno-centrism, which is a very strong expression moral relativism[166]. Instead, MacIntyre's ethical enquiry based on human metaphysical biology can secure moral objectivity because the concept of the human-*qua*-human flourishing (the good) as the human *telos* is transcendental in all human cultures. An act that is good enhances *eudaimonia* and is objectively good in every human culture. To avoid moral relativism, an ethical theory requires a substantive instead of formally agreed universal to base its enquiry[167]. Thus, evaluation of ethical theory in MacIntyre based on metaphysical biology against the ethical naturalism in Wiredu, and consensual ethics in Habermas reveals that, to secure objective moral rationality moral enquiry should be anchored in metaphysics. Otherwise, ethical

---

[165] Mathew T. Eggemeier, "A post-Secular Modernity? Jurgen Habermas, Joseph Ratzinger, and Johann Baptist Metz on Religion, Reason, and Politics", in *The Heythrop Journal*, XLVIII (2011), p. 5.

[166] Jürgen Habermas, *The Liberating Power of Symbols: Philosophical Essays*, p. 34.

[167] Kevin Schilbrack, "Rationality, Relativism and Religion: A Re-Interpretation of Peter Winch", in *Sophia*, 48 (2009), p. 411.

IN HONOUR OF KWASI WIREDU

enquiry that is not anchored in metaphysics easily slides into moral relativism.

Conclusion

This study has critically analysed moral enquiry in the philosophical thoughts of Wiredu, Habermas and MacIntyre. We have started by a one after another study of the ethical theories in the thoughts of each of the thinkers. The study proceeded to a comparative analysis of their ethical theories under three main themes, namely, establishment of universal elements for the possibility of intersubjective moral enquiry, identification of a principle for universalization of morality, and inter-contextual (cultural) moral enquiry and its challenges. The study ends with interrogation of the ethical theories in Wiredu, Habermas and MacIntyre about the problem of moral relativism. Each of their theories is found to have internal weaknesses that lead to moral relativism. For example, discourse ethics in Habermas inevitably leads to moral relativism since emphasis is not laid on moral content but on the process of debate that culminates in consensual agreement on what is the good. Similarly, Wiredu's ethical naturalism cannot guarantee moral objectivity, largely due to the fact that it is not anchored in metaphysics, and MacIntyre's ethical enquiry based only on social teleology leads to moral enquiry that is community bound, leading to moral relativism.

However, MacIntyre's moral enquiry progresses from a foundation on social to metaphysical teleology. Thus, he finally bases his ethical enquiry on metaphysical teleology such that his ethical naturalism is a metaphysical biology. Therefore, the ethical enquiry in MacIntyre is found to be a stronger alternative to challenge moral relativism than consensual ethics in Habermas and ethical naturalism in Wiredu. From the analysis of the ethical enquiry in the three thinkers, we can conclude that to avoid sliding into moral relativism, an ethical enquiry should be anchored in metaphysics. Although the moral theories of Wiredu, Habermas and MacIntyre have individual internal weaknesses, we should laud the three for the originality of thought and for the contribution of their theories to political and social life. Their theories all enshrine a very important social and political value i.e., the participation in public life in the determination of common good. For example, Wiredu articulates the concept of consensual democracy, Habermas strongly expounds the theory of public sphere, and MacIntyre proposes an inclusive-participatory political life in the local community.

Bibliography

AFOLAYAM, A. and FALOLA T., eds. *The Palgrave Handbook of African Philosophy*. USA: Palgrave Macmillan, 2017.

BARNES, H. trans. *Sartre's Being and Nothingness* (New York: Philosophical Library, 1956), 626-27.

BUTLER, J., HABERMAS J., TAYLOR C. and WEST C. *The Power of Religion in the Public Sphere*, Edwardo Mendieta and Jonathan Vanantwerpen, edits. New York: Columbia University Press, 2011.

EGGEMEIER, M. T. "A post-Secular Modernity? Jurgen Habermas, Joseph Ratzinger, and Johann Baptist Metz on Religion, Reason, and Politics", in *The Heythrop Journal*, XLVIII (2011).

HABERMAS J. *The Theory of Communicative Action: A Critique of Functionalist Reason*, Vol. 2., Thomas McCarthy, trans. Boston: Beacon Press, 1981.

HABERMAS J. *Moral Consciousness and Communicative Action*. Massachusetts: MIT Press, 1990.

HABERMAS J. *Postmetaphysical Thinking*, William M. Hohengarten, trans. Massachusetts: Massachusetts Institute of Technology Press, 1992.

HABERMAS J. *On the Pragmatics of Communication*, Maeve Cooke, ed. Massachusetts: MIT Press, 1998.

HABERMAS J. *Religion and Rationality: Essays on Reason, God and Modernity*, Edwardo Mendieta, edit. London: Polity Press, 2002.

HABERMAS J. *The Liberating Power of Symbols: Philosophical Essays*, Peter Dew, trans. Massachusetts: MIT Press, 2001.

HALDANE, J. "Ethics, Religion and Relativism" in *The Review of Metaphysics*, Vol 6, 1 (Sep, 2006).

HALLEN, B. *A Short History of African Philosophy*. Indiana: Indiana University Press, 2002.

MACINTYRE, A., *Secularization and Moral Change*. London: Oxford University Press, 1967.

MACINTYRE, A., *A Short History of Ethics*, 2nd edit. London: Routledge, 1967.

MACINTYRE, A., *Which Justice, Whose Rationality?* 2nd edit. London: Duckworth, 1988.

MACINTYRE, A., "Epistemological Crisis, Dramatic Narrative, and the Philosophy of Science", in *The Task of Philosophy: Selected Essays*, Vol. I. Cambridge: Cambridge University Press, 2006.

MACINTYRE, A., *Three Rival Versions of Moral Enquiry*. London: Duckworth, 1990.

MACINTYRE, A., "Antecedents of Action" in *Against the Self-Images of the Age: Essays on Ideology and Philosophy*. Indiana: University of Notre Dame Press, 1978.

MACINTYRE, A., *Dependent Rational Animals*: *Why Human Beings Need the Virtues. 2nd ed.* London: Duckworth, 1999.

MACINTYRE, A., "Can One Be Unintelligible to Oneself?" in *McKnight and Stchedroff*, (1987). 23-37.

MACINTYRE, A., *After Virtue, 3rd ed.* London: Bloomsbury, 1981.

MACINTYRE, A., *Ethics in the Conflicts of Modernity: An Essay on Desire, Practical Reasoning, and Narrative*. London: Cambridge University Press, 2016.

MCCARTHY, T. *The Critical Theory of Jürgen Habermas*. Massachusetts: MIT Press, 1978.

MOLEFE, M. *An African Philosophy of Personhood, Morality and Politics.* Switzerland: Palgrave Macmillan, 2019.

RATZINGER, J. *Without Roots: The West, Relativism, Christianity, Islam.* New York: Basic Books, 2007.

SCHILBRACK, K. "Rationality, Relativism and Religion: A Re-Interpretation of Peter Winch", in *Sophia*, 48 (2009).

TRIGG, R. "Religion and the Threat of Relativism" in *Religious Studies*, Vol. 19, 03 (September 1983).

WIREDU, K. *Cultural Universals and Particulars: An African Perspective.* Bloomington and Indianapolis: Indiana University Press, 1996.

Philosophy and the Political Problems of Human Rights in Africa: A Reflection on Kwasi Wiredu

Dr. Ochieng' G. Ojwang', Department of Philosophy and Religious Studies Kisii University, Kenya

Abstract

Philosophy as a human attempt to understand the human situation in a fundamental way in order to gain wisdom was not devoid of the African tradition. According to Wiredu, the accumulated wisdom of what might be called the collective mind of our societies, handed down through tradition, both verbal and behavioural, including aspects of arts, rituals and ceremonial had philosophical aspects of human rights. By virtue of being human, Wiredu asserts that a person has a union of three elements: Principle of life (*Okra*), the blood principle (*Mogya*) and personality principle (*sunsum*). In the possession of these three elements, a person has intrinsic value that is situated in a network of kinship that generates rights and obligations which must be respected by all. These rights are natural to all as pronounced by the ancient Greek philosophers, Sophocles and Aristotle and later in the medieval period philosophers, Thomas Aquinas, Thomas Hobbes and the seventeenth century philosopher, John Locke. Nonetheless, the political establishments of the current African states have contributed to abuse of human rights against article 19 of Universal Declaration of Human Rights which states that "Everyone has the right of opinion and expression." In Africa, civil, political, economic, social and cultural rights are depended on the ruling regime. From independence, most African states have evolved from one-party to multi-party democratic systems, which later brought divisions to the people in society while the earlier was characterized by authoritarianism. We therefore need to infuse philosophy in governance in Africa, in order to sensitize leaders to respect and protect human dignity, freedom and equality, and more so to realize that any civilization should be pegged on the reflection on the concept of human rights.

Key words: Africa, dignity, government, human rights, Ubuntu.

Introduction

This section discusses the concepts of philosophy and the political problems of human rights in Africa in light of Kwasi Wiredu. Since Greek Hellenization, the term "*philosophy*" has been seen to be derived from a combination of two Greek words, namely *philia* (love) and *Sophia* (wisdom) meaning "love of wisdom." You may therefore, define philosophy as "love of wisdom." However, the word "philosophy" is frequently translated as "the love of wisdom," it represents an important meeting of languages of the world. It derives from *Sbyt*, which means "wise teachings" in *Mdw Ntr*, which is related to Egyptian word *Seba* (meaning "to teach" or "to be wise"). To teach (*seba*) is to open the door (*seba*) to the mind of the pupil (seba) in order to bring in light, as from a star (seba). Egyptian concepts concerning the topic under consideration are precise: *Seba*: "*to teach*" at *seba*: "school," literally "house of teaching. This word underwent a change as a result of the ancient Greek habit of changing the *Mdw Ntr* "b" to "*ph*" or, in English, "f."[168], hence philosophy.

---

[168] Theophile Obenga, "Egypt: Ancient History of African Philosophy" in Kwasi Wiredu. *A companion of African Philosophy,* USA: Blackwell Publishing, 2004), 34.

We have to emphasize that philosophy is done a *priori*. Fundamentally, philosophy is an argumentative discipline. It makes use of logic to draw robust conclusions from logically sound premises. The intellectual aim of philosophizing is to achieve *reflective equilibrium*[169]. The philosopher accomplishes this by synthesizing, incorporating, and balancing all of our instant intuitions, significant insights, painstakingly derived findings, and creative speculations. The goal of the philosopher is to dispel contradictions, resolve paradoxes, and, when necessary, offer appropriate premises. The goal is to develop a broad grasp of the relationship between mind, language, and the world, as well as of the relationships between emotion and reason, fact and value, being and truth.

The concept of human rights is now a familiar entity across the world, since all people have the same basic legal rights, regardless of their gender, colour, nationality, ethnicity, language, religion, or any other distinction. Human rights cover a wide range of rights, such as the freedom from slavery and torture, the right to life and liberty, the freedom of speech, the right to a job and an education, among many more. The goal of strategic communication initiatives for recruiting, fund-raising, and mobilization is to engage the general public in human rights concerns. However, according to Clapham [170], the concept of a 'human rights culture' also means different things to different people. Others view it as making sure that everyone is treated with respect for their innate dignity and worth as people. Others interpret this as requiring judges, law enforcement, and immigration officials to defend the rights of terrorists, criminals, refugees, and other undesirable individuals at the expense of the

---

[169] Neil Tennat, *Introducing Philosophy, Introducing Philosophy: God, Mind, world and Logic*, (London: Rutledge 2015) 4.

[170] Andrew Clapham, *Human Hights, A Very Short Introduction*, (New York: Oxford University Press Inc. 2007), 2.

safety of the general public. In a way, the tension is inherent on how human rights safeguards function.

Human rights are important because they prevent governments and other actors from pursuing practical goals at the price of a particular people's welfare and the smooth operation of a democratic society based on the rule of law. Human rights can really help to safeguard people from the 'tyranny' of the majority, despite the fact that at times they may appear to be anti-majoritarian. But as we shall see, human rights legislation does allow for security needs to be taken into consideration, with the exception of the outright prohibition on torture.

Although they are not native, international human rights live in the hearts of supporters. The concepts that make up human rights arise via agitation after conflict and disaster are formalized in legal documents. Human rights travel in a nonlinear manner, channelled through filters and guided by translators, from declarations and conventions into the conscience of common people. Nongovernmental organizations primarily act as channels for dissemination of human rights as they work to build support bases for their causes. The goal of strategic communication initiatives for recruiting, fund-raising, and mobilization is to engage the general public in human rights concerns. [171]

The Nexus between Philosophy and Human Rights

Human rights are rights, and rights apply to all people. They are moral rights that inevitably call for legal recognition. In fact, the law frequently recognizes them. My explanation of what human rights will be based on how both the philosophy of human rights and the law, particularly with regard to its attributes, understand them. However, the definitions of "moral rights" and "human

---

[171] Joel R. Pruce, *The Mass Appeal of Human Rights*, (Cham, Switzerland: Palgrave Macmillan 2019), 9.

rights" are not the same. Human rights are moral privileges that one has only by virtue of being a person in the state. According to Plato[172],that cities exist to provide the good life for their citizens, and that means their helping the citizens so far as possible to avoid making mistakes. Thus, *Magnesia*, the best city of the Laws, was built by philosophers as a kind of machine to produce bliss that, without the city and its institutions and philosophy, would and could not exist at all.

Andrew Clapham[173] also contends that many who approach the subject of human rights turn to early religious and philosophical writings. According to their interpretation of human rights, all people possess certain fundamental and unalienable rights simply because they are people. In different communities, this conclusion has existed in a variety of forms. Although the historical development of the idea of human rights is frequently linked to the development of Western philosophical and political principles, another viewpoint might point to Confucian, Hindu, or Buddhist traditions as having similar values regarding mass education, self-fulfilment, respect for others, and the desire to contribute to others' well-being. He further argues that it is possible to interpret religious writings like the Bible and the Koran as establishing both duties and rights.

From Hammurabi's Code[174] in ancient Babylon (circa 1780 BCE) to the natural law traditions of the West, which built on the Greek Stoics and the Roman law notions of *jus gentium* (law for all peoples), some of the earliest codes make reference to the need to

---

[172] Ferrari G R. *The Cambridge companion to Plato's Republic* (Cambridge: Cambridge University Press 2007) 38.

[173] Andrew Clapham, *Human Rights: A very short introduction*, 2.

[174] Hammurabi code is a Babylonian legal text composed during 1755–1750 BC. It is the longest, best-organized, and best-preserved legal text from the ancient Near East. It is written in the Old Babylonian dialect of Akkadian, purportedly by Hammurabi, sixth king of the First Dynasty of Babylon.

2 of KWASI WIREDU

protect human freedom and human dignity[175]. The acceptance of a few universally true ideas and norms of behaviour is a feature shared by all of these codes. These moral principles undoubtedly influence human rights thinking and can be considered as forerunners of or alternative manifestations of the concept of human rights, although the relationship is not as direct as is commonly claimed.

It will suffice here to examine some early historical references to the genuine concept of rights (as opposed to decency) and the scepticism they have elicited.

Beginning with the *Gorgias*[176], Socrates asserts that he is (possibly) the only true statesman in history because he alone has his fellow citizens' best interests at heart and goes about securing those interests by telling them what they need to hear rather than make them happy, using Parthenons, walls, and dockyards. Socrates is understood here to be the only leader who ensures that the rights of all the citizens are protected. In Book 2[177], Socrates starts to build a nice city as an analogue for the good (and thus just) person or soul to aid him in finding justice. The first city he builds is one that Glaucon calls a "city of pigs" because of the austere lifestyle, Socrates imagines its residents live in. Socrates once more draws a line between himself and the rest, just as he did in Book 1: he considers this form of city to be the "true" one. Since Socrates has not yet established any human political institutions in the Republic, not even an army, the "city of pigs" bears some resemblance to the city of Magnesia in the Laws or possibly to that combined with the depiction of life in the age of Cronus in the myth of the *Politicus*. It is my argument that Plato was aware of the rights of all citizens when it comes getting

---

[175] Andrew Clapham, *Human Rights: A very short introduction*, 5.
[176] Plato, Gorgias 521d–522a.
[177] Plato, Gorgias 521d–522a.

justice as we shall see later that justice is one of the supreme rights which must be enjoyed by all citizens.

In *Nicomachean Ethics*[178], Aristotle asserts that the most noble is that which is justiest, and best is health; but pleasantest is it to win what we love. The question of whether happiness is something that can be learned, developed via habit or some other type of training, or whether it arrives as a result of divine providence or again through chance is raised for this reason. Now, if the gods have given anything to man, it makes sense that they would have given happiness as well, since it is the best of all human qualities. In article 10[179] of *Nicomachean* Ethics, Aristotle believes that a truly good and wise man always makes the most of the circumstances that come his way, just as a good general uses the army under his command and a good shoemaker utilizes the hides that are provided to him, as well as all other craftsmen. And if that's the case, a joyful person can never become unhappy; however, he won't be blessed if he experiences circumstances similar to Priam's[180].

The traditional Western explanation of the history of human rights has been argued by some to have flaws. Early legal developments in the field of human rights are credited to the 1215 Magna Carta, a pact made between English King John and the Barons who objected to the king's imposition of taxes. However, despite the fact that this agreement guaranteed a freeman's right to not be "arrested, detained in prison, or deprived of his freehold, or outlawed, or banished, or in any way molested...except by lawful judgment of his peers and the law of the land," this guarantee was

---

[178] W. Ross, (translator), *Nicomachean Ethics, book* 1 article 8, (Focus Publishing/R. Pullins Company 2002).

[179] W. Ross, (translator), *Nicomachean Ethics, book* 1 article 10, (Focus Publishing/R. Pullins Company 2002).

[180] Priam is the embodiment of Aristotle's idea that beauty and nobility shine through (dialampei to kalon) (EN I. 10, 1100b31-33) even in the most unfortunate circumstances.

merely a right to jury trial given only to men who owned property. Nonetheless, according to Andew Claphan[181], the rights contained in the *Magna Carta* were not human rights, but rather political settlements. Human rights belong to all human beings and therefore, cannot be restricted to a select group of privileged men. He asserts that the *Magna Carta* ends up being a fairly bad example of a human rights statement from a modern standpoint.

According to Locke, no one is allowed to "take away or impair the life, or what tends to the preservation of the life, the liberty, health, limb, or goods of another" because everyone "is bound to preserve himself so when his own preservation is not threatened everyone should" as much as he can... preserve the rest of mankind."[182] Men can be prevented from violating the rights of others and from hurting one another in this way. Every man has the right to execute the rule of nature and punish the wrongdoer. Locke recognizes the impossibility of this "strange doctrine," but he maintained that persons must remain in their natural state unless they agree to join "some political society" through moral consensus. This is asserted by Greg Foster[183] who argues that the goal of Locke's theory of moral consensus was not simply to make society a mere political coalition, by showing groups that had a mutual interest in peaceful relations. Such a society would fall apart into civil war every time some religious prophet came along to lead the faithful of his group in a struggle against the heathens and blasphemers of other groups.

Locke therefore saw the civil government as the remedy for men acting as their own judges to enforce the law of nature. He considered this, with respect to the exercise of political power, not only will the common good always take precedence over self-

[181] Andrew Clapham, *Human Rights: A very short introduction,* 5.

[182] Verry Chappell, *The Cambridge companion to Locke*, (New York: Cambridge University Press 1994), 202.

[183] Greg Foster, *John Locke's Politics of Moral Consensus,* (Cambridge: Cambridge University Press 2005), 5.

interest but, also, government will have to be constituted in such a manner as to rule out a Hobbesian Sovereign or a divinely instituted monarch who retains an interest that is distinct and separate from that of his subjects[184]. As a result, a social contract that was voluntarily entered into grants the government the right to enforce laws as long as it upholds the confidence that has been placed in it. According to Locke, if the populace allowed the government to exercise arbitrary or total control over their "lives, liberties, and estates" then governmental authority would be forfeited and return to the populace.

Any person may have a private will (*volonteparticuliere*), and his private interests (*interetparticulier*) "may dictate to him very differently from the common interest," according to Jean-Jacques Rousseau's Social Contract. Rousseau asserts that, "whoever refuses to obey the general will shall be compelled to it by the entire body: this, in fact, only forces him to be free." Very early in human history, according to Rousseau's hypothetical scenario, people began to work and collaborate occasionally with one another. This was the beginning of a long golden age that saw the appearance of family units and patriarchal authority but not yet of private property. Hus- bands and wives, parents and children dwelled together under one roof, experiencing the "sweetest sentiments" known to human beings, "conjugal and paternal love." Each family resembled a "little society" in which members were united by mutual affection and liberty. There was commerce among the different families; human faculties, social rituals, and a sense of morality evolved somewhat, all contributing to "the happiest and most durable epoch" in human

---

[184] Verry Chappell, *The Cambridge companion to Locke*, (Cambridge: Cambridge university Press, 1994), 228.

history, an interim period ''between the indolence of the primitive state and the petulant activity of egoism.' [185]

According to Rousseau, "Man loses his natural liberty by the social contract, and an unlimited right to all that tempts him, and that he can obtain; in exchange, he acquires civil liberty, and proprietorship of all that he possesses." The Social Contract, published in 1762, was a prelude to the French Revolution of 1789, and the principles it represented have had a significant impact on people all over the world as they have sought to define the rights of the rulers and the governed.

We must acknowledge that the communitarian society he envisions in *The Social Contract is*, above all things, the one in which civic obligations and responsibilities take precedence over personal freedoms and rights. Citizens voluntarily bond and dedicate themselves to the welfare of everybody, and they are prepared to suffer for their political community. Their good deeds are amply rewarded. They flourish as people and reach their greatest potential in terms of reason and morality by being devoted to their community, exercising self-control, and being patriotic.[186]

Other thinkers have undoubtedly helped us to understand how important it is to uphold human rights and dignity in the modern world. For instance, the German philosopher Immanuel Kant argues that one should respect others, because it is commanded by the formula of humanity based at the bottom, the same as the Categorical Imperative. In all of Kant's published works, the

---

[185] Jean - Jacques Rousseau, *The Social Contract and The First and Second Discourses*, Edited and with an Introduction by Susan Dunn, (New Haven: Yale University Press, 2002), 7.

[186] Jean - Jacques Rousseau, *The Social Contract and The First and Second Discourses*, Edited and with an Introduction by Susan Dunn, (New Haven: Yale University Press, 2002), 9.

word "dignity" is used 111 times. In the *Groundwork[187]*, he makes the claim that someone is an end in himself in virtue of freedom and capacity of morality. Hence 'end in itself' is a normative expression with four additional places where Kant refers to *"Menschenwürde"* (human dignity) rather than the more common *"Würde der Menschheit"* (dignity of humanity). Thus, in the realm of ends, everything has either a price or a dignity. What has a price is such that something else can also be put in its place as its equivalent; by contrast, that which is elevated above all price, and admits of no equivalent, has a dignity

Oliver Sensen[188] also discovered two notes for meditation and one lecture. He claims that there are eighteen published texts with at least one reference to dignity. He arranged these pieces according to how frequently the word "dignity" is used, and the formula of humanity expresses what the Categorical imperative says in relations to ends or using the language of ends.

Humanity is the centre focus of Kant, he stresses this in the second formulation of the categorical imperative, "Act so as to treat humanity whether in your person or that of any other as an end never as mere means". The foundation of this principle is the intrinsic value of persons. Thus, persons are centres of value they should be with dignity consistent with their intrinsic value. Thus, persons have intrinsic value; they should never be treated as expendable objects. To treat people as if they were mere means is to deny them personhood. According to this principle to act morally is to respect personhood of person. Kant says that this principal is at the bottom, the same as the categorical imperative

---

[187]Allen W. Wood *Groundwork for the Metaphysics of Morals Immanuel Kant* Edited and translated by with essays by J. B. Schneewin, (New Haven, Yale University Press, 2002), 52.

[188] Oliver, Sensen, *Kant on human dignity* (Berlin: De Gruyter, 2011), 112.

which he argues is a *priori* and indeed there is, at least prima facie, little to say in favour of Kant's teleological considerations[189]. From the above discussion, we can argue that the concept of human rights is universal to all human being including Africans. This argument is, to some extent, valid if by "human rights" one means the set of normative standards enshrined in the International Bill of Rights, which is made up of the Universal Declaration of Human Rights, the International Covenant on Civil and Political Rights, and the International Covenant on Economic, Social, and Cultural Rights, among other human rights instruments, given that the West was instrumental in their adoption, their justification is clear. But even when seen from this particular angle, the standards have worth outside this particular context because they were adopted by the most diverse international body at the world level. The fact that human rights are a reflection of the universal search for human dignity, however, provides a deeper explanation for the claim of universality which includes the African continent.

African Conception of Human Rights

What do we mean by Africa or Afrocentricity? Ali Mazrui[190] asserts that we can only locate this by discussing four elements which lead towards the Afrocentric perspective. They are: Firstly, Africa as being subject rather than object. Secondly, and related to it, is Africa as being active rather than passive. Thirdly, Africa as being cause rather than effect. Fourthly, Africa as being centre rather than periphery. And finally, Africa as being *maker of history* rather than *incident in history*. Thus, sometimes the term used is *Africana*, meaning the Blackworld as a whole. But this

---

[189] Christoph Horn and Dieter Schönecker (edts) *Groundwork for the Metaphysics of Morals*, (Berlin Walter de Gruyter, 2006) 45.

[190] Rene Laremont (edt), *Africanity Redefined, Collected Essays of Ali A. Mazrui volume* I (Asmara, Africa World Press 2000) 21-22.

term should be meant to refer to Global Africa as the sum total of firstly the continental Africa and secondly, the diaspora of enslavement, which was created by the dispersal caused by the horrors of enslavement; and thirdly, the diaspora of colonialism, caused by the destabilization and long -term consequences and disruptions of the colonial era.

In African context, the human rights are intrinsic to the individual and the society at large since an individual person is not in isolation. Regarding the African story of human rights, there is no interrogation of this concept without discussing ontological progression of African person, since we conceive of the movement of the individual human child into personhood, and beyond, as essentially a journey from an it (foetus in the womb) to an it (buried body). Thus, in all these stages there was respect when treating the individual person, such that even a dead body was treated with respect as we usher them into the world of the ancestors. There were if any minimal human rights abuse in the traditional African communities, and in response to the growing trend of human rights abuses in contemporary Africa, Kwasi Wiredu[191] comes to the conclusion that these abuses cannot be "rationalized by appeal to any legitimate part of African traditional politics". One of the greatest issues modern Africa faces is how to design a political structure that would respond to both current advances and reflect the best conventional ideas about human rights (and other ideals). Educating oneself about traditional life and ideas is a fantastic place to start.

Francis Deng[192] argues that in the Dinka thought, because God created all of humankind, every human being, no matter what his race or religion, has a sanctity and moral or spiritual value that must be respected. To mistreat him is to mistreat God, and doing

---

[191] Kwasi Wiredu, *Cultural Universals and Particulars in the Philosophy* (Indiana University Press 1996)116,.

[192] Francis Deng Human Rights in the African Context, in 501 in *A Companion to African Philosophy Edited* by Kwasi Wiredu (Blackwell Publishing Ltd 2004) 502.

so will result in a curse. The Dinka perspective is noteworthy in that it holds that upholding the rights of one person eventually serves the interests of everyone. This is also asserted by Wiredu[193] on the Akan people claiming "every one is the offspring of God; no one is the offspring of the earth." Implied in this formulation is the right of each person to the dignity bestowed upon him or her as God's creature.

Among the Luo community of South Nyanza, there is expressed kinship value. According ABC Ochola Ayayo[194], kinship value is a value of relationship actually or putatively traced through parental links and recognized for social purposes. He asserts that kinship value is a universal value found in all societies. Among the Luo community, kinship value is stressed more to the patrilineal or cognatic kinship which sometimes we call the patrilineal value. Nonetheless, the "cognatic" value derives from the parental love of persons descended from the same ancestor, both from male and female. The value of parental and brotherly love among the Luo is very strong that a Luo will call all who are related to the father's brother's sons as his fathers, and those related to his mother's sisters as his mothers. The same is true for his father's brother's sons as his brothers. This kinship value came into being out of respect for each other and with responsibilities to assist and protect one another person from abuse and exploitation.

We have to note that since a child's journey, or ontological progression, takes place in time, a word might also be in order regarding the nature of time in the African thought. Time's movement was generally from the present to the past, so that the more of a past one has, the more standing as a person one also has. In this regard, a remark to the effect "I am looking forward to my own past" would be a remark well placed within the

---

[193] Kwasi Wiredu, *Cultural Universals and Particulars,* 1996, 157.

[194] A.B.C. Ochola Ayayo, *Traditional ideology and Ethics among Southern Luo,* Scandinavian Institute of African Studies, Uppsala, 1976. 37-38.

thought system of the community with members who respect each other and hold each other with dignity.

By virtue of being human, Kwasi Wiredu asserts that, a person had a union of three elements: Principle of life (*Okra*), the blood principle (*Mogya*) and personality principle (*sunsum*)[195]. In the possession of these three elements, a person has intrinsic value which is situated in a network of kinship that generates rights and obligations which must be respected by all. This is also asserted by Appiah[196] that an individual is composed of a body (*Nipadua*) produced from the mother's blood (the *mogya*), a unique spirit (*Sunsum*), which is the primary carrier of one's identity, and a third entity (*okra*). At conception, the father is the source of the *Sunsum*. The *okra*, a kind of life energy that only leaves the body when a person breathes their last, is sometimes identified with breath, as were the Greeks and the Hebrews, and is frequently said to be sent to a person at birth as the bearer of their *Nkrabea,* or destiny, from *Nyame*. In contrast to *okra*, the *Sunsum* may leave the body while a person is still alive. It may do this, for instance, while sleeping, with dreams supposed to represent the impressions of a person's *Sunsum* on its nightly peregrinations.

And one of the ways to act is on that recognition and joining the task of transforming the individual into a true person, in other words, a moral being or bearer of norms. For example, for the married, the notion of person is the notion of moral arrival, a notion involving yardsticks and gradations, or, more simply, involving an expectation that certain ways of being or behaving in the world may be so off the mark as to raise important questions regarding the person-status of their doers. Thus, Shaban

---

[195] Kwasi Wiredu, *Cultural Universals and Particulars,* 1996, 158.

[196] Kwasi K. Appiah, "Akan and Euro-American Concepts of the Person" in African Philosophy: New and Traditional Perspectives. Edited by Lee M. Brown. (Oxford: Oxford University Press, 2004): 28

Roberts[197] *"Wa miguu miwili huwaje wa miine"* (How does a person turn into a beast) is a call for all human beings to act in accordance with and respect to all despite their political social and economic status, humanity and dignity should be the norm. Shaban Roberts assertion is complemented by Kwasi Wiredu[198] that through the possession of an *okra, mogya* and *sunsum*, a person is situated in a network of kinship of relation that generate a system of rights and obligations; hence, *wa miguu miwili hawezi kuwa wa miguu miine* (the two legged cannot be four legged) because of the obligation.

This is the basis of the Ubuntu philosophy that the person is only a person through others, without respect for others and community then, he/she will be leaving like a monster. According to Ogude[199], Ubuntu does not simply confer high importance on the community over the individual, but it refers to the individual's experience in reintegrating into a greater community. Ubuntu then revitalizes those connections not just between the livings, but also between the living and the living dead. Ubuntu is an ethic, a moral imperative, a moral virtue expected of all humans wherever they are found. This is the significance of native informants' insistence that the term *"muntu,"* which designates a human person, implies the idea of an excellence attaching to what it designates in other words, that it does not merely refer to people who are thought of as simple existences. It makes the most sense to view the development of a single human infant into adulthood and beyond as essentially a voyage from one of it to another.

The ethical salvation for the collective and the individual, in this regard, is in the present now, not in some imagined and maybe unreachable future. Immortality can only reach so far into

---

[197] Bin Roberts, *Shaban, utubora Mkulima.* (Diwani ya Shaban No 8. London: Evans brothers) 21.

[198] Kwasi Wiredu, *Cultural Universals and Particulars,* 1996, 158.

[199] James Ogude, *Ubuntu and the reconstruction of the community,* (Bloomington: Indiana University Press, 2019), 34

ancestor ship because there are no theoretical foundations for the kind of extended future in which survival in perpetuity of the human is possible. This situation is the outcome of traditional society's mentality being more empirical in nature. One makes decisions based on what is already known and not on how time will unfold. Of course, it would be lovely if everyone could attain immortality beyond the ancestral stage, but actual observation of the passage of time does not support that conclusion; therefore, human rights should be for everyone living in the present.

Thus, human rights in Africa, though not explicitly documented, are reflected in our DNA[200] as, Mbiti[201] writes:

> In traditional life, the individual does not and cannot exist alone except corporately. He owes his existence to other people, including those of past generations and his contemporaries. He is simply part of the whole. The community must therefore make, create, or produce the individual; for the individual depends on the corporate group... Whatever happens to the individual happens to the whole group, and whatever happens to the whole group happens to the individual. The individual can only say: "I am, because we are; and since we are therefore I am." This is a cardinal point in the understanding of the African view of man.

Mbiti therefore is propagating a socio-centric view of personhood, in which the status of an individual is determined through cultural criteria, is quite evident from the assertion that a society "makes, creates or produces the individual."

---

[200] Deoxyribonucleic acid (abbreviated DNA) is the molecule that carries genetic information for the development and functioning of an organism. DNA is made of two linked strands that wind around each other to resemble a twisted ladder a shape known as a double helix.

[201] John Mbiti, *African Religion and Philosophy*, (London, Heinemann. 1969) 108– 109

Problems with Human Rights in Africa

The history of human rights abuse in Africa is far much contested due to her pre-literate past or lack of "history" in the argument of Hegel that concerns the nature of the evidence available about the society's past. According to Hegel[202] slavery, with its inducement to sell, rather than kill, captured enemies was a norm; thus, humanity was not part of Negros lives. Nonetheless, of course, Hegel had no access to the empirical data that supports such viewpoints or the body of evolutionary theory that explains the relevance of the data. However, as has previously been mentioned, he would have had no trouble in principle accepting them.

It is my argument that since there was lack of evidence from Hegelian perspective about Africa, we cannot consider Africa's past to be "unhistorical" partly because they were pre-literate. Historical evidence was not only pegged on documentation, but orally transmitted, and a document was equated with the written word. However, Ali Mazrui[203] argues that in the face of such a conception of history, three lines of defence were open to Africa. One was to accept the paramount position of written documents and then proceed to demonstrate that Africa does have documentary testimony for much of its precolonial history. The second line of defence was to establish the validity of oral evidence for historical work. The third line of defence was to try and cast doubts on the validity of written evidence, in an attempt to show that countries which have massive written documentation of their history are no more certain about their past than those which do not have such evidence since the written evidence sometimes arises from misinformation as the case of Hegel.

---

[202] 'McCarney, Joseph, *Routledge Philosophy Guide Book to Hegel on history,* (Routledge, *2000*)142, 2000

[203] Rene Laremont (edt), *Africanity Redefined, Collected Essays of Ali A. Mazrui volume* I 4.

The documentation of the violation of Human rights in Africa has been documented by those who faced the violations or discrimination themselves and their descendants. It is my strong conviction that whoever suffers human right abuse in most instances will give the right information on their experiences, even if they are orally transmitted. Having said that, human rights violation in Africa started with the Berlin Conference of 15th November, 1884 – 26th 1885 also known as Congo conference or West Africa conference. For part of the colonizers' defining role is that as human beings they are superior to the inferior (African) human beings they colonize. This kind of double standard would negate any theoretical basis for a universal humanism. This continued during World War I (1914–1918), which included local battles for control, and drew Africans into European conflicts. This process continued during the World War II (1939–1945) in which Africans were involved in the line to defend their colonizers[204].

Though the historical slavery was abolished, the need for labour in the colonies continued. This problem was addressed in Sierra Leone, for example, by paying local leaders to recruit workers to what, in practice, constituted forced labour migration. Throughout the colonial period, Africans were forcibly dispossessed of their land, such as with the Land Apportionment Acts (1930, 1931) in Rhodesia. This was still the highest violation of Africans in colonial Africa.[205]

In South Africa, the minority ruled and segregated against blacks, according to Toyin Falola[206], after 1910, the white minority government used and abused power to benefit a select few at the

---

[204] John Middleton and Joseph C. Miller, *New Encyclopaedia of Africa*, Volume 4 Nairobi–Symbol, New York: Thomson Gale), p. 301.

[205] John Middleton and Joseph C. Miller, *New Encyclopaedia of Africa*, Volume 4 Nairobi–Symbol, New York: Thomson Gale), p. 302

[206] Toyin Falola, *Key Events in African History: A Reference Guide*, (Greenwood Press Westport, 2002) 200-201,

detriment of the majority dominated South Africa's history. In 1910, there were 1.2 million white people, 150,000 Indians, 500,000 Coloured people, and more than 4 million Africans in South Africa. Only the white population were taken into account while determining citizenship advantages and rights. Now securely in power, white minority governments enacted numerous legislation intended to segregate society along racial lines. The apartheid system was the eventual result.

In the meantime, the mining business generated enormous affluence that was primarily experienced by white English speakers. Although thousands of Afrikaners went to the cities as their prosperity declined, they remained primarily farmers. The government satisfied the demands of the Afrikaners because they were white community members and more than half of the electorate, but only at the expense of Africans, Indians, and Coloured people. Africans suffered numerous changes that faced South Africa's politics and economics that occurred after 1910. South Africa's rulers and the white minority population possessed extensive authority over its domestic affairs because the country was a dominion within the British Empire. The Afrikaners persisted in advancing their own nationalism and were hostile toward the English-speaking people. The English-speaking people looked for ways to increase their riches and influence. Both diminished Africans' demands.

Falola illustrates his argument by empirical evidence of the of the segregation laws which were enacted as follows:

> The Mines and Works Act (1911) reserved jobs for whites in mines and on railroads.

> The Natives' Land Act (1913) restricted Africans to just 7 percent of the South African land, in reserves of just 22 million acres.

> The Defence Act (1920) set up a White Active Citizen Force, with legal rights for its members to defend themselves.

The Native Affairs Act (1920) established separate managements and judicial systems for reserves.

The Natives (Urban Areas) Act (1923) restricted the access of blacks to white urban places. Blacks were required in the cities only for their labour. Black townships were to be created away from white areas. Pass laws were used to restrict the entry of blacks to the cities.

The Native Administration Act (1927) gave the government absolute authority in dealing with the Africans who lived outside the Cape Province. The British governor could appoint and dismiss African chiefs, define land boundaries, and relocate people. Such laws contradicted the universal declaration of human rights that creates a room whereby all human beings are treated with respect and dignity.

Post-colonial Africa Human Rights Abuse

Despite independence, the political establishments of the current African states have contributed to abuse of human rights against article 19 of Universal Declaration of Human Rights which states that "Everyone has the right of opinion and expression ..." However, in post-colonial Africa, civil, political, economic, social and cultural rights depend on the ruling regime.

From independence, most African states have evolved from one-party to multi-party democratic systems, of which the later has created divisions in society while the earlier was characterized by authoritarianism. Algeria, for instance Abde-laziz Bouteflika, a moderate who won Algeria's presidential elections in April 1999, attempted to start mending the rifts between the military-backed regimes and the Islamist groups. Despite allegations of cheating and corruption, Bouteflika's victory signalled a genuine shift in government policy. Bouteflika was more forthright about the misery Algeria had endured during its internal conflict than had his predecessors, even going so far as to subtly acknowledge government involvement in some of the "disappearances." Bouteflika also ordered the release of several Algerians who had been detained throughout the conflict as a show of his sincerity.

Bouteflika suggested a "Civil Harmony law," which was adopted by the general public in September 1997 in response to the AIS's peace measures. To put the past behind them, Algerian law required an amnesty for Islamist rebels who surrendered within six months and who had not committed murder or rape. The penalties for murderers and rapists would be less severe.

Nonetheless, the government of Algeria has often refused to grant permits to those groups it opposes, particularly those sympathetic to the Islamist movement. Freedom of religion is not protected in Algeria. The sole recognized and permitted religion in the nation is Islam. However, the government typically permits other religious organizations to function covertly. Despite governmental restrictions, there are Catholic churches that welcome worshipers each and every Sunday. The security forces through government have not attempted to shut these churches down. Other people belonging to various religious organizations frequently get together in one another's houses. Islam is a core subject covered in all of the schools' curricula. There are no permitted private religious schools. Evangelizing is forbidden. Mosque operations are under the direction of the Ministry of Religion[207].

In Angola, both the government and National Union for the Total Independence of Angola (UNITA), are guilty of countless violations of human rights. Numerous residents have been displaced and hundreds have died as a result of battles between government and UNITA forces. According to some reports, UNITA supporters, criminal suspects, and those who disregard police instructions have all been the targets of extrajudicial

---

[207] Wilson Center Marina Ottaway Algeria: The Enduring Failure of Politics, *https://www.wilsoncenter.org/article/algeria-enduring-failure-politics*

murders and torture carried out by government security personnel. Hundreds of people have been jailed and arrested for political grounds, while government opponents have vanished. At the moment of the arrest, many people are beaten. According to Amnesty International, four young people allegedly asphyxiated to death in police detention in Luanda in November 1999 after being violently abused[208].

In Rwanda, in 1973, a military coup dissolved the National Assembly and abolished all political activities. In 1978, the Rwandans went again to the polls. President Juvénal Habyarimana, the leader of the National Revolutionary Movement for Development (MRND), was elected president. He promised to eliminate the widespread corruption and to transform Rwanda from a one-party state to a multiparty democracy. President Habyarimana was re-elected in 1983 and 1988. Despite his promise to allow more freedom and justice, Habyarimana and his Hutu followers kept themselves in power by fanning the flames of ethnic hatred against the Tutsi minority.

In 1990, the Uganda-based Rwanda Patriotic Front (RPF), made up of ethnic Tutsi Rwandan exiles, invaded Rwanda, claiming to fight for greater justice. In 1992 peace talks began. In April 1994, the airplane carrying President Habyarimana was shot down. The Tutsi RPF was blamed for the attack, although it was almost certain that the extreme members of Habyarimana's own party shot down his plane, most likely to halt the peace talks. The government, using the attack as an excuse, organized a mass slaughter of the Tutsi population. Military troops and militia groups began killing all Tutsis, as well as Hutu political moderates, precipitating one of the worst genocides in history.[209]

---

[208] John Middleton and Joseph C. Miller, *New Encyclopedia of Africa,* 370- 376.

[209] Andrew Lewis 104, *Silent Accomplice: The Untold Story of France's Role in the Rwandan Genocide,* London R. B. Tirus London, 2007). 104,

Because the RPF remains the ruling and only political party, citizens do not have the right to challenge their government. Numerous human rights abuses are reportedly committed by the security forces, in the form of extrajudicial killings, torture and beating of suspects, and arbitrary arrest and detention. The government occasionally takes some steps to punish the perpetrators. The number of disappearances has been increasing, and credible reports identify some of the missing persons as being former Hutu insurgents trying to return to their homes in the northwest region.

Although some Hutus are unfairly targeted by government forces, Hutus are also guilty of attacks and human rights violations against innocent Tutsis.

Insurgent Hutu militias, which include members associated with the 1994 genocide continue to commit hundreds of killings targeting Tutsi refugees from the Democratic Republic of the Congo, Hutu governmental officials who work with the Tutsis, local Hutu politicians who also work with the Tutsis, and those Hutus who refuse to support the insurgents' cause. These actions have increased the friction between the Hutu population and the government. Prison conditions are harsh. Overcrowding is a major problem, and sanitary conditions are extremely poor. Thousands of persons have died while in custody in the past few years. Following the genocide, more than 100,000 alleged killers were being held in prisons across Rwanda, overwhelming the justice system in coping with the investigations of the crimes and putting the accused on trial[210].

In Kenya, during the then KANU government, despite the zeal with which President Moi and his ruling party had, the Kenya Africa National Union (KANU), pursued economic reforms, little was done in those years to address Kenya's ongoing human rights

---

[210] Andrew Lewis 104, *Silent Accomplice: The Untold Story of France's Role in the Rwandan Genocide.* 191.

problems. There were reports of police harassment, excessive use of force/ torture, and deaths in custody. Refugees from neighbouring countries and migrant workers had also been targeted by police who harassed them, they also faced threats of relocation to rural camps and arbitrary deportation. Moreover, all the governments in post-colonial Kenya have been found to have violated human rights. From the British colonial era through the administrations of Presidents Jomo Kenyatta, Daniel arap Moi, and Mwai Kibaki, including during the 2007–2008 post–election violence, there are report documents on extensive human rights violations and other injustices committed in Kenya[211]. The TJRC commission suggested criminal prosecutions, financial compensation for victims, institutional reforms, and amnesty in exchange for the truth for offenders who did not seriously violate human rights. The document is "an official record of the state's complicity in serial human rights violations, a state whose institutions are frequently exposed as corrupt and in callous disregard for the fundamental human rights of citizens"[212].

It is clear that despite the apparent universal acceptance of the human rights message, there is still discord over what constitutes a human right and how rights should be implemented. Clearly a starting point should be the enforcement at the national level and the Kenyan case is not different. Kenya embarked on an ambitious trajectory as soon as it gained its independence, hoping to shed its reputation as a developing nation and become more like Western democracies. Kenya has discovered that it must contend with the same challenges as its neighbours, and in some ways, it has prevailed. The Kenyan case nevertheless serves as a cautionary tale for those who assert that the realization of human rights is a natural consequence of economic prosperity. Nonetheless, all the

---

[211] Kenya Truth, Justice and Reconciliation Commission (TJRC). (2013). Report of the Truth,Justice and Reconciliation Commission Vol. 1. Nairobi: TJRC.

[212] Ndungu, C. G. (2014). "Lessons to be Learned: An Analysis of the Final Report of Kenya's Truth, Justice and Reconciliation Commission," ICTJ Briefing. New York: International Centre for Transitional Justice.2014), 5.

governments since independence have had their share of challenges when handling opposition leaders and more so the supporters when it comes to regional development. There are several cases where people are imprisoned without fair trials and the conditions in the prisons are worse, this including women prisons.

According Alice Macharia[213], there are no fixed standards of accommodation for women in Kenyan prisons, but in most cases, they are held inside stone-walled buildings divided into cells holding around 50–70 inmates. Those with children live with them therein. She further argues that initially, there were no beds for prisoners, but currently, the situation has improved, with all female prisoners at Lang'ata having beds. However, there continues to be a shortage of appropriate bedding in all the prisons. The day-to-day routine of the women's prison is focused principally on the containment of convicted offenders. Across Africa the refugee[214] status has been a perennial problem due to wars which have engulfed Africa causing instabilities in many countries. Besides, there have been many refugees who cross the borders into neighbouring countries or cross the sea into other continents raising a concern on the state of their countries' affairs as the holders of rights.

Michael Addaney[215] on the plight of the refugees argues that despite their predicament, climate refugees are not legally recognized and protected by international law. As a result, it is

---

[213] Alice Macharia, *Rights of the Child, Mothers and Sentencing*, (New York: Rutledge, published 2021) 70.

[214] The term 'refugee' offers legal protection based on a defined conceptualization under the 1951 Geneva Refugee Convention. However, there is no agreement over the definition and the legal treatment of persons forcibly displaced by climate change. Currently, they are treated as economic migrants, resulting in barriers to entering crossing international borders legally.

[215] Michael Addaney, Michael Gyan Nyarko, Elsabé Boshoff (Editors), Governance, Human Rights, and Political Transformation in Africa "The Legal Challenges of Offering Protection to Climate Refugees in Africa".333-334

unclear what legal protections exist for climate refugees on a global scale and in particular, Africa. This calls into question whether the current regional and international institutions for protecting refugees could be put to use. Governments have a misperception that refugees contribute to an increase in crime especially in urban areas. Consequently, the majority of African governments are unfriendly to refugees in general. Due to the arbitrary application of international and national protection regimes, the experiences of refugees in particular are typified by a high level of helplessness in cities like Cairo, Nairobi, Johannesburg, Kampala, and Khartoum. The AUs reticence to implement a policy response to protect climate refugees in the continent is reinforced by these developments.

Current Debates of Human Rights in Africa (A Case of LGBTQ)

There seems to be a lot of pressure from the western community to African societies to accept the LGBTQ[216] community and people of other sexual orientation as right holders which is true, when it comes to them being human beings. This community has a long history of activism and development. Fighting for recognition and rights, it started to become more prominent in the late 20th century (more especially, the 1990s). The legalizing of homosexuality, the acceptance of same-sex unions, and the greater awareness of transgender concerns are just a few of the critical milestones that have been reached over time, most notably in the United States of America. What is the meaning of LGBTQ, the following discussion will be of help.

Lesbian, these are females who are attracted to other females romantically, emotionally, or sexually. Some girls might have

---

[216] The LGBTQ community is made up of diverse individuals who identify as lesbian, gay, bisexual, transgender, and queer/questioning.

crushes on other girls, just like some may have affections for boys. Lesbians are significant members of the LGBTQ community and they demonstrate that love and relationships may exist between people of the same gender.

Gay, these are men who are attracted romantically, emotionally, and/or sexually to other men. Similar to how boys may develop feelings for girls, some boys may have feelings for other boys. They form relationships and have the capacity for love, just like any other individuals.

Bisexual, these are persons who are attracted to both men and women romantically, emotionally, and/or sexually. Bisexual people can connect with and feel affection for anyone, regardless of the person's gender. As a result, individuals could find themselves attracted to someone who is either of the same gender as them or of a different gender.

Transgender people are those whose gender identity does not match the gender they were given at birth. For instance, a transgender woman is someone who was assigned a male gender at birth but identifies as a female, and a transgender man is someone who was given a female gender at birth but identifies as a male. In order to live as the gender they identify with, transgender people may change their name, use alternative pronouns, and, in certain circumstances, receive medical treatment.

Queer is a catch-all phrase that refers to those who do not fall into the lesbian, gay, bisexual, or transgender classifications. People who are still figuring out who they are, who feel their gender or sexuality defies conventional gender or sexuality categories, or who just prefer to use a more inclusive phrase may use it. It's vital to keep in mind that various people may interpret the term "queer" differently and use it to describe their particular experiences.

When the letter Q appears at the end of the phrase LGBT, it can occasionally also denote inquiry. This phrase refers to someone who is unsure of their gender identity or sexual orientation.

Intersex, this is a term used to describe someone who has one or more natural sex traits, such as chromosomes, internal reproductive organs, or genitalia, that aren't in line with conventional ideas of what it is to be male or female. Do not conflate an intersex trait with transgender identity. Intersex people are given a gender at birth, either male or female, and it's possible that this choice does not correspond to the child's gender identification. Not every intersex person considers themselves to be a member of the LGBTQIA+ group.

Asexual, is an individual who lacks sexual attraction as described by this adjective. A term that is sometimes abbreviated as "ace," it can also refer to people who are demisexual, which means they do feel some sexual attraction, gray sexual, which refers to people who might not strictly fall under the definition of asexual, and aromantic, which refers to people who feel little to no romantic attraction and/or have little to no desire to enter into romantic relationships.

Nonebinary, this adjective refers to a person who utilizes a variety of adjectives to identify themselves and whose gender is neither male nor female. Other phrases include agender, bigender, genderfluid, and many others. None of these phrases have exactly the same meaning, but they all refer to gender experiences that go beyond being either male or female.

+Plus, the word "plus" is used to refer to all gender identities and sexual orientations that words and letters are unable to fully encompass.

Discussing gender and sexuality must be done so with an acceptance, respect, and open attitude. It's important to foster an environment where people can be honest to themselves and receive love and understanding because everyone's feelings and identities are particular to them.

The argument the west advances is that by understanding and embracing the diversity within the LGBTQ community, we can foster a society that appreciates and celebrates individual differences, creating a more inclusive and compassionate world for everyone. This is due to continued constant homophobic attack on them. According to Erick Russell[217] the roots of hegemony and violence run far deeper than epithets, bashings or stigmatization; they are fixed on acts of removal and tokenization, such as those seen in the corpus. Pinkwashing is nothing more than a political gimmick because it is used to support the case for far greater overt and immediate antagonism toward others rather than for the equality or betterment of LGBTQ people. There is a homophobic mirror in such discursive practices and among those who accept the pinkwashed message since it takes tacit support for an underlying cycle of violence and inequality to accept the commodification of one group in order to further exclude another.

Debate

LGBTQ touches on human rights sexuality and more so human families, as right holders, we need and must recognize them as human beings who are part of humanity, though with different sexual orientation from the traditional gender differentiation. However, the way young people are being inducted into LGBTQ+ communities is worrying. The west has stuck to the recognition of the LGBTQ+ community and are using financial institutions to encourage African states to give them the space in African countries. A case in point is the letter by the Congress of United States directing the World Bank to stop aid to Uganda because of

---

[217] Eric Louis Russell, *The Discursive Ecology of Homophobia Unraveling Anti-LGBTQ Speech on the European Far Right,* 257, (Library of Congress Cataloging in Publication Data, 2019) 257.

the anti LGBTQ+ law[218]. The letter categorically instructs the World Bank director to stop financial aid to Uganda because of

---

[218] Congress of United States, Washington DC 20510. July 25, 2023

Ajay Banga
President, World Bank Group
1818 H Street, NW
Washington, D.C. 20433
Dear Mr. Banga,
As Members committed to protecting the rights of LGBTQ+ people globally, we urge you to immediately postpone and suspend all current and future lending to Uganda until the recent Anti- Homosexuality Act, signed by President Yoweri Museveni on May 29, 2023, is struck down. While we undoubtedly support efforts to promote long-term economic development and poverty reduction in Uganda, the recent law mandates state-sponsored discrimination and violence against LGBTQ+ individuals, creating a humanitarian crisis that plainly violates World Bank stated policies. We join more than 170 international organizations in urging you to act swiftly so that the World Bank is a leader among multilateral development banks (MDBs) in condemning this egregious and unjust law that threatens LGBTQ+ people across Uganda. The Anti-Homosexuality Law 2023 (AHA) requires all people in Uganda to report to the police any person reasonably suspected of engaging in the "offense of homosexuality." It significantly increases already harsh criminal penalties to life in prison or death and also criminalizes those who advocate for and provide certain forms of social support to LGBTQ+ people. It disqualifies LGBTQ+ people from certain types of employment and prohibits landlords from renting housing to LGBTQ+ people. In response, the World Bank issued a brief statement saying that "the Act is not consistent with the values of non-discrimination and inclusion that the institution upholds." Given these egregious human rights violations against LGBTQ+ people and allies outlined in the AHA, the World Bank's initial response is insufficient.
This law starkly contradicts the World Bank's stated values of inclusion and shared prosperity. In 2016, the World Bank approved a new Environmental and Social Framework (ESF) that included provisions on inclusion and non-discrimination. However, the AHA goes against the principles and requirements of this policy by prohibiting LGBTQ+ people from sharing in the benefits and opportunities of Bank-financed projects. Further, the law even directs those implementing these projects to report any beneficiary they have reason to believe may be LGBTQ+ to the police.
Actively promoting the protection of LGBTQ+ communities is beneficial for the economic and social development of countries and regions, opening further investment opportunities. Studies conducted at both the international and country-specific levels have shown that greater inclusion of sexual and gender minorities in the workforce benefits the economy at large. However, regardless of economic outcomes, the World Bank is a global standard-setter among MDBs and should promote the highest levels of inclusivity and equity in its

President Museveni's stand and the law he ascended to punish all those publicly announcing or caught having sex with the same gender.

The question is, should aid to Africans be intercepted and pegged on acceptance of the LGBTQ community members? And what has sexuality which is just a percentage of our lives got to do with our political and economic debates? Sex, defecation, and giving birth are the only activities which fulfil the sphincter law. Why then should we celebrate people because of their sexual orientation which is a private thing in public? Is being a member of LGTQ community an achievement? We don't have a universal culture because of our cultural and social differences across the globe. And differences need to be appreciated when it comes to sexual orientation, not imposing other people's sexual orientation to others. In African context for instance, there cannot be sexual intercourse between people of the same gender and our sexuality which is public leads to family to family unit which connects one to the previous generation and help brings another t generation

projects and policies, including in countries where LGBTQ+ individuals face repressive legal and social conditions. We urge you to demonstrate that under your leadership, the Bank will prioritize the protection of LGBTQ+ individuals and will not tolerate draconian laws that degrade their rights.
We stand with Ugandan activists, international humanitarian organizations, and the LGBTQ+ community and insist that the Bank take swift action to postone and suspend all lending to Uganda until the law is struck down. Continuing to lend money to Uganda and implement projects in the country would signal to the Ugandan Government, other governments considering similar laws, and LGBTQ+ people around the world that the World Bank does not truly value inclusion and that its commitments to non-discrimination are disingenuous. The World Bank can and must do better. We urge the Bank to stand up for the principles and values it claims to uphold by swiftly and publicly suspending all forms of financing, current and future, to the Government of Uganda pending the outcome of legal challenges to the law.
Sincerely: (Joyce Beatty: Member of Congress, Steven Horsford: Member of Congress, Mark Pocan: Member of Congress, Al Green: Member of Congress, Brad Sherman: Member of Congress, Brad Sherman: Member of Congress, Wiley Nickel: Member of Congress, Jan Schakowsky: Member of Congress, James P. McGovern: Member of Congress, Dina Titus: Member of Congress: Eleanor Holmes Norton Member of Congress)

and prosperity of humanity, there is no way we can reproduce if we encourage same sex marriage. In African societies, sex is a sacrosanct act which must be treated with dignity and it was and still is expected that copulation is from different gender. According to Augustine Shutte[219] good sex is sex symbolic. It is core-meaning for it is a union, intimacy sharing, community of the fullest kind. It also carries the meaning for cooperative creativity, and it's for personal growth and the community. He argues that sexual partnership is face-to-face affair and sexual partners must be friends concerned with a common value. Thus, in sexual friendship, this common value is naturally the child. The question is, what is the agenda of the LGBTQ community? Is it to discourage procreation so as to reduce the population of Africans?

Again, what is biological or natural about lesbianism or gaysm? As long as lesbian couples will still go for menstrual cycle, they are still women, and as long as gay couples will go for anal reconstructive surgery, they will still be men since their anus is not meant for the act of procreation. Then there are arguments that the lesbians and gay couples are allowed to adopt a child. Well, whose child are they adopting? The child they are adopting is from a union between a male and female whom in one way or another they loath (from an egg of a woman fertilized by sperm from a man) that means the LGBTQ agenda is definitely self-contradictory. In the African context, marriage is one of the ontological stages of the development of an African person, it's a stage of detachment from once biological family and attachment to another person of the opposite sex to form a family. It is a stage of procreation and production of wealth for one's family and the security of the children. Sex and marriage are for the communal sustainability from one generation to the next. The point of marriage for men and women alike is thus to make their sexual

---

[219] Augustine Shutte, *Ubuntu, An Ethic for a New South Africa*, (Cape Town, Cluster Publications, 2001) 92-93

powers and express their desire for personal growth and that of the community. Augustine Shutte[220] further argues that in this community, they seek for each other is one that is essentially open to and can be shared in by their child. Since this child is the natural focus of their friendship with each other, so it should be their intention in marrying.

We have to understand that in the African context, before the coming of the missionaries, most marriages were polygamous by nature and it should be clear that polygamy was not meant for men to have multiple sexual partners, but it was meant for every child to have a father figure and every woman to have a husband. This is true to all Abrahamic religions too. A case in point is my in-law Mzee Mogaya who married more than 10 women and sired more than 54 children whom he educated. When he came to visit me to see where his daughter is married (Pauline Mogaya) who is the first born of the seventh wife, he categorically advised Pauline to respect me and my mother. He asserted that he has given out 28 girls for marriage and none of them has walked away from their marriage. Is he a sinner for marrying many women and siring children he has since been responsible for? From the Christian perspective, he is, but from the African perspective he is real man. After the missionaries came, they insisted on one man one woman as a form of marriage, this has seen many women becoming single mothers. Now they are again preaching same sex marriage which others consider to be a gift from God, tomorrow it will be men and animals as long as the intercourse will not lead to veterinary attention, what a contradiction? The same religion cannot teach contradictory message about marriage, it's against logic. To think critically and logically, we need accurate and well supported beliefs. But, just as important, we need to be able to reason from those beliefs to conclusions that logically follow from them. Unfortunately, illogical thinking is all too common in human

---

[220] Augustine Shutte, *Ubuntu, An Ethic for a New South Africa*, 94

affairs including full acceptance of the LGBTQ's arguments and family rights.

There is a problem with the argument that individual autonomy and sexuality is private matter, and we should not publicly talk against induction of our children into the LGBTQ+ community in Africa. Take a case where a secondary school going girl or boy is introduced into LGBTQ community using money and food, it becomes a child abuse to introduce a child or a young person who has been brought up by his/her parents as a boy or a girt into an LGBTQ community at a tender age without being informed of the consequences of actions related to such relationship. This account for the deformation of a children whom, the families and societies have taken care of to train and nurture into a particular culture and gender. It's infringing the child's right, which results into human rights violation of both the children and their parents. Even if they are adults, the people involved are being dishonest to go against nature and biological orientation as from their birth. Nonetheless, People should also realize that sexuality is a public conception, but sex is a private matter which we cannot interfere with if it is between two consenting adults, but try to use money to influence people into a particular sexual orientation is unwarranted.

As the debate of LGBT continues, the question is, are we note selling our dignity in the name of being in the global community? We are peddling individual autonomy, which is a direct attack on the self-worth of Africans and cultural values. Whose right are we protecting, whose values are we propagating? Simon Wale[221] on the needs for roots asserts that those who keep masses on subjection by exercising cruelty deprive them at once two vital foods; liberty and obedience for it is no longer within the power of such masses to accord their inner consent to the authority to which they are subjected.

---

[221] Simone Waile,L *The need for roots; the Prelude to a Declaration of Duties towards Mankind*, (London: Routledge) 13

The Way Forward for Africa and Conclusion

From the previous arguments, all the evidence points to the fact that most of the cultural degradation in Africa is due to what we term as "Global/Universal" culture, due to the influence of the west. This is illustrated by George Ritzer[222] that culturally, the globalists give great importance to the rise of a global popular culture, a culture that is common to large numbers of people and most, if not all areas of the world. However, sceptics reject the idea of a common global popular culture, including and especially one dominated by the United States. To them, the whole idea of such a culture has been exaggerated. We therefore need to infuse philosophy in governance in Africa, to sensitize leaders to respect and protect human dignity, freedom and equality, and more so to realize that any civilization should be pegged on the reflection on the concept of human rights in the context of Africans and above all to control the appetite of her population from excess cultural borrowing.

We can therefore see that LGBTQ agenda is a form of colonialism which is not only a political imposition but also a cultural one. Gravely affected are areas of our religions and systems of education and thought. The system of education introduced by colonialism consists of the fact that our education was delivered in the medium of one foreign language or another. It therefore results to total up rootedness from our cultures and practices. Up rootedness is not just a military conquest, money power and economic domination, it can also be mental and cultural influence from the foreign culture. However, today money is being used to influence our young ones from universities, colleges and even from high schools to be involved in LGBTQ agenda. As argued by Somone Weil[223] money destroys human roots wherever it is

---

[222] George Ritzer, *Globalization: A basic text*, (United Kingdom: John Wiley & Sons 2010) 36.

[223] Simone Waile, *The need for roots; the Prelude to a Declaration of Duties towards Mankind*41

able to penetrate, by turning desire for gain into the sole motive. Why should we have purely lesbian or gay clubs in the big cities across Africa? The sole motive is to uproot Africans from their sexuality which will always lead to communal development.

We as African philosophers though studied in foreign languages, sometimes, we are influenced by foreign understanding of realities. For example, the African who has studied philosophy in English has likely become cognitively westernized to a significant extent not voluntarily but as a result of historical events. He might have lost some of his African identity to some degree. Whether the philosophy was taught in Africa is irrelevant. This is where Kwasi Wiredu [224] insists that we need consensual, that consensus does not entail total agreement, it in fact presupposes diversity and since issues do not always polarize along lines of strict contradictoriness, dialogue can function to produce compromises by means of smoothing edges, leading to a willing suspension of disagreement, making possible agreed actions without necessarily agreed notions. This means, unanimity about what is to be done, not about what ought to be done and not unanimity in intellectual and ethical belief. Thus, members with diverse opinions can reach agreement on what is to be done without forsaking their opinions about what is true or false. Africans should use African conceptual resources to inform their approaches to solving problems. When it is possible, they must incorporate African inputs, whether in logic, epistemology, ethics, or metaphysics.

In Africa today, we are looking for political and social structures that are best suited to the demands of rapid development, but we are also re-evaluating and changing our African culture in response to modern circumstances, more specifically, in response to a foreign influence that first came to us in the form of colonialism, which is still being violently resisted in some parts

---

[224] Kwasi Wiredu Wiredu, K. 2010. The state and civil society in Africa. Pp. 1055–66 in H. Lauer and K. Ayidoho (eds), *Reclaiming the Human Sciences*. Volume 2. (Legon-Accra Sub-Saharan Publishers, 2010). 1055-66)

of Africa. I might be accused of entrenching African "ethnocentrism", but we have to realize that ethnocentric tendencies must be epistemic (intellectual) and behavioural attitude which varies among individuals. VY Mudimbe[225] asserts that epistemological filiation maintains and sustains anthropology as a system of knowledge and as a developing science and thus cultural ethnocentrism explains ideological changes and struggles in the history and practices of the social science discipline. We therefore have to assert ourselves in the world today against the pressure to succumb to the western ideology on LBGTQ and other western cultural relativism.

Wiredu[226] asserts that an African philosopher must let his voice be heard on the question of what mode of social and political organization is best suited to our conditions and he must take active part. Since development does not mean merely the acquisition of technology with its associated material benefits, it means also the securing of such conditions as shall permit the self-realization of men as rational beings. However ambiguous the term ideology is, we must as Africans seek that which can lead to the development of the individual person and the community, and this is what I refer to Ubuntu philosophy, we shall discuss this in the next page.

One way in which a man can lose his soul is by being prevented from trying to think for himself, or even more terribly, by being rendered unable to think for himself. In Africa nowadays, people mobilize the population for rapid development and force their pet preconceptions down the throats of their countrymen in order that their actions might seem to have support of the masses. But in the African context, there was responsibilities in behaviour after

---

[225] V.Y Mudimbe, *The invention of Africa: Gnosis, Philosophy and the order of knowledge*, , Bloomington, Indiana University Press,1998) 19.

[226] Kwasi Wiredu, *Philosophy and African Culture*, , London Cambridge University Press), 1980, 52.

initiation. This is asserted by Ivan Karp and D.A. Masolo[227] that adult responsibilities are seen to be part and parcel of the rights achieved through initiation. That many of those responsibilities are shaped, embodied and created through marriage, though they may be accepted with ambivalence. And we must understand that ambivalence in marriage is not the bride's and the groom's alone. The bride family must relinquish their child, while the groom's family accepts as stranger into their home. This culmination with the idea of extending the same responsibilities to the community and children to control their appetite for cultural borrowing.

As man lives in a complex world and he is in constant endeavour to understand the world he lives in and therefore philosophers have to engage in discussion on the quest for the good of man. This good should improve the society and this will eventually lead to change. Since change is inevitable, it should be managed carefully to produce a good society. This is majorly so since there is a lot of influence from modern conditions. This is in line with the philosophy of Nyerere[228], that all human beings are equal and should be treated as such (*binadamu wote ni sawa*), meaning that all human beings should have equal opportunities and rights. And this should be coupled with *utu* (dignity) and *haki* (justice). Nyerere asserts that we have to work towards a position where each person realizes that his rights in the society. And we have to establish social organization which reduces personal temptation, above the level of a minimum.

Philosophers should examine their African cultures and identify the strengths and weaknesses of these cultures. They should appreciate the good things and try to change the bad in a logical manner. They should however not consider their cultures inferior and abandon them. Additionally, Wiredu calls for independence/

---

[227] Ivan Karp and D.A. Masolo *African Philosophy and Cultural Inquiry*, Indiana university Press, Bloomington, 2000, 139

[228] Nyerere, J.K., *Fredom and Unity*. Oxford University Press, 15, 17. 1966

autonomy in evaluating ideas. Philosophers should not succumb to communal pressure.

As African philosophers, we need to insist on the teaching of the Ubuntu philosophy or African humanism. We have to realize that Ubuntu philosophy is a living Philosophy of Africans, it is a philosophy of the past, a present and a project of the future, because it enhances the triad nature of human living in this world: connecting the living human beings to the environment and to the world of the ancestors. It is in the lived and living experiences of human beings inherent in everyone which places people on equal plane. Extreme wealth by few individuals, leaving the vast majority poor, destroys the Ubuntu which in essence lead to the violation of human rights and by extension the protection, promotion and respect of the right to be a human being.

Ubuntu calls for the respect and fair treatment of all human beings regardless of their economic, political or religious affiliations. Radical ideologies also violate the principles of Ubuntu which are necessary for the peaceful coexistence of people of different cultures and societies in the world. *Ubuntu is not the Cartesian cogito ergo sum* (I think therefore I am), but an existential *cognatus sum, ergo sumus* (I am related therefore we are). Therefore, all human beings are related and should be respected in the spirit of Ubuntu, and should be taken as an end to themselves, not as a means to paradise by destroying that humanity.

Bibliography

ADDANEY, M. et al. *Governance, Human Rights, and Political Transformation in Africa,* Switzerland: Palgrave Macmillan 2020.

APPIAH, K., "Akan and Euro-American Concepts of the Person" in African Philosophy: *New and Traditional Perspectives.* Edited by Lee M. Brown, Oxford: Oxford University Press, 2004.

AYAYO, O., *Traditional ideology and Ethics among Southern Luo*, Scandinavian Institute of African Studies, Uppsala, 1976.

CHAPPELL, V., *The Cambridge companion to Locke*, Cambridge University Press, 1994.

CLAPHAM, A., *Human Rights: A Very Short Introduction*, Oxford, University Press Inc., New York, 2007.

CONGRESS OF UNITED STATES, Washington DC 20510. July 25, 2023 to the President, World Bank Group 1818 H Street, NW Washington, D.C. 20433.

DENG, F., "Human, Rights in the African Context", *A Companion to African Philosophy*, Edited by Kwasi Wiredu, Blackwell Publishing, 2004.

FALOLA, T., *Key Events in African History: A Reference Guide*, Greenwood, Press Westport, 2002.

FERRARI, G., *The Cambridge companion to Plato's Republic*, Cambridge University Press 2007.

FOSTER, G., *John Locke's Politics of Moral Consensus*, Cambridge, Cambridge University Press 2005.

HORN, C. and SCHÖNECKER D. (edts). *Groundwork for the Metaphysics of Morals*, Berlin, Walter de Gruyter 2006.

KARP, I. and MASOLO D.A., *African Philosophy and Cultural Inquiry*, Bloomington: Indiana University Press, 2000.

KENYA TRUTH, JUSTICE AND RECONCILIATION COMMISSION (TJRC). (2013). Report of the Truth, Justice and Reconciliation Commission Vol. 1. Nairobi: TJRC.

LAREMONT, R., (edt). *Africanity Redefined Collected Essays of Ali A. Mazrui volume I*, Asmara. Africa's Word Press. 2000.

LEWIS, A., *Silent Accomplice: The Untold Story of France's Role in the Rwandan Genocide*, R. B. Tirus London, 2007.

MACHARIA, A., *Rights of the Child, Mothers and Sentencing*, Rutledge, published 2021.

MBITI, J., African Religion and Philosophy, London, Heinemann, 1969

MCCARNEY, J., *Routledge Philosophy GuideBook to Hegel on history*, London: Reutledge, 2000.

MIDDLETON J. and. MILLER J. C., *New Encyclopedia of Africa*, Volume 4 Nairobi–Symbol, Thomson Gale.

MUDIMBE, V.Y., *The invention of Africa: Gnosis, Philosophy and the order of knowledge*, Bloomington, Indiana University Press, 1998.

NDUNGU, C. G., (2014). "Lessons to be learned: An Analysis of the Final Report of Kenya's Truth, Justice and Reconciliation Commission," *ICTJ Briefing*. New York: International Centre for Transitional Justice.2014, p. 5).

NEIL, T., *Introducing Philosophy: God, Mind, world and Logic*, London, Rutledge, 2015.

NYERERE, J. K., *Fredom and Unity*. Oxford University Press, 15, 17. 1966.

OBENGA, T., "Egypt: Ancient History of African Philosophy" in Kwasi Wiredu et. Al. A *companion of African Philosophy*.

OGUDE, J., *Ubuntu and the reconstruction of the community*, USA, Indiana University Press, 2019.

PLATO, Gorgias 521d–522a

PRUCE, J. R., *The Mass Appeal of Human Rights, Palgrave Macmillan*, Cham, Switzerland, 2019.

RITZER, G., *Globalization: A basic text*, United Kingdom, John Wiley & Sons, 2010.

ROSS, W., (translator). *Nicomachean Ethics,* book Focus Publishing/R. Pullins Company, 2002.

ROUSSEAU, J. J., *The Social Contract and The First and Second Discourses,* Edited and with an Introduction by, New Haven, Yale University Press, 2002.

RUSSELL, E. L., *The Discursive Ecology of Homophobia Unraveling Anti-LGBTQ Speech on the European Far Right*, Library of Congress Cataloging in Publication Data, 2019.

SENSEN, O., *Kant on human dignity*, Berlin: De Gruyter, 2011

SHABAN, B. R., Utubora Mkulima, Diwani ya Shaban No 8. London: Evans brothers.

SHUTTE, A., Ubuntu, An Ethic for a New South Africa, Cape town, Cluster Publications, 2001.

WAILE S., The need for roots; the Prelude to a Declaration of Duties towards Mankind, Routledge, London 2002

WILSON CENTER MARINA OTTAWAY ALGERIA: The Enduring Failure of Politics, https://www.wilsoncenter.org/article/algeria-enduring-failure-politics

WIREDU, K., *Cultural Universals and Particulars*, Indiana University Press, 1996.

WIREDU, K., *Philosophy and African Culture*, London, Cambridge University Press. 1980, 52.

WIREDU, K., *The state and civil society in Africa*. Pp. 1055–66 in H. Lauer and K. Ayidoho (eds), Reclaiming the Human Sciences. Volume 2. Legon-Accra Sub-Saharan Publishers, 2010.

WIREDU, K., "The Akan Concept of Mind" in *Ibadan Journal of Humanistic Studies,*

WOOD, A., *A. Groundwork for the Metaphysics of Morals Immanuel Kant*, Edited and translated by with essays by J. B. Schneewin, New Haven, Yale University Press, 2002.

One Moral Obligation One Universal Morality: A Critique of Kwasi Wiredu's Cultural Universals and Particulars[229]

Crispin Ong'era Isaboke, Chuka University Department of Humanities, Chuka, Kenya. Crisaboke@yahoo.com

Abstract

Being a rational animal, a human being is by nature a moral agent. In spite of having the ability to distinguish between good and evil, he is also conscious of the fact that he has the obligation to do that which is right and avoid that which is wrong. Moreover, every culture since time immemorial has defined itself with quite distinctive qualities that not only include beliefs, customs and knowledge but also morals, art and other attributes specific to that culture. The African continent, ipso facto, is comprised of numerous ethnic nationalities with varying qualities, for instance, language and greetings. Her culture is not a homogeneous culture due to use of different languages and traditions. Nevertheless, all African peoples share quite a lot in terms of cultural traits. These traits distinguish Africa from the rest of the world and therefore define what we may refer to as the African culture. Social values, religious beliefs, moral and political values, as well as economic and aesthetic values add to the richness of the African culture. Africa's diversity of cultures does not therefore destroy the underlying principle of shared similarities, for example, the morals they uphold, love and respect for human dignity and respect for the aged. Each African culture looks at reality from their perspective and this influences the extent to which they

---

[229] G. W. F. Hegel, *The Philosophy of History,* J. Jibree trans. (New York: Dover, 1956), p. 99.

become objective in that regard. The aim of this paper is to reflect on the universality of African morality by arguing that the diversity of African cultures is not an impediment to moral objectivity and universality. The paper argues that an African is a human being and therefore rational by nature; he has the obligation to do good. Moral values are therefore natural and must be universal, thus there is need to transcend cultural particularities and arrive at genuine objectivity founded on authentic subjectivity.

Key words: cultural universal, particulars, moral obligation, Africa.

Introduction

Kwasi Wiredu, a Ghanaian, is one of the renowned African philosophers who is highly regarded for his project known as "conceptual decolonization" in contemporary African systems of thought. By conceptual decolonization he means a re-examination of the present-day African epistemic formations in view of accomplishing two objectives. First, he intends to destabilize any disagreeable and unpleasant aspects of tribal culture embedded in modern African thought to make that thought more viable; and, second, he undertakes to dislodge unnecessary Western epistemologies that are to be found in African philosophical practices. In the dichotomy of universalism in philosophical discourse and African philosophy in particular, Wiredu argues against the negative influence of colonial experience, which was largely dehumanizing in its exploitative nature in view of raising African thinking to the same level as that of the West, given the fact that the human being is one and an African is not an exception. More importantly, his elucidation of the compatibility of cultural particulars and universals was of paramount significance in the search for African identity.

Be that as it may, it must be borne in mind that the intellectual discourse of the West on Africans had been ignited by Hegel's argument that Africa "is no historical part of the world; it has no movement or development to exhibit. Historical movement in it – that is in its northern part – belongs to Asiatic or European World...."[230]. By way of explanation, this simply means that an African has no reason, and by virtue of that has no capacity to attain intellective knowledge, he has no morals. Simply put, the misconception was that an African cannot think. What can be deduced from this is that an African and development cannot be referred to in the same sentence; the two are seen as contradictories. As a consequence, Hegel would argue further to say that "Africa is the unhistorical, undeveloped spirit, still involved in the conditions of mere nature, and which had to be presented here only as on the threshold of the World's history."[231]. With this thinking, philosophy and Africa would only seem a contradiction. The West conceived rationality as a preserve of Western civilization whereas Africans were seen as primitive and alien to reason.

It is against this background that African scholars had to respond to in defense of the existence of philosophy in Africa in the pre-colonial period and even after. In his article, "Towards an African Concept of Law," Abiodom emphasizes that "the significant role played by Western scholarship and erstwhile Western imperial lords in presenting and treating the African people as inferior and deserving of external control, necessitates that African scholarship in post-colonial era, should be active in the deconstruction of this negative and battered identity."[232]. Effectively, it is a duty of African scholars to counter such

---

[230] Hegel, 99.

[231] Abiodom Balogun, "Towards an African Concept of Law" African Journal of Legal Theory, 2007, p. 1.

[232] Ademola Kazeem Fayemi, "Cultural Universals and Particulars in Kwasi Wiredu's Philosophy, Trames 3, p. 259-276.

misleading and demeaning mentality against Africans which would only place Africans in the same level as brutes. Kwasi Wiredu is one such scholars who contributed immensely to this debate. Wiredu, therefore, considers conceptual decolonization as an imperative in contemporary African philosophy; it is something that must be done. This refers to the elimination from our thought of modes of conceptualization that came to us through colonization and remain in our thinking owing to inertia rather than to our own reflective choices. He avers that colonialism has caused a widespread involuntary intermixing of Western and African intellectual categories in the thinking of contemporary Africans, and this makes it a bit difficult for the deconceptualization. Our present concern is on his conception and criticism of cultural universals and particulars in relation to ethics and morality. He critically examines the cultural universals in relation to particulars with the intention of demonstrating that the two are not incompatible as the Western scholars had viewed them.

Cultural Universals and Particulars

It is worth to note that Wiredu wrote a book dedicated to cultural universals and particulars, in which he argues on the particularity and universality of the human nature. Cultural universals on the one hand "denies cultural relativism and ethnocentrism maintained by Western anthropological scholarship"[233] while cultural particulars is the view that all philosophies are cultural philosophies, hence, there is no philosophical datum of any given culture which is applicable to other cultures. In essence, Wiredu disagrees with Western scholarship in the thinking that African cultures do not transcend their cultural viewpoints to arrive at objective and universal truths acceptable across cultures. Incidentally, the west is presented as

---

[233] Fayemi, p. 259-276.

one homogeneous and universal culture while Africa is presented as a fragmented continent whose cultures are many and unrelated; and therefore, do not communicate with each other. This is the context within which we consider the two cultures; the Western culture and the African culture; yet an African is an individual rational being just like any other human being. On the contrary, Wiredu holds the view that it is not impossible to arrive at universally relevant concepts which can at the same time be disentangled from the contingencies of culture. Consequently, due to the universality of universal concepts, they are able to be known in diverse cultural establishments.

As a consequence, cultural particulars and universals are just but orientations in the search for African self-identity; "…the general deducible impression is that there is a dichotomy and incompatibility between the perspective of African scholars on cultural universalism and particularism as related to the quest for identity."[234] In essence, this explains why Wiredu discusses the paradox of universalism and particularism in the human nature and demonstrates that it is possible to arrive at concepts of universal relevance. Concepts are intelligible within various and diverse cultural groups due to their universals. The intelligibility of these concepts across cultures is due to their universality and objectivity. They cannot be reduced to the mere particular perceptibles that are unknowable. According to him, there are universals and particulars in philosophy, religion and culture.

In Wiredu's opinion, therefore, whereas universals are founded on the human nature which is common to all human beings, particulars ensue from certain accidental or non-essential variations in culture. Undoubtedly, each particular culture will exhibit certain particular qualities that are specific to that culture alone. He says: "universal is what is general, and what is general

[234] Kwasi Wiredu, "The Akan Concept of Mind" *Ibadan Jounal of Humanistic Studies,* 3, p. 113-134.

is what can be instantiated, i.e. what can have an instance."[235]. To say that a universal is what is general is to imply that it has been abstracted from the particular and can, therefore, be instantiated. For instance, the concept "cow" is a universal concept which is only abstracted from a particular cow; for which reason it can refer to any particular cow. As evidence of cultural universals, he cites intercultural communication; the fact that one culture can communicate with another and vice-versa. Effectively, human beings share in rationality which makes them the same: "the assumption behind his argument is that the entire human race shares some fundamental categories and criteria of thought in common."[236]. Therefore, the differences and particularities brought about due to nurture cannot be wished away. Central to these differences and particularities rests the universal human nature.

There are elements in each culture of particularity in spite of the fact that there are also elements of universality. Wiredu rightly observes that "…being a human person implies having the capacity of reflective perception, abstraction, deduction and induction. In their basic nature, these mental capacities are the same for all humans; irrespective of whether they inhibit Europe, Asia or Africa…"[237]. What defines a human being does not require these differences of race, culture, religion etc. Rationality is what constitutes humanity. A human being is a rational animal. Particulars, so to say, include specific practices that distinguish cultures from one another e.g. all people become hungry but the potential food sources defined as edible vary across all cultures. Particulars, therefore, include specific practices that distinguish cultures from one another, for instance, although people of all cultures get hungry at one point or another, whatever is defined

---

[235] Fayemi, p. 259-276.

[236] Wiredu, 1996:23.

[237] D.A. Masolo, *African Philosophy in Search of Identity* (Nairobi: East African Educational Publishers Ltd., 1995), p. 207.

as food and therefore good for human consumption may vary across all cultures. Yet these are not essential to humanity.

On the contrary, universals are those things or aspects that are common to all societies; based on physical and environmental needs.

Be that what it may, Wiredu views cultural universals as not incompatible with cultural particulars. He rightly observes that universals are ultimately based on human nature, which is common, whereas particulars stem from some accidental variations in culture. At the moral level, the moral law, which is the expression of the human rational nature, is universal. It also follows as a matter of logical necessity that all human actions must ensure from and be guided by the moral law. In point of fact, "the primary significance of knowledge...lies in its guidance of action, for knowing is for the sake of doing."[238]. This is the reason why knowledge for Wiredu depended on whether action can be derived from it or not. Moreover, he sees knowledge as na apprehension of the future as qualified by values which action may realize[239]. Accordingly, emphasis is laid on the necessary relations between knowledge and values we look forward to. The critical question is "is morality universal? This question can only be adequately answered by examining the human nature to establish whether morality ensues from it.

Human Nature: Source of Universal Morality

It goes without saying that the human nature is universal and is the foundation of universals, according to Wiredu, who emphasizes that this nature is common. On the contrary,

---

[238] Masolo, p. 207.

[239] Kwasi Wiredu, "The Moral Foundations of an African Culture," *Person and Community (Ghanaian Philosophical Studies), Kwais Wiredu and Gyekye (eds.)* (Wahington, D.C.: The Council for Research in Values and Philosphy), p. 217.

particulars ensue from certain accidental variations in culture. Thus, it is deducible that the particulars need be compatible with the human nature and in that way they can transcend particularity to reach levels of universality. The human nature is expressed at the moral level through the moral obligation, a dictate of reason, which states that good ought to be done. This is a dictate of reason, which also implies that evil ought not to be done. Does this apply to all human beings? The truth is that it does. Thus, what is good does not depend on circumstances of race, religion, tribe or of any kind; and, what is evil does not depend on any circumstances. The morally good is good irrespective of even the mind that affirms or denies it.

What the above means is that good and evil are objective and by that fact universal. They do not depend on the mind that either affirms or denies them. Any argument to the effect that good and evil are relative necessarily denies the moral law, and as a result denies humanity. The one reason for this is that all human beings share the same nature, rationality. This rationality is expressed at the moral level through the moral obligation, according to which good ought to be done and evil avoided. According to Wiredu, morality refers to the motivated pursuit of sympathetic impartiality. This in effect means that one's conduct must manifest a genuine concern for the interest of others at all times.

Whereas it is true that what different cultures hold as moral may not necessarily be what is universally good, it is a fact that cannot be denied that the human nature is one, and it entails morality. Hence, whatever these cultures hold to be true ought to be true. It is for this reason that the moral law is the first principle of morality and from which morality flows.

Any human act, therefore, must not only flow from this first principle but must also be consistent with it for it to be morally good. Any act done freely but which is in contradiction with the moral law is evil by that fact alone. This applies to all culture since the human being is one by virtue of their essence, which is rationality, and through which the human person orders his action. Thus, regardless of one's culture, morality must transcend culture to attain levels of universality and objectivity that is an expression of humanity. Morality is human yet the human culture is one, identified with rationality. Whatever we call cultures is a product of nurture rather than nature and hence, the reason for all the differences in the way these cultures express themselves is nurture. Essentially, if nurture is not guided and directed by reason or nature, it will result in relativism, the thinking that the human mind is not the same and therefore, what is good for one culture need not be good in another culture, which is not the case. It is deducible from the this that "morality in the strictest sense is universal to human culture. Indeed, it is essential to all human culture. Any society without a modicum of morality must collapse."[240]. In addition, morality is "the observance of rules for the harmonious adjustment of the interests of the individual to those of others in society."[241]. In Wiredu's understanding, this is a minimal concept of morality, although he goes further to argue that "a richer concept of morality even more pertinent to human flourishing will have an essential reference to that special kind of motivation called the sense of duty."[242]. In essence, this implies that morality must take into account both the general conformity to the demands of common interests as well as to those motivated or driven by an imaginative and sympathetic identification with the interests of other people, even if this was to demand a sacrifice of the interests of an individual: "…a certain minimum of altruism is absolutely essential to the moral motivation."

To put emphasis on the fact that morality has its foundation in the human nature, Wiredu argues that among the Akans of Ghana, just like it is the case in all human societies, "…it is a

---

[240] Wiredu, "The Moral Foundations…, p. 217.
[241] Wiredu, "The Moral Foundations…, p. 217.
[242] Wiredu, "The Moral Foundations…, p. 217.

human being that has value: *onipa na ohia.*[243]. Thus, in spite of the fact that man is not an absolute being, he is (or has) an absolute value that gives him a certain dignity that must always be respected. Furthermore, this could also mean that all value flows from human interests and find meaning in them. On this, Wiredu makes morality dependent on others' interests and in a sense erodes the true meaning of morality. Nevertheless, the fact that he considers both the interests of others and those of the individual is something that goes a long way in incorporating African socialism to morality. In the true spirit of an African, one is happy when their actions are of greater good to the other. This explains further why human fellowship is at the heart of human needs, underscoring African socialism. Wiredu emphasizes that "one important implication of the founding of value on human interests is the independence of morality from religion in the Akan outlook: what is good in general is what promotes human interests."[244]. On this, he clearly and rightly detaches what is moral from what is religious and maintains that what is morally right need not be religiously right; so morality cannot be subservient to religion. Morality is personal and for this reason one must take personal responsibility for what they do.

In this, "…Wiredu explores the possibility of establishing ethical or moral universalism. His basic consideration in this regard is to find out such a principle of conduct that without its recognition, the survival of human society in a tolerable condition would be inconceivable."[245]. More importantly, he distinguished between custom and morality where he viewed customs as a contingent fact of particular social formations and broadly constitute such things as usages, traditions, conventions,

---

[243] Wiredu, "The Moral Foundations…, p. 218.

[244] Fayemi, p. 259-276.

[245] Fayemi, p. 259-276.

etiquette, fashions, aesthetic standards, taboos and even folklores[246].

However, the two cultures, African and Western, are in conflict with regard to some of the cultural particulars (moral). The contingence implied here is they cannot be universally evaluated since there are no universal principles for the same. It can, therefore be inferred that the rightness or wrongness of such rules is dependent on culture and so vary from one culture to another. But, one may ask, to what extent can this be the case?

The definition of morality as "...the motivated pursuit of sympathetic impartiality," signifies that one's conduct must be reflective of a due concern for the interests of others. That is to say that one's conduct must bring good to others and by that virtue it is good. Essentially, this assertion is more or less characteristic of Immanuel Kant's categorical imperative which states that "act only on that maxim that you will at the same time will that it becomes a universal law of reason." Apparently, even Kant argues that to know that one acts from the motive of duty, one must ask themselves if their action would be good if done to them; if not, then it cannot be a universal law, and hence, the act is evil and must not be done. Nevertheless, while Kant does not include the other as a factor to consider in determining the morality of an act, Wiredu seems to invoke some emotions by appealing to the interests of others and gives them an equally central role to play in the same. Wiredu says, "sympathetic impartiality represents a fusion of impartiality and sympathy: the impartiality is what the moral rules embody, and the sympathy is what the moral motivation evinces."[247] "Values such as truthfulness, honesty, justice, chastity, etc. are aspects of sympathetic impartiality and do not differentiate morality from culture to culture." These values are cherished across cultures since they are not culture-

---

[246] Kwasi Wiredu, *Cultural Universals and Particulars* (Bloomington: Indiana University Press, 1996), p. 23.

[247] Ibid., p. 31.

specific. They transcend culture to attain levels of objectivity and universality. They are irreducible to one culture or another. However, "the contingencies of cultures may only introduce some variations of details in the definitions of some of these values".

Conclusion

From the above exposition, it is clearly evident that Wiredu's defense of the compatibility of cultural universals and particulars is a significant move in the history of African thought. As he observes, it was not only wrong and demeaning for the West to see equate particularities of the human nature to African thought while elevating their own and placing it at the level of universality and objectivity; it was also demeaning and a misrepresentation of Africans. The truth remains that a human being is defined by rationality and this rationality is expressed at the level of morality through the moral obligation. This obligation knows no race, religion or tribe, it knows no culture; it is itself a culture, one human culture. It cannot be logical, therefore, for anyone to argue that rationality is a preserve of the West while an African is reduced to mere emotion. It is a fact that human nature is universal although it can be influence by different environments; and this is the cause of what are called (many) cultures, which are a product of mere nurture rather than nature. Universals are founded on the human nature while particulars proceed from and are guided by it. In a nutshell, morality is universal due to its firm foundation in the one universal human nature and all (societies) stand due to their moral considerations. The human person has an inherent dignity which must never be wished away; he has an absolute value.

Bibliography

ABIODOM B. "Towards an African Concept of Law" African Journal of Legal Theory, 2007.

HEGEL, G. W. F. *The Philosophy of History*, J. Jibree trans. New York: Dover, 1956.

KAZEEM, F. A. "Cultural Universals and Particulars in Kwasi Wiredu's Philosophy, Trames 3, 259-276.

MASOLO, D.A. *African Philosophy in Search of Identity.* Nairobi: East African Educational Publishers Ltd., 1995.

WIREDU, K. *Cultural Universals and Particulars.* Bloomington: Indiana University Press, 1996.

WIREDU, K. "The Moral Foundations of an African Culture," *Person and Community (Ghanaian Philosophical Studies), Kwais Wiredu and Gyekye (eds.).* Washington, D.C.: The Council for Research in Values and   Philosophy.

WIREDU, K. "The Akan Concept of Mind" *Ibadan Jounal of Humanistic Studies, 3.*

A Critical Analysis of Kwasi Wiredu's Compatibility of Religion and Morality

Oliver Babirye Najjuma, LSOSF, Full-time Lecturer at Tangaza Institute of Philosophy, and Part-time Lecturer at the Apostles of Jesus Institute of Philosophy and Theology (AJIPT), Nairobi – Kenya.
obabirye@tangaza.ac.ke

Abstract

There is no doubt that religion is a dominant concern of humanity. This concern has led many to conclude that it is within the circles of religion that human beings can live morally. Despite this, it is very difficult to define or describe religion. We can attribute this difficulty to the fact that, different people practice a great diversity of religions. This is evident in the different rituals and ceremonies associated with each religion. Secondly, the concept of religion is broad; it does not only focus on the universally accepted religions of Judaism, Christianity and Islam but also African religion, whose ideas of religion, spirituality, and ethics has gone unappreciated by religious scholars. Kwasi Wiredu points out that even some authors who reckon that African life is full of religion hardly have a word in African languages that translates the word religion. Briefly, religion is something growing, dynamic, essential, personal and broad in scope. It also has many constitutive elements, like, metaphysical beliefs, moral teachings, psychological attitudes, legends, traditions, written scriptures, ceremonies, music and poetry. From Wiredu's perspective, an attempt to define religion sometimes implies a certain kind of attitude. For example, where a religion postulates a Supreme Being, an attitude of unconditional reverence and worship comes in. A further condition is the one, which introduces an ethical dimension into the definition. This implies that, essential to any religion is a conception of moral uprightness. Thus, what is morally right is what is in accord with the Supreme Being. Although this view of ethics is not universal, it is particularly popular among different religions. A major question that arises then is whether religion is a field of convergence or divergence of thought among the peoples and cultures of the world. The main task of this paper therefore is to examine whether the two terms of morality and religion are compatible. Apart from Wiredu, we shall consider other philosophers' views on the two concepts in comparison with Wiredu's stance.

Keywords: Kwasi Wiredu, Religion, Morality, and Compatibility

Introduction

Looking at the two terms religion and morality, it is evident that the central issue arising from them is their relationship with each other. The close interweave between them is reflected not only in the universally accepted regions of Judaism Christianity and Islam but also within African traditional religions. This article will attempt to clarify on the two terms in order to establish whether they are compatible. This article comprises of three sections. The first section focuses on deepening our understanding of religion and morality. The second section elucidates Kwasi Wiredu's compatibility of religion and morality plus his stance bolstered by African perception. In the third section, we shall focus on the critical analysis of religio-moral compatibility.

General Understanding of Religion and Morality

Religion

The word religion is derived from the Latin verb *religare,* which means 'to bind together'. Thus, the Latin noun *religio* referring to obligation or reverence is based on religare, and so *religio* and its English derivation religion connote a 're-binding', that is, to bind together that which might otherwise fall apart. According to Dr. Hemanta Kumar Kalita, religion in a literal sense is a principle of unification and harmonization. It is not a mere believe of Almighty, rather is an activity, behavior and conviction, a kind conduct which contemplates the inner order of soul[248]. Religion works for personal and social integration of values and for a general orientation of personal human existence.

Religion from Paul Tillich's perspective is the state of being grasped by an ultimate concern, a concern which qualifies all other concerns and in which the answer to the question of the meaning of life is entailed. The ultimate concern is that which demands complete surrender of the person who faithfully accepts the Ultimate[249]. Apart from Paul Tillich, other philosophers have attempted a definition of religion. According to Immanuel Kant, "religion is the recognition of all our duties as divine commands."[250]. Schleiermacher's view is that, "the essence of religion consists in the feeling of absolute dependence, alternatively, the essence of religion is piety, a feeling of

---

[248] Hemanta Kumar Kalita, (2018). *A Philosophical Approach to Religion and Culture,* International Journal of Science and Research (IJSR) ISSN (Online): 2319-7064 Index Copernicus Value (2016): 79.57 | Impact Factor (2015): 6, p. 391

[249] Philip A. Pecorino. (2001). *Philosophy of Religion.* Queensborough Community College https://www.qcc.cuny.edu/socialscienceppecorino/Phil-of-religion-text/default.htm, p. 3.

[250] Wood, Allen W. (2020). "Religion and Reason." Chapter. In *Kant and Religion,* p. 1–26. Cambridge Studies in Religion, Philosophy, and Society. Cambridge: Cambridge University Press. doi:10.1017/9781108381512.002.

immediate self-consciousness of absolute dependence on a divine entity."[251].

Briefly, most religions including African religions, address the metaphysical questions concerning the origin and nature of the universe, the meaning of human nature and ultimate reality and the presence of purpose in the universe. This is obvious in Dr. Philip Pecorino's definition that religion is an organized system of belief that generally seeks to understand purpose, meaning, goals, and methods of spiritual things. These spiritual things can be God, people in relation to God, salvation, after life, purpose of life and order of the cosmos[252]. What one draws from the above attempts to define religion, is that religion has been a dominant concern of humankind. Yet despite such a concern, it is very difficult to define or describe religion due to the fact that, it is growing, dynamic, elemental, personal and broad in scope.

Morality

Although some philosophers focus on the differences between molarity and ethics, basing on their etymological sense, in this work we shall look at them as one. The term 'moral' comes from the Latin word *mores,* which means custom or rules. Ethics originated in speculation on the good life. The Greeks systematized it into a part of philosophy and called it ethics from a Greek word *ethos,* which means custom or character[253]. From such a context, ethics is also known as moral philosophy. This is the same also with Britannica's article on ethics, they consider the

---

[251] Schleiermacher, Friedrich D. E. (1928). *The Christian Faith* H. R. Machintosh and J. S. Steward, Trans. Edinburgh: T. & T. Clark, p. 42.

[252] Philip A. Pecorino. (2001). *Philosophy of Religion.* Queensborough Community College   https://www.qcc.cuny.edu/socialscienceppecorino/Phil-of-religion-text/default.htm, p. 7.

[253] Milton Gonsalves, A. (1989). *Fagothey's Right and Reason,* Ethics in Theory and Practice Ninth Edition Prentice Hall, p.22.

terms to be the same as moral philosophy[254]. Its purpose is to study this fact of experience, that men distinguish right from wrong and have a feeling for the ought. Precisely, the philosophers use the term 'ethics', to refer to a philosophical study of morality, that is, morality understood as a set of social rules, principles, norms that guide or are intended to guide the conduct of people in a society, and as beliefs about right and wrong conduct as well as good or bad character.

Kwasi Wiredu's Compatibility of Religion and Morality

Kwasi Wiredu's Biography

Kwasi Wiredu was born in Kumasi, in the Ashanti Region of Ghana, in 1931. He belonged to the Akan community of Ghana. He studied at the University College of the Gold and Oxford University. He lectured at the University of Ghana, and it is at that university that he advanced to professorship, which he exercised also in the University of South Florida. He died in 2022[255]. Some of his works are; *Philosophy and an African Culture: The Case of the Akan* (1980), *Cultural Universals and Particulars: An African Perspective* (1996). It is important to note that Kwasi Wiredu's life was greatly influenced by Western philosophy. His philosophical stance below conspicuously attests to this observation.

---

[254] Grannan, Cydney. "What's the Difference Between Morality and Ethics?". *Encyclopedia Britannica*, 1 Sep. 2016. https://www.britannica.com/story/whats-the-difference-between-morality-and-ethics. Accessed 29 March 2023.

[255] Kwasi Wiredu, https://www.ug.edu.gh/sites/default/files/documents/Professor%20Kwasi%20Wiredu.pdf.

Kwasi Wiredu's Philosophical Stance

With the background of Western philosophy, Kwasi Wiredu came to find out about African traditions of thought through his own individual efforts. He discovered that after African countries attained political liberation, decolonization became an immediate and overwhelming preoccupation. As one of Africa's foremost philosophers, Kwasi Wiredu was not an exceptional in the task of decolonization. He got involved with a project he termed 'conceptual decolonization' in contemporary African systems of thought. This term entailed a re-examination of the current African epistemic foundations. Specifically, he intended to deconstruct the unnecessary Western epistemologies found in African philosophical practices. Basing on Wiredu's understanding, "it is a duty, of philosophy in any society to examine the intellectual foundations of its culture. It should take the form of reasoned criticism and, where possible, reconstruction. No other way to philosophical progress is known than through criticism and adaptation"[256]. His struggle of decolonization is also reflected in his views concerning religion and morality as we shall see in the following section.

Wiredu's Stance Bolstered by African Perception

In order to establish the compatibility of religion and morality, we need first to deepen our understanding of African religion and African morality, enriched with Wiredu and other African philosophers. Consequently, this becomes our concern in this part of our article.

Religion from African Perception

It is important to note from the beginning that we are viewing African religion as one religion and the African continent

---

[256] Kwasi Wiredu, (1980). *Philosophy and an African Culture: The Case of the Akan.* Cambridge University Press. p.20.

as a whole. The rationale behind this is to introduce classical African religious ideas, before the arrival of Christianity and Islam in Africa, and to establish them as the significant forerunners of much of continental African thought. In *The Encyclopedia of African Religion*, Molefi Kete, make as a starting point the unity of African religion, although he is quite aware of the diversity of expressions of that religion, much like one would see in Christianity, Judaism, Buddhism, and Islam. African religion dramatizes its unity in the universal appeal to the spirits that animate all of nature[257]. From his perspective, African religion has withstood the worst of human brutality and cruelty against other humans yet it has some beliefs and aspects of life and knowledge that are consistent across the continent. Africans are deeply spiritual people despite the multiple deities and ancestral spirits in African traditional religions. This is evident in some of their notable features. We shall have a glimpse of some, as a sign that Africans are not exceptional in the matters of religion.

The Hierarchy of Beings

Both Wiredu and Gyekye explain that the traditional Akan people of Ghana believe in a hierarchy of beings, with God, the Supreme Being, at the apex. After God, in a descending order, are found various kinds of spirits. Some of these spirits are believed to reside in some parts of nature, notably trees, mountains, animals and rivers. After these spirits, is the human species, which is, in turn, followed by lower animals, vegetation, and the rest of inanimate objects, in a descending order. Africans integrate this religious worldview into every aspect of life[258].

---

[257] Molefi Kete Asante & Ama Mazama, Eds. (2009). *Encyclopedia of African Religion*. Sage Publications, U.S.A. p. XXI.

[258] Stephen Nkansah Morgan & Beatrice Okyere-Manu *The Belief in and Veneration of Ancestors in Akan Traditional Thought: Finding Values for Human Well-being.* ORCID ID https://orcid.org/0000-0002-4480-7952 ORCID ID: https://orcid.org/0000-0003-2735-9227.

John Mbiti expressed the same while talking about ontology. He stressed that; Africans have their own ontology, but it is a religious ontology and to understand their religions we must penetrate that ontology. He divided it into five categories: "First God, as the ultimate explanation of the genesis and sustenance of both man and all things. Secondly, spirits, consist of extra-human beings and the spirits of men who died a long time ago. Thirdly, man, including human beings who are alive and those about to be born. Forth, animals and plants, or the reminder of biological life. Fifth, phenomena and objects without biological life"[259]. All these reveal that, the idea that a creator exists is at the base of African reality. In fact, African people have lived with the name of a Supreme Deity longer than any other people have. The first humans who responded to the unknown with the announcement of awe originated on the African continent. The names of Bes, Ptah, Atum, Ra, Amen, Khnum, Set, Ausar, and Auset, Omukuru, Nyankopon, are among the oldest names for divinities in the world[260]. Wiredu expresses the same, that Onyame is one among several names for the supreme being in Akan. Another frequent one is Onyankopon, which means The Being that is alone Great[261].

The African Supreme Being, however, rarely plays a role in the daily activities of the people. No one would even think of knowing this being or trying to know him as "a personal savior." The Abrahamic deity of Judaism, Christianity, and Islam is quite different from the African God of Yoruba, Zulu, and Gikuyu. This is evident in Wiredu's views while elaborating on the character of the Akan belief in the Supreme Being. He expresses that there is

[259] John Mbiti, (1969) *African Religions & Philosophy.* Heinemann Educational Publisher, p. 15-16.

[260] God: African Supreme Beings. "Encyclopedia of Religion". Retrieved March 20, 2023, from Encyclopedia.com: https://www.encyclopedia.com/god-african-supreme-beings.

[261] Kwasi Wiredu, (1996). *Cultural Universals and Particulars; An African Perspective.* Indiana University Press, p.46.

no attitude or ritual of worship directed to that being. He adds that, they regard him as good, wise and powerful in the highest. He is the determiner of human destiny as of everything else. But in all these they see no rationale for worship. Thus for them neither is the Akan conception of morality based logically or even psychologically on the belief in the Supreme Being[262]. Questions like these arise in the minds of the Africans concerning the personal nature of God. Who could fathom the possibilities of the Creator being involved on a personal level with humans? How could one have a personal relationship with God? How could God be a dictator in human life? Thus, the myths, are designed in most of the African communities to approximate the nature of the God of Gods.

Ancestors appear more important on a daily basis than the Supreme Deity. It is the ancestors who must be feared, who must be appeased, and to whom appeals must be directed; they are the ones who must be invoked and revered because they are the agents of transformation. A person's life can change drastically if he or she does not pay proper homage to the ancestors. Some ancestors are more powerful than others, but all are essentially concerned about the well-being of the society[263]. The number of gods and goddesses varies from culture to culture. The Baganda people of east-central Africa have twenty or more deities. Many populations regard the earth, sun, and moon as gods. In the Congo River region, the most densely wooded part of Africa, the forest itself is a deity, or else a mysterious other world where spirits

[262] Kwasi Wiredu, (1996). *Cultural Universals and Particulars; An African Perspective*, p. 46-47.

[263] Molefi Kete Asante & Ama Mazama, Eds. (2009). *Encyclopedia of African Religion*, p. XXIV.

dwell[264]. Such a belief was not only to emphasize the religious aspect of Africans but also a way of conserving the environment.

The Attributes of The Supreme Deity

The nature of God in the Akan belief system can be deduced from the qualities ascribed to Him. They refer to him as the Supreme Being, who occupies the summit of the hierarchy, and the ultimate creator of all that there is[265]. The Akan supreme being, Onyame, has many other names. Some of these names indicate Onyame's most worthy attributes, such as Amosu (Giver of Rain), Amowia (Giver of the Sun), and Amaomee (Giver of Plenitude)[266]. Akan religion is polytheistic. This is evidenced in the existence of many minor deities, who exercise powers over believers but are in turn subordinate to Onyame. Apart from the Akan, other Africans refer to God as the moulder, the bringer of rain, the one who thunders from afar. He is the one who gives life, the ancient of days, and the one who humbles the great.

While talking about the attributes of God it is important to note there are other aspects relevant to religion. For example, from Mbiti's perspective, names of people have religious meanings in them; rocks and boulders are not just empty objects, but religious objects; the sound of the drum speaks a religious language; the eclipse of the sun or moon is not simply a silent phenomenon of nature, but one which speaks to the community that observes it, often warning of an impending catastrophe[267]. Conclusively, despite the Akan's mentality of the Supreme Being, the African vision of God shapes people's consciousness of the

---

[264] "African Mythology." U.X.L Encyclopedia of World Mythology. Retrieved March 20th, 2023, from Encyclopedia.com: https://www.encyclopedia.com/african-mythology.

[265] Stephen Nkansah Morgan & Beatrice Okyere-Manu *The Belief in and Veneration of Ancestors in Akan Traditional Thought: Finding Values for Human Well-being.*

[266] J. B. Danquah, (1968). *The Akan Doctrine of God: A Fragment of Gold Coast Ethics and Religion,* second edition London: Cass, p.4.

[267] John Mbiti, (1969). *African Religions & Philosophy,* p. 15.

world and of themselves. It provides a hermeneutical key for understanding the world and the reason for the existence of political, economic, social, moral, cultural, and religious events.

Morality from African Perception

It is worth noting that, if we are to trace the ethics of a society, we cannot ignore the fact that, it is rooted in the ideas and beliefs concerning what is right or wrong, what is a good or bad character, and the social relations and attitudes considered important by the members of the society. It is evident then that African societies being organized and functioning human communities have ethical systems, like, ethical values, principles, rules that ground their social and moral behaviour. It is with such a background then that we can view some of them.

Morality Based on Personhood, or Good Character

Many African scholars, specifically John Mbiti, would sum up morality in these two phrases; "A person is a person through other persons" or "I am because we are and, since we are, therefore I am"[268]. While these phrases imply that one needs others in order to exist and have a certain identity, they also convey a normative outlook, particularly, personhood and selfhood. In the journey of the individual toward personhood, the community plays a vital role both as catalyst and as prescriber of norms. The emphasis here is that in order to transform what was initially biologically given into full personhood, the community has to step in, since the individual by himself, cannot go through the transformation independently. The implication of this is that, personhood has to be achieved, and it is the sort of thing at which individuals could fail[269]. Kwasi Wiredu summarizes it that, one's basic aim as a moral agent should be to become a complete person

---

John Mbiti, (1970). *African Religions and Philosophy.* New York: Doubleday, p.141.

Kwasi Wiredu, (1996). *Cultural Universals and Particulars; An African Perspective,* p. 58.

or a real self. An individual is not a person in the fullest sense unless she or he has shown a responsiveness to those ideals in confirmed habits of life[270].

Discourses or statements about morality turn out therefore, to be discourses or statements essentially about character. When a speaker of the Akan language wants to say, "He is immoral", or "He is unethical", he expresses it as, "He has no character"[271]. The same applies to the Baganda, when they talk of an immoral person; they are referring to a person without good character. African ethics is, thus, a character-based ethics that maintains that the quality of the individual's character is most fundamental aspect of moral life.

Morality Based on Right and Wrong Actions

While the previous section discussed personhood, or good character, this one focuses on right action. The standard here is that; actions are right insofar as they promote communion or harmony. According to Gyekye, "what is morally good is not that which is commanded by God or any spiritual being; what is right is not that which is pleasing to a spiritual being or in accordance with the will of such being"[272]. Traditional African ethics is rooted, rather, in humanism, that is, in that which leads to the betterment or well-being of humanity or the community. Thus, in Akan moral thought the sole criterion of goodness is the welfare or well-being of the community. This is what we see in Wiredu's point of view that, to the traditional Akan, what gives meaning to life is usefulness to self, family, community and the species. Therefore, nothing transcending life in human society and its

---

[270] Gyekye, Kwame, "African Ethics", *The Stanford Encyclopedia of Philosophy*. Fall 2011 Edition. Edward N. Zalta (ed.), URL = <https://plato.stanford.edu/archives/entries/african-ethics/>. Accessed on 12th march 2023.

[271] Gyekye, K. (1995). *An essay on African Philosophical Thought: The Akan Conceptual Scheme*. Philadelphia Temple a University Presses, p. 131.

[272] Kwasi Wiredu, (1996). *Cultural Universals and Particulars; An African Perspective*, p. 57.

empirical conditions enters into the constitution of the meaning of life[273]. Life thus, is another category in African discussion of right action, specifically in distinguishing the permissible from the impermissible. Africans prioritizes the principle that actions are right insofar as they promote vitality. Any action thus which increases life or vital force is right, and whatever decreases it is wrong.

Before finalizing with this part, there is a need to revisit our concern whether religion is a field of convergence or divergence of thought among the peoples and cultures of the world. According to Kwasi Wiredu;

> "a particular case which is of considerable intellectual interest is the question of the legitimacy or illegitimacy of polygamy, it is well known that in Africa and some other parts of the world polygamy is regarded as a legitimate marriage arrangement. On the other hand, the Christian missionaries who came to Africa 'to save' our souls, perceiving the practice to be incompatible with their own norms of good conduct, condemned it as immoral and worked assiduously to eradicate it. They have had a measure of success in this. But there has been a certain superficiality about that success which has been responsible for a kind of ethical schizophrenia in the consciousness of many of our people".[274]

From that example, religion can lead to divergence. When religion is used to discard or demoralize a cultural practice without enough explanation, it takes such a direction. The best way to convergence in such a practice is to teach people first and show them the dangers of polygamy before discarding it. Once people are convinced of the dangers such as poverty, sexual

---

[273] Kwasi Wiredu, (1996). *Cultural Universals and Particulars; An African Perspective.* Indiana University Press, p. 69.

[274] Kwasi Wiredu, (1996). *Cultural Universals and Particulars; An African Perspective, p. 62.*

transmitted diseases, to mention but a few, then the religious aspect of the two becoming one, monogamy, will have no issues.

To sum up this part, it is important to pay attention to Wiredu's words while talking about the word moral and its cognates. He stressed that:

> "the word moral and its cognates are frequently used with such a broad signification as to cover matters under custom, tradition, or even convention. Thus in discussing the morals of a given people, one may mention such things as their rules of marriage and sexual conduct generally, their manner of organizing mutual aid, their way of defining and evaluating success in life, their system of reward and punishment. Considerations of this kind should certainly reveal a lot about their values, but the point is that not all those values would be moral values.[275]

By considering those views, some values in Akan community like the beauty of speech, greeting the audience before addressing them, cannot be compared with the rule of truth-telling, due to its unconditional imperativeness. To trifle with such an imperative is to be immoral in a very strict sense, yet this is not the case with those other values with their conditional nature.

A Critical Analysis of Religio-Moral Compatibility

The previous sections have exhausted the general understanding of religion and morality, Kwasi Wiredu's compatibility of religion and morality, Wiredu's stance bolstered by African perception. In this section, we shall base on that knowledge, to analyze critically their compatibility. However, before reaching that target, we shall pay attention to the origin of

---

[275] "Morality and Religion". *Encyclopedia of Religion.* Encyclopedia.com. (March 20, 2023). https://www.encyclopedia.com/morality-and-religion.

the tension between the two terms and this will entail surveying the modern thought about religion and morality.

The Origin of The Tension Between Religion and Morality

The terms morality and religion, at a closer interval signal two related but distinct ideas. The distinction is based on the fact that, morality pertains to the conduct of human affairs and relations between persons, while religion primarily involves the relationship between human beings and a transcendent reality. Accordingly, some think that, this distinction between religion and morality is a relatively modern one. Although tension between religion and morality is already evident in the writings of Plato and other Greek philosophers, the popular modern conception that religion and morality are separate phenomena is probably traceable to the Enlightenment[276].

Thinkers of the Enlightenment period, reflecting on Europe's fatigue with centuries of religious strife, sought to elaborate ethical theories based on reason. As a result, there was an establishment of the assumption that the norms governing conduct, morality, and ethics were separable from matters of religious belief. This also led to a number of efforts to explain the relationship between morality and religion. Thinkers like Kant exemplified the views of those who believed that religion and morality are mutually necessary: despite such a view, he was willing to criticize religious excesses and fanaticism, he was convinced that belief in a God who rewards the righteous and punishes the wicked was necessary to ensure full moral commitment[277].

Other thinkers took the position that religion signified the effort to strengthen morality by adding to its ordinary social

---

[276] Ibid.

[277] Terrell Carver, Ed. (1991). *The Cambridge Companion to Marx.* Cambridge University Press, p. 131.

sanctions a concocted series of supernaturally mediated rewards and punishments. Such a mentality, grounded a sequence of cruel critiques of traditional religion. Since morality could be understood in rational terms, it gave the impression that the use of religious sanctions to support moral conduct was appropriate only where primitive or morally weak persons were involved. Consequently, some thinkers within the same period questioned the usefulness of religion. One of them is Karl Marx who viewed religion as the effort to support the moral norms and codes of the ruling groups, and at the same time veiling worldly wrongs with the false allure of otherworldly rewards. He emphasized that religion is "the opiate of the people" because it dulls their minds and makes them uncritical of the wretched conditions in which they live[278].

Some thinkers like Friedrich Schleiermacher, Rudolf Otto, sought to develop an abiding place for religion independent of its moral significance. This reaction is evident also in Soren Kierkegaard's *Fear and Trembling,* where he discerned a teleological suspension of the ethical. He elaborates that, the ethical life is 'universal' in so far as it comprises the laws, customs and institutions of a particular society. On this understanding of 'the universal', Abraham's being a single individual who is 'higher' than the universal amounts to the idea that he considers his own private, individual relation to God to have priority over his duties as a social creature and a good citizen[279]. Accordingly, following the teleological suspension of the ethical implies that morality is essentially subordinated to religious concerns. Kierkegaard's direction was totally different from philosophers like Hegel, who stressed that, morality must ultimately be subordinated to the ethical life of one's society.

---

[278] Soren. Kierkegaard, (1941). Fear *and Trembling. The Sickness Unto Death.* Walter Lowrie, Trans. Princeton University Press, p. 110.

[279] W. Hegel, (1977). *Phenomenology of Spirit.* Trans. A. V. Miller, Oxford: Oxford University Press, p. 352

Thus, for Hegel, "wisdom and virtue consist in living in accordance with the customs of one's nation"[280].

The Relevance of Morality

The tension between religion and morality leads one to the important question of; Why should one be moral? Though sometimes this question is ignored, some philosophers have tried to answer it. Some focus on the obvious long-term interest and welfare of the moral agent. Others pay attention to the benefits of being a morally upright person and the disadvantageous part of being an immoral one. Others have rejected this approach claiming that one's decisions to be moral must rest on a respect for moral reasoning requiring no further justification. Still others, rejecting the two ideas, have stressed the importance of various metaphysical or religious views in grounding, explaining, and justifying commitment to the moral life and we shall give our priority to this last one. Thinkers holding to this view have argued that, without at least some metaphysical or religious basis moral striving makes no sense. This basis may range from the minimal belief that morality is not pointless or futile, that one's efforts do make a difference, to the stronger belief that, however much it may appear true that good people suffer for their commitments, moral acts and dispositions are acknowledged and rewarded[281].

Thus, the question "Why should one be moral?" returns ethics to basic matters of religious belief. This development comes with surprise, due to the fact that it was anticipated strongly in the works of Kant. Kant held a different view in his *Groundwork for the Metaphysics of Morals*. In that book, he emphasized that moral commitment must be autonomous. This idea is summarized in his formula of autonomy which states that,

---

[280] "Morality and Religion". *Encyclopedia of Religion.*

[281] Immanuel Kant, (2002). *Groundwork for the Metaphysics of Morals*. Allen W. Wood, Ed. Yale University Press New Haven and London, p. 120.

"Act only so that, the will could regard itself as at the same time giving universal law through its maxim or the idea of the will of every rational being as a will giving universal law"[282]. Nevertheless, Kant's later writings, especially the *Critique of Practical Reason* and *Religion within the Limits of Reason Alone*, focused largely on questions concerning philosophy of religion. In these writings, Kant developed the position that, to make sense, moral striving requires belief in a morally intentioned governor of the universe and this was Kant's moral proof for the existence of God. He adds that the moral law must postulate the existence of God and the immortality of the soul as the necessary conditions of the possibility of the *Summum Bonum*[283]. He advocates for the two still as the postulates of pure practical reason.

A Critique on Wiredu's Stance

The question "why should one be moral" is not an exceptional in African thought. The response to this question is evident in the way Africans view morality. Wiredu for example, points out that in Akan moral system, morality originates from considerations of human welfare and interests, not from divine pronouncements. Actions that promote human welfare are good, while those that detract from human welfare are bad. African morality from such a perspective is a humanistic ethics, a moral system that is preoccupied with human welfare. Wiredu, in protesting against Kant's postulate of acting out of duty, emphasized that, "human well-being is an irreducible presupposition of all morality"[284]

---

[282] Thomas Kingsmill Abbott, Trans. (2016). Critique of Practical Reason. in '*The Collected Works of Immanuel Kant*' Delphi Classics.

[283] Kwasi Wiredu, (1996). *Cultural Universals and Particulars; An African Perspective, p. 64.*

[284] Kwasi Wiredu, (1996). *Cultural Universals and Particulars; An African Perspective, p. 47.*

This may not pose a challenge to some philosophers; however, it is important to suggest a recap on the African cosmology of which the Akan are part of. Akan cosmology posited the existence of a Supreme Being, Onyame, Onyankopon, 'The Being That Is Alone Great'. African myths frequently describe numerous lesser deities who assist the Supreme Being in performing diverse functions in the created world. Human spirits and nature spirits. Individuals, who have died, usually ancestors in particular lineages, are the human spirits. These spirits play a role in community affairs and ensure a link between each clan and the spirit world. Natural objects, such as rivers, mountains, trees, and the sun as well as forces such as wind and rain, represent the nature spirits. Africans integrate this religious worldview into every aspect of life.

The Akans while talking about the Supreme Being acknowledge that He is good in the highest sense, He disapproves of evil, but to their mind, the reason why people should not do evil, is not because, He disapproves of it, but rather because it is contrary to human well-being, which is why He disapproves of it in the first place[285]. The conclusion one can draw is that, despite the humanistic origins of morality in traditional Akan societies, the role of the supernatural, that is, God and the other spiritual beings, is not completely absent. Gyekye acknowledges this, when he notes that God and other spiritual beings, even though they are not the people's source of morality, do, in a way, act as their motivation to act morally, or influence how people respond to moral norms. Since some of these sanctions derive from the Akan system of religious beliefs, it follows that religion cannot be completely banished from the practice of morality.

---

[285] Gyekye, Kwame, (2011 Edition) "African Ethics", *The Stanford Encyclopedia of Philosophy.*

Conclusion

Although Immanuel Kant is not an African and he is seen as an example of those biased Europeans who denied philosophy to Africans. His metaphysical answer to the question 'why should one be moral' bridges the gap, which was created concerning morality and religion. Apart from the appeal to personal and community well-being, plus a respect for moral reasoning which requires no further justification. Various metaphysical or religious views which ground, explain, and justify commitment to the moral life are highly recommended. Thus, without at least some metaphysical or religious basis, moral striving makes no sense. In order to make sense out of moral striving, a belief in a morally intentioned governor of the universe is necessary. This however, remains an open field of study, some may reject such a conclusion basing on the idea that people can behave morally without being religious. Some Africans including Wiredu may also reject the compatibility of religion and morality basing on the fact that, the word religion is not limited to a belief in a Supreme Being regarded as the architect of the world order, but also a way of life based on those ideas. Others may base on the idea that; African religion is not a revealed religion like other worldly religions. Such a description makes African ethics seem independent of religion and thus autonomous. However, basing on African cosmology, ontology, and beliefs, we cannot deny that, the two terms work hand in hand for the wellbeing of the community. A critical study on Africans' character, behaviour, their responses to moral norms and rules, reveals that one cannot take it for granted that such molarity is independent of religion.

Bibliography

DANQUAH, J. B., *The Akan Doctrine of God: A Fragment of Gold Coast Ethics and Religion*, second edition London: Cass,1968.

GONSALVES, M. A., *Fagothey's Right and Reason*, Ethics in Theory and Practice Ninth Edition Prentice Hall, 1989.

GRANNAN, C., "What's the Difference Between Morality and Ethics?". Encyclopedia Britannica, 1 Sep. 2016. https://www.brita nnica.com/story/whats-the-difference-between-morality-and-ethics. Accessed 29 March 2023.

GYEKYE, K., *An essay on African Philosophical Thought: The Akan Conceptual Scheme*. Philadelphia Temple a University Presses, 1995.

GYEKYE, K., "African Ethics", The Stanford Encyclopedia of Philosophy Edward N. Zalta (ed.), URL = https://plato.stanford.edu/ archives/entries/african-ethics/, 2011.

HEGEL, W., *Phenomenology of Spirit.* Trans. A. V. Miller, Oxford: Oxford University Press,1977.

HEMANTA K. K., *A Philosophical Approach to Religion and Culture,* International Journal of Science and Research (IJSR) ISSN (Online): 2319-7064 Index Copernicus Value (2016): 79.57 | Impact Factor (2015): 6.391, 2018.

KANT, I., *Groundwork for the Metaphysics of Morals.* Allen W. Wood, Ed. Yale University Press New Haven and London, 2002.

KIERKEGAARD, S., *Fear and Trembling. The Sickness Unto Death.* Walter Lowrie, Trans. Princeton University Press. 1941.

KINGSMILL, T. A., Trans. *Critique of Practical Reason.* in *'The Collected Works of Immanuel Kant'* Delphi Classics, 2016.

MBITI, J., *African Religions & Philosophy.* Heinemann Educational Publisher, 1969.

MBITI, J., *African Religions & Philosophy.* New York: Doubleday, 1970.

MOLEFI, K. A. & MAZAMA, A., Eds. *Encyclopedia of African Religion.* Sage Publications, U.S.A. 2009.

NKANSAH, S. M. & OKYERE-MANU, B., *The Belief in and Veneration of Ancestors in Akan Traditional Thought: Finding Values for*

Human Well-being. ORCID ID https://orcid.org/0000-0002-4480-7952 ORCID ID: https://orcid.org/0000-0003-2735-9227.

PECORINO, P. A., *Philosophy of Religion*: online Text book. Queensborough Community College https://www.qcc.cuny.edu/socialscienceppecorino/Phil-of-religion-text/default.htm, 2001.

SCHLEIERMACHER, F. D. E., *The Christian Faith* H. R. Machintosh and J. S. Steward, Trans. Edinburgh: T. & T. Clark, 1928.

TERRELL C., Ed. *The Cambridge Companion to Marx.* Cambridge University Press, 1991.

WIREDU K., *A Companion to African Philosophy.* Blackwell Publishing, 2004.

WIREDU K., *Cultural Universals and Particulars; An African Perspective.* Indiana University Press, 1996.

WIREDU K., *Philosophy and an African Culture: The Case of the Akan.* Cambridge University Press, 1980.

WOOD, A. W., "Religion and Reason." Chapter. In *Kant and Religion*, 1–26. Cambridge Studies in Religion, Philosophy, and Society. Cambridge: Cambridge University Press. doi:10.1017/978110 8381512.002, 2020.

"African Mythology." U.X.L Encyclopedia of World Mythology. *Encyclopedia.com*. March 20th, 2023, https://www.encyclopedia.com.

"Morality and Religion". Encyclopedia of Religion. *Encyclopedia.com*. March 20th, 2023, https://www.encyclopedia.com.

"God: African Supreme Beings." Encyclopedia of Religion. *Encyclopedia.com*. March 20th, 2023, https://www.encyclopedia.com.

A Critique of Kwasi Wiredu's Humanism and Impartiality

Dr. Sabas Kimani, Full-time Lecturer at The Catholic University of Eastern Africa (CUEA), Part-time Lecturer at Tangaza University, and Apostles of Jesus Institute of philosophy and Theology (AJIPT), Nairobi – Kenya. skimani@tangaza.ac.ke

Abstract

This article offers a critical reflection on Kwasi Wiredu's moral theory. On the one hand, the article is concerned with the meta-ethical question regarding the nature of moral properties, specifically, whether they are natural or supernatural. On the other, we shall reflect on one facet of Wiredu's normative theory, namely, whether morality is best captured by partiality or impartiality in the African tradition. Through regards to meta-ethics, this article reflects that Wiredu's rejection of a supernaturalist foundation of African ethics is unsatisfactory; we contend that he does not offer a satisfactory defense of physicalism. We shall conclude by observing that a plausible meta-ethical theory, either physicalist or religious, is yet to be elaborated within the African tradition. Secondly, we argue that Wiredu's normative theory is characterized by a feature impartiality that is at odds with much of African moral intuitions. Assertions like 'charity begins at home' seem to suggest that African ethics should be read in terms of partiality rather than impartiality.

Keywords: (Humanism, Impartiality, Kwasi Wiredu)

Introduction

A prominent issue that has dominated the enterprise of African philosophy since its inception in written form is the question of how to define African identity. The anthology *Person and Community: Ghanaian Philosophical Studies*[286] was a ground-breaking intellectual project that played a huge role in exposing the world of philosophy to topics in African philosophy. Three salient philosophical contributions caught the attention of readers: Kwame Gyekye's statement of an under-explored conception of democracy qua consensus[287]; Gyekye's influential moral-political theory of 'moderate communitarianism' a defense of human rights[288]; and Kwasi Wiredu's moral theory of 'sympathetic impartiality'[289]. The first two philosophical accounts have received some considerable critical engagement in the literature[290]; the latter, however, has not received as much critical attention. We reject two aspects of Wiredu's moral theory, that is we problematize humanism a secular interpretation of morality that dominates African moral theorization a thesis that human nature is a source and foundation of all moral value; and we reject Wiredu's interpretation of morality in terms of sympathetic impartiality insofar as it departs from the evidence that recommends partiality as the best interpretation of African ethics. This article proceeds as follows. Firstly, briefly familiarize the reader with Wiredu's ethical theory and meta-ethical position, humanism. Secondly, we consider Wiredu's 'welfarism', and also make a rough sketch of how an African theory of welfare might look. Finally, we illuminate Wiredu's principle of right action qua

---

[286] This is a book that was edited by Kwame Gyekye and Kwasi Wiredu.

[287] Gyekye Kwame, Beyond *Cultures: Perceiving A Common Humanity, Ghanaian Philosophical Studies.* (Accra: The Ghana Academy of Arts and Sciences, 2004), p. 243.

[288] Gyekye, Beyond culture, p. 101-104.

[289] Gyekye, Beyond culture, p. 193-204.

[290] Gyekye's moral-political theory, 'moderate communitarianism' has shaped and influenced debates in the African moral-political discourse.

sympathetic impartiality in the form of the golden rule as we problematize his humanism and impartialism.

Wiredu's Ethical Theory

According to Wiredu's ethical theory, it has previously been subjected to critical consideration. Thad Metz, an expert of Ubuntu, critically discusses Wiredu's moral theory of sympathetic impartiality as an instance of utility in African moral discourse. However, he does not give a detailed account as to the nature of the 'utility' in question, but he simply assumes that it is more or less the same as the Western utilitarian account[291]. Metz also criticized Wiredu's impartialism and rejects the golden rule as indeterminate as a principle of right action[292]. we offer a more extensive critique here by drawing on the African tradition to support partiality. More recently, Okeja applies sympathetic impartiality to a quest for a global ethic but does not give an extensive critical engagement of this theory[293].

Wiredu's moral theory focuses on his humanism and impartiality. we challenge humanism precisely because we hold the intuition that African ethics is best captured by appeal to some religious consideration following the thinking of John Mbiti and others[294]. Here, we are contented merely to demonstrate that Wiredu did not provide a good philosophical reason for believing that morality cannot be grounded on religious considerations or that it ought to be grounded on physical ones. With regards to impartiality, we argue that African moral intuitions like 'charity

---

[291] Metz Thad, Human Dignity, Capital Punishment and An African Moral Theory: Toward A New Philosophy of Human Rights. *Journal of Human Rights*, 2010, 9: p. 81-99. http://dx.doi.org/10.1080/14754830903530300.

[292] Metz Thad, *Two conceptions of African ethics in the work of D.A. Masolo*. 2013 in the Quest 25: p. 141-161.

[293] Okeja U. *Normative Justification of a Global Ethic: A Perspective from African Philosophy*. (New York: Lexington Books 2013).

[294] John Mbiti, *African religions and philosophy*, (New York: Doubleday 1970), p. 56.

begins at home' appears to imply that morality in African thought may best be captured in terms of partiality, a moral consideration that is at probabilities with Wiredu's moral principle of 'sympathetic impartiality'.

Christine Korsgaard distinguishes three senses a philosopher might have in mind when dealing with moral theorization. Firstly, one could be after a principle of right action (normative theorizations. Here a philosopher specifies a ground norm or a principle that specifies what all im/permissible actions have in common – a theory of right action. Secondly, one could be after an answer to the question 'what makes a life go well?' In this sense, one is looking for that property in virtue of which life will be considered choice worthy. Lastly, one could simply be concerned about questions of what is a good character. For the purposes of this analysis, I will limit myself to the first sense of moral theorizations i.e. a theory of right action. In what follows, I give the reader a sense of Wiredu's meta-ethical theory and afterwards, I procced to discuss his normative theory.

Wiredu's Humanism

By 'meta-ethics' we mean an account about the nature of moral properties, whether they are physical or spiritual[295]. To claim that moral properties are 'physical' amounts to the position that physical properties are natural and as such can be accessed by appeal to scientific methods. To claim that moral properties are 'spiritual' amounts to the claim that they are supernatural and as such one has to rely on methods that are beyond science, such as intuitions. According to Wiredu he held the view that the best way to understand morality in the African tradition is in terms of some physical property. He denies that morality can be grounded on any spiritual foundation and therefore argues that "the will of

---

[295] We shall not here consider 'non-naturalism' since there is no one who defends such a view in the African literature.

God, not to talk of that of any other extra-human being, is logically incapable of defining the good"[296].

Elsewhere, he explicitly states that: "But in fact, I deny that Akan moral thought is supernaturalistic to any extent"[297]. This means that, morality cannot be grounded in any supernaturalistic considerations or properties. To argue that morality cannot be grounded in spiritual considerations does not mean that God and ancestors play no role at all, it is rather to deny that this role may be foundational. Hence, it is common then that extra-human entities can be considered to play a supportive role[298]. This role is generally exemplified in taboos that appeal to some extra-human authority. Even in this light, Wiredu insists that these taboos can be explained purely in rational terms[299].

Wiredu refers to his naturalistic ethics in terms of 'humanism'. In other words, the physical property that grounds or informs morality is some aspect of human nature. He articulates his humanism by appeal to his native (Akan) language 'Onipa na ohia'. He translates this sentence to mean "that it is a human being that has value" and observes that the original language is more illuminating than English as he argues:

> The word "(o)hia" in this context means both that which is of value and that which is needed. Through the first meaning the message is implied that all value derives from human interests and through the second that human fellowship is the most important of human needs[300].

---

[296] Kwasi Wiredu, *Moral Foundations of An African Culture*. In: Wiredu K & K Gyekye (eds) *Person and community: Ghanaian philosophical studies, 1*. (Washington DC: The Council for Research in Values and Philosophy 1992), p. 194.

[297] Kwasi Wiredu, *Cultural Universals and Particulars: An African Perspective*. (Indianapolis: Indiana University Press 1996), p. 234.

[298] Kwasi Wiredu, *Cultural Universals and Particulars*, p. 245.

[299] Kwasi Wiredu (1996) Reply to English/Hamme. *Journal of Social Philosophy* 27: p. 234- 243. http://dx.doi.org/10.1111/j.1467-9833.1996.tb00248.x.

[300] Kwasi Wiredu, *Cultural Universals and Particulars*, p. 195.

In another place he observes that "the first axiom of all Akan axiological thinking is that man or woman is the measure of all value"[301]. The first meaning is crucial in terms of capturing Wiredu's meta-ethics. All moral value, according to him, is a function of human nature, specifically, human interests. We can only derive morality from some facts connected with human beings or their interests. Simply put, 'humanism' is the doctrine that some aspect of human nature is the source and foundation of all moral value; and by implication without humanity there would be no morality. It is therefore fitting that his metaethical position is captured as humanistic and not supernaturalistic.

Wiredu's Theory of Right Action

To articulate Wiredu's principle of right action, we begin by clarifying how Wiredu understands morality. Wiredu talks about strict morality and he contrasts it with custom, and sometimes he refers to this distinction in terms of ethics, moral philosophy proper, and an ethic, custom[302]. The latter, custom, is concerned with questions of human interaction at a contingent level, and is not universal and can change over time[303]. An ethic or custom is concerned with questions of how to raise children, rules regarding weddings and married life, how to bury the dead, greetings and so on[304]. Strict morality, on the other hand, offers principles that inform human interaction that is both essential and universal, without which human existence is in jeopardy. He characterizes strict moral rules as "intrinsically obligatory"[305].

---

[301] Kwasi Wiredu, *Cultural Universals and Particulars*, p. 65.

[302] Kwasi Wiredu, *On the idea of a global ethic*. Journal of Global Ethics 2005 1: p. 45-51. http://dx.doi.org/10.1080/17449620500106636.

[303] Kwasi Wiredu, *Cultural Universals and Particulars*, p. 237-238.

[304] Kwasi Wiredu, Social Philosophy in Postcolonial Africa: Some Preliminaries Concerning Communalism And Communitarianism. (South African Journal of Philosophy 2008) 27: p. 332-339. http://dx.doi.org/10.4314/sajpem.v27i4.31522.

[305] Kwasi Wiredu, *Cultural Universals and Particulars*, p. 68.

Consequently, an ethic may recommend that people should not eat with their hands and an ethics requires that people be truthful. The choice of whether people eat with their hands, spoons or whatever kind of utensil does not threaten the continuance and quality of life. But if people were to abandon the institution of honesty and truth as a matter of accepted norm, the whole human project would be threatened[306]. We may now enquire as to the basic norm that grounds morality according to Wiredu.

We contend, to construe Wiredu's moral theory in terms of welfare or that it defends some version of welfarism. 'Welfarism' is the claim that well-being "is the only value which an ethical theory needs to take seriously, ultimately and for its own sake"[307]. For example, Wiredu, in his very first articulation of his moral theory, claims that "by our lights, human well-being is an irreducible presupposition of all morality ... every moral endeavor is a certain kind of quest after human well-being"[308]. In addition, he continues to claim that "[e]very Akan maxim about the specifically moral views that I know ... postulates the harmonization of interests as the means, and the securing of human well-being as an end, of all moral endeavor"[309].

Wiredu's reference to well-being as an irreducible proposition of all morality implies that it is a foundational or basic norm upon which all morality is grounded. In other words, it is a fundamental moral property against which we can assess moral actions or characters. One can safely assume that since it is fundamental or basic, all other values reduce to it. In other words, freedom or equality are good because they lead to well-being. Wiredu's language of capturing well-being as an end and harmonization of interests as a means also captures his welfarism.

---

[306] Kwasi Wiredu (2005) On the idea of a global ethic. Journal of Global Ethics 1: p. 45-51. http://dx.doi.org/10.1080/17449620500106636.

[307] Sumner L., Welfare, *Happiness, And Ethics*. Oxford: Clarendon Press 1996), p. 3.

[308] Kwasi Wiredu, *Cultural Universals and Particulars*, p. 64.

[309] Kwasi Wiredu, *Cultural Universals and Particulars*, p. 65.

To refer to well-being as an end is to claim that it is a final good, the very essence or goal of morality; in other words, actions are right or wrong insofar as they produce or lead to well-being or wrong if they detract from it.

It is not entirely clear whether Wiredu is using the phrases 'human well-being' and 'human interests' as interchangeable or whether he thinks that satisfaction of human interests leads to welfare[310]. Either way, this does not quite help us to understand what Wiredu has in mind when he talks about well-being. This consideration is crucial given that Wiredu does not tell us what he means by either well-being or by human interests. This lack of conceptual and theoretical clarity and elaboration does not help the case of moral philosophizing in the African tradition. Clarity with regards to welfarism, what he considers to constitute human well-being, is crucial for Wiredu since lack thereof has the potential to cast in a negative light an otherwise promising account because much of 'welfarism' as captured in terms of utilitarianism has not had a good philosophical record; it thus becomes urgent for a philosopher to distinguish his kind of welfarism[311].

We admit that Wiredu is not alone in being vague about what he means by wellbeing. However, we are not aware of any thoroughgoing account of welfare in the African tradition[312]. We do however think that in the light of certain claims made by African scholars, in general, and, Wiredu specifically, it is justified to construe welfare in terms of basic human needs fulfilment[313]. A close reading of Wiredu strongly suggests that he

---

[310] Kwasi Wiredu, *Moral Foundations of An African Culture*. In: Wiredu K & K Gyekye (eds) *Person and Community: Ghanaian Philosophical Studies*, 1. Washington DC: The Council for Research in Values and Philosophy 1992), p. 194.

[311] Menkiti I., On the Normative Conception of a Person. In: Wiredu, K (ed) companion to African philosophy. (Oxford: Blackwell Publishing, 2004), p. 36.

[312] Gyekye K. *Beyond Cultures: Perceiving A Common Humanity, Ghanaian Philosophical Studies*. (Accra: The Ghana Academy of Arts and Sciences,2004), p. 67.

[313] Gyekye K. *Beyond Cultures*, p. 78-79.

conceives of well-being in these terms. Two aspects of Wiredu's humanism in particular support the argument that he conceives of welfare in terms of basic human needs fulfillment. First, the centrality of needs emerges from the fact that human beings are conceived as essentially and continuously self-insufficient; secondly, we can deduce the centrality of needs from the imagery of the Siamese crocodile. This figure typically invoked in Akan moral thought with two heads and one stomach underscores the need for harmony as central to social existence.

According to Wiredu he articulates his humanism by appealing to an *Akan adage* that has dual meanings. That is on one hand, a human being, individually, is characterized as a bearer of moral value; and, on the other, it is characterized by natural inadequacy that necessitates human fellowship. A human being is understood simultaneously as a being of value and of need. An insight that flows from this maxim is that though a human being is a bearer of value, he, however, requires the context of a vigorous human interaction to develop into full humanity. Human fellowship, it is correct to suppose, is essential for her functioning as an ordinary human being. In light of the human inadequacy mentioned above, it is not surprising Wiredu argued that:

> Self-reliance is of course understood and recommended by the Akans, but its possibility is predicated upon this ineliminable residue of human dependency. Human beings, therefore, at all times ... need the help of their kind.[314]

The idea here is that a human being individually is continually and essentially insufficient to the task of survival, personal development and moral development. This natural insufficiency of a human being positions her as one who always stands in need of the help of fellow human beings. One interesting consequence that follows from this thought is that it completely repositions how one may think about self-interest. It appears that

---

[314] Kwasi Wiredu, *Cultural universals and particulars: an African perspective.* (Indianapolis: Indiana University Press, 1996), p. 293.

a moral theory entailed in this account cannot adhere with anything like ethical egoism. On this account, to truly talk of self-interest is to always implicate one in relation with others between whom there is always co-dependency[315]. Considerably without these relations, one's sense of self both descriptively and normatively would be compromised. In this sense, we need other human beings to discover ourself as a human being, to function ordinarily as a human being and to flourish as a moral agent.

The second clue is found in one of the profound ethical symbols in the Akan culture of a crocodile with two heads and one stomach[316]. Wiredu invokes this art motif to elaborate on his moral philosophy[317]. We think it is also instructive of needs as a central tenet to this notion of well-being. In this line, human beings at bottom have the same interests, and without finding ways to balance or adjust conflicts, the human society is jeopardy. This ethical symbolism communicates needs. Further, African scholars have observed that African moral thought is grounded in duties that are best explicable by appeal to needs rather than to rights as is the case typically in the West. For example, Thad Metz, in his ground-breaking paper on African ethics, captures the following intuition as salient below the Sahara arguing that:

> A greater percentage of Africans think that one is morally obligated to help others, roughly to the extent that one can and that others need, with rights not figuring into the analysis of how much one ought to transfer wealth, time or labor.[318]

Kwame Gyekye, a fellow Ghanaian African philosopher and former colleague of Wiredu at the University of Ghana also

---

[315] Kwasi Wiredu, *Moral foundations of an African culture*. In: Wiredu K & K Gyekye (eds) Person and community: Ghanaian philosophical studies, 1. Washington DC: The Council for Research in Values and Philosophy 1992).

[316] Kwasi Wiredu, *Moral foundations of an African culture*.

[317] Kwasi Wiredu, *Cultural universals and particulars*, p. 290.

[318] Metz T. (2013) *Two conceptions of African ethics in the work of D.A. Masolo.* Quest 25, p. 141-161.

understands African thought to be grounded in the notion of needs rather than rights. He observes that "A shared humanity, conceived as a universal family of humankind, mandates, not a rights-based morality it mandates rather a kind of moral outlook animated by the awareness of the needs and interests of others and demonstration of sensitivity to those needs[319]. The view from these scholars is that Afro-communitarian societies are not rights-based, but may be understood as based on duties that are responsive to others' needs. Subsequently, there is some agreement among African scholars that well-being is a function of fulfilling human needs. It is for this reason that African ethics is sometimes compared to or even captured in terms of care[320].

Thus far, we have made sense of Wiredu's humanism, and we have proceeded to elaborate on what he considers to be the ultimate good, welfarism qua human needs fulfilment. We proceed now to focus on his principle of right action. Wiredu calls this principle sympathetic impartiality, which he understands to be tantamount to the golden rule[321]. These principal functions, to harmonize or adjust human interests to the effect of securing human well-being. Why do human interests need to be adjusted or harmonized? The reason is found in the art motif of a crocodile with two heads alluded to earlier. A message that is communicated by the two heads is the idea "although human beings have a core of common interests, they also have conflicting interests that precipitate real struggles … the aim of morality …

---

[319] Gyekye K. *Beyond cultures: perceiving a common humanity, Ghanaian philosophical studies.* (Accra: The Ghana Academy of Arts and Sciences 2004), p. 91.

[320] Ramose, *Ecology through ubuntu.* in: Murove (ed) *African ethics: an anthology of comparative and applied ethics.* (Pietermaritzburg: University of Kwa-Zulu Natal Press, 2009), p. 89.

[321] Kwasi Wiredu, *Cultural universals and particulars*, p. 170.

is to harmonize those warring interests through systematic adjustment and adapting"[322].

Wiredu gives several articulations of how he understands the golden rule. In some instances, he represents it positively: "Let your conduct at all times manifest a due concern for the interests of others a person may be said to manifest a due concern for the interests of others if in contemplating the impact of his actions on their interests, she puts herself imaginatively in their position"[323]. And in some, negatively way he argues: "Do not do unto others what you would not that they do to you"[324]. It is also important to note that Wiredu equates the golden rule to what he refers to as sympathetic impartiality[325]. Wiredu informs us that the principle of sympathetic impartiality requires us to "be willing to put oneself, as the saying goes, in the shoes of others when contemplating an action"[326]. In another place, he states: "Pure morality that is, those requiring of the individual an impartial regard for the interests of others motivated by a certain minimum of altruism is the most indispensable"[327]. He refers to this principle as a test of what might be permissible or impermissible action. To exemplify how the moral test functions, he evaluates a custom among the Akans that required some people to be killed so as to accompany and continue to serve their departed king in the hereafter.

---

[322] Kwasi Wiredu, *Moral Foundations of An African Culture*. In: Wiredu K & K Gyekye (eds) *Person and Community: Ghanaian Philosophical Studies*, 1. Washington DC: The Council for Research in Values and Philosophy 1992), p. 197.

[323] Wiredu K (1996) Reply to English/Hamme. Journal of Social Philosophy 27: p. 234-243. http://dx.doi.org/10.1111/j.1467-9833.1996.tb00248.x

[324] Wiredu, Moral *foundations of an African culture. In: Wiredu K & K Gyekye (eds) Person and community: Ghanaian philosophical studies, 1.* (Washington DC: The Council for Research in Values and Philosophy, 1992), p. 45.

[325] Ibid.

[326] Kwasi Wiredu, *Cultural universals and particulars*, p. 237.

[327] Kwasi Wiredu, (2005) On the idea of a global ethic. Journal of Global Ethics 1: p. 45-51. http://dx.doi.org/10.1080/17449620500106636.

This moral test or principle requires one to impartially imagine oneself in another's position and see whether they would welcome the action or outcome in question. With regards to the king, he should put himself in the position of a servant and consider whether he would be willing to be put to death so as to accompany and serve his king in the afterlife. Wiredu informs us that the king qua servant's position would probably not accept such a position. It is crucial to note that that this moral theory has two aspects: on the one hand, there is some kind of moral psychology captured either in terms of sympathy/ empathy; and, on the other, there is the element of impartiality. Through regards to sympathy (empathy), Wiredu claims that it is the root of all moral virtue. It is the second aspect of impartiality that we will subject to scrutiny, as we think it misses what is at the heart of African thought. Below, we start by critically reflecting on humanism.

Rejection Of Humanism

At the level of meta-ethics, humanism remains a stubborn feature of African moral thought[328]. Human-centered axiological approaches like the one advocated by Wiredu are problematic for various reasons. To interpret moral value exclusively in terms of human interests involves an untenable anthropocentrism and may also imply speciesism. Elsewhere we argue that this kind of approach is parochial and chauvinistic[329]. In this article, we question Wiredu's meta-ethical presupposition that the foundation of morality is best conceived in physicalist terms, namely, as grounded in some human property (humanism) as opposed to some spiritual (religious) considerations. We argue

---

[328] Dzobo K (1992) Values in a changing society: man, ancestors and God. In: Gyekye K & K Wiredu (eds) Person and community: Ghanaian philosophical studies, 1. Washington DC: Council for Research in Values and Philosophy.

[329] Gyekye K. *Beyond cultures: perceiving a common humanity, Ghanaian philosophical studies*. (Accra: The Ghana Academy of Arts and Sciences, 2004), p. 37.

that Wiredu has not offered us convincing philosophical reasons to the effect that physical properties do a better job at accounting for morality than religious (spiritual) considerations in the African tradition.

Wiredu reports that his humanism flows from some Akan adage that says that human beings are bearers of all moral value or implies that all moral value is derivable from human beings. It might be anthropologically true that Akan people do actually believe that all moral value derives from human beings, and surely a philosopher may ground his philosophy in such anthropological moral data. But as philosophers, our task is not just to analyses what some anthropological-moral data implies with regards to question of morality; more is needed. It is one thing for some claim to be anthropologically true, but quite another for it to be philosophically plausible. The philosophical standard requires that we demonstrate the veracity of the claim in question that 'human beings are bearers of all moral value'; it is not enough to merely analyze its implication we need reasons and/or evidence to the effect that what Akans actually believe is philosophically true. The whole enterprise of philosophy, so far as we understand it, is based on subjecting and justifying claims on the basis of rational argumentation.

Unfortunately, like many who advocate humanism, Wiredu does not give us a positive argument to defend humanism[330]. He simply assumes that merely because it is believed by Akans it must be true. Before, he thinks that by simply arguing that African ethics is not supernaturalistic he can secure the alternative, which is naturalism. Nevertheless, all we have from Wiredu is a supposition and not an argument. He claims that "[o]ne important implication of the founding of value on human interests is the independence of morality from religion in the Akan outlook"[331]. If it is true that morality is strictly definable by an appeal to human

[330] Kwasi Wiredu, *Cultural universals and particulars*, p. 194.

[331] Kwasi Wiredu, *Cultural universals and particulars*, p. 196.

interests, it indeed implies a kind of independence between it and religion. Nonetheless this line of reasoning begs the question; is morality purely grounded in human interests? This more pressing philosophical question is left unattended.

Further, Wiredu makes interesting claims about God. He observes, "On the Akan understanding of things, indeed, God is good in the highest; but his goodness is conceptually of a type with the goodness of a just and benevolent ancestor, only in his case quality and scale are assumed to be limitless"[332]. Wiredu appears to be drawing a conceptual distinction between moral goodness and God's goodness. There are two senses of the notion of 'good' at play. One is purely moral and the other is that of God; but unfortunately, Wiredu does not undertake any conceptual analysis to distinguish the difference that is at least obvious to him; once again the reader is left to wonder what Wiredu has in mind such a difference is merely asserted and never demonstrated.

The best Wiredu gives us to sustain the conceptual difference between moral goodness and God's goodness is to claim that the latter's is like that of an ancestor, and this kind of elaboration only complicates matters. For a human being to qualify as an ancestor after they die, they should have lived a good life i.e., a life that promoted human interests[333]. Therefore, metaphysically, an ancestor in some important sense is a human being who has since joined a higher sphere of existence because of their moral achievements. On the other hand, God does not achieve his goodness; it appears to be a property of his very nature, or so it is commonly believed. Thus, to make sense of the kind of goodness of God in terms of the goodness of ancestors appears to be problematic; the one is acquired and the other is

---

[332] Mkhize N. *Ubuntu and harmony: an African approach to morality and ethics.* In: Nicolson R (ed) *persons in community: African ethics in a global culture.* (Pietermaritzburg: University of KwaZulu-Natal Press, 2008), p. 78-83.

[333] Kwasi Wiredu, *Cultural universals and particulars*, p. 248.

inherent. One question lingers in our mind like an uncomfortable thumb that why is God's goodness inadequate to ground morality? Is God's goodness distinct or opposed to human goodness? All we are satisfied to make out in this particular channel is that Wiredu has not demonstrated to us that morality is indeed a function of human nature; and he has not even begun to demonstrate that God cannot ground morality in the African tradition. Besides, if these observations are true then the question of whether morality is physical or spiritual is still an open question in the African tradition.

Impartiality in Wiredu's Philosophy

We proceed now to present three aspects of African culture that recommend partiality as the best interpretation of an African moral tradition contrary to Wiredu's principle of right action: the high regard usually accorded to the family, ancestor veneration and the normative concept of personhood qua a good person. We will not elaborate on all these cultural items to make my argument; to build a strong case it suffices that we appeal to the notion of personhood, which is a central feature of African moral thought. If impartiality does not cohere with this notion of personhood that will be sufficient grounds to reject it. But for the sake of a non-African audience, we will give a brief discussion of the other two aspects of African culture that also endorse partiality: family and ancestor veneration.

Wiredu construes his principle of right action in terms of sympathetic (empathetic) impartiality. This comes with the implication that morality in the African tradition is best construed as impartial. I begin my analysis with how the notion of a family appears to imply partiality. A family unit is usually accorded a high status, morally speaking, within the African tradition. It is interesting to note that the family is reported as the best school for moral education[334]. It is also interesting to note that many African scholars articulate their moral theories in light of analogies drawn from how a family works or ought to work[335]. Furthermore, a scholar like Augustine Shutte who defends a 'Thomist' understanding of ubuntu observes that a family is seen in the African tradition as intrinsically good[336].

In another place, he introduces the idea of partiality by using the idea of permeable boundaries since he is opposed to what he calls 'bounded reason'. He states: "Thus *motho ke motho ka batho* is the maxim that prescribes permeable boundaries"[337]. It is interesting that whatever else this comment amounts to, it begins by validating boundaries, thus affirming partiality; nonetheless insightfully, he further informs us that the boundaries in question are permeable. In other words, one is urged to avoid moral myopia and parochiality by thinking that one's partiality considerations exhaust what morality is all about. A moral agent must recognize that she is not only her own person and a member of a family; moreover, she is also a member of different communities: her tribe, nation, country, continent and the world. It is for this reason that her moral sensitivity and sensibility must be as wide as the world is, but all this 'wide' moral responsibility must be interpreted from an agent's locus of focus, that is, from a perspective that is entirely her own. Simply put, though she has immediate duty to herself and family, all things equal, she also has a duty to the community (humanity) at large.

---

[334] Behrens K., *African philosophy thought and practice and their contribution to environmental ethics.* (Johannesburg: University of Johannesburg, 2011), p. 46.

[335] Augustine Shutte, Ubuntu: *An ethic for a New South Africa.* (Pietermaritzburg: Cluster Publications,2001), p. 29.

[336] Kwasi Wiredu, (2008) Social philosophy in postcolonial africa: some preliminaries concerning communalism and communitarianism. South African Journal of Philosophy 27: p. 332-339. http://dx.doi.org/10.4314/sajpem.v27i4.3152.

[337] Kwasi Wiredu, (1999) Society and democracy in Africa. New Political Science 21: p. 33-44. http://dx.doi.org/10.1080/07393149908429850.

IN HONOUR OF KWASI WIREDU

It is not only the high prize attached to the family that buttresses the view that African ethics is best read as partiality. Another interesting source for defending a partialist thesis is the ubiquitous practice of ancestor veneration among African communities. Ramose informs us that "[the concept of community in the African philosophy of Ubuntu (Botho-humanness) is comprised of three tiers, namely, the living, the living-dead ('ancestors') and the yet to be born. Life is wholesome and just if harmony prevails in these tiers of community[338]. On this view, one can't sufficiently talk of an African community until they have spoken about ancestors or the living-dead. The 'living-dead' are not 'gods', as in entities to be worshipped; strictly speaking, they are human 'persons' who have since joined a supernatural realm of God because they have lived morally worthy lives[339]. Precisely because they are 'persons', it is inappropriate and a sign of confusion to speak of 'ancestor worship' hence it is appropriate to talk of ancestor veneration/reverence[340].

It is for this reason that some ancestor rituals only involve family members, or that even if the whole community is involved, some parts of the ritual are held in private. It is this partialist consideration from the ubiquitous ancestor veneration we wanted to bring to the fore. We are appealing to this idea of ancestors since it is a commonly held view that extra-human beings reinforce morality[341]. This far, we have roughly discussed two aspects of African culture that somehow lend evidence to the idea that African moral thought is best interpreted as partialist. We

---

[338] Menkiti I. *On the normative conception of a person.* In: Wiredu, K (ed) companion to African philosophy. (Oxford: Blackwell Publishing, 2004), p. 347.

[339] Menkiti I. *On the normative conception of a person,* p. 348.

[340] Ramose M. *African democratic tradition: oneness, consensus and openness*: a reply to Wamba-dia Wamba. Quest 6: (1992), p. 62-83.

[341] Menkiti I. *Person and community in traditional African thought.* In: Wright L (ed) *African Philosophy, An Introduction.* (Lanham, MD: University Press of America 1984), p. 245.

proceed now to make my argument for partiality by considering the concept of personhood.

Personhood and Partiality

We now make an argument to the effect that African moral thought is best construed in terms of partiality. One central notion in African morality is that of 'personhood'. The notion of 'personhood' in this instance is normative insofar as it is a claim about what constitutes a good person or a moral exemplar i.e., a human being characterized by moral virtue[342]. This notion of personhood is concerned with how one has conducted oneself relative to the relevant moral norms and standards; it evaluates one as a moral agent[343]. It is in this sense of personhood that appears to characterize African moral thought. The notion of personhood we are appealing to here is generally considered to be a fundamental or defining feature of African moral thought[344]. It is also interesting to note that a talk of personhood which implies a perfectionist or self-realization ethics is reported to be a dominant interpretation of ethics[345]. With regards to this notion of personhood Gyekye states:

> In Akan cultures, then, much is expected of a person in terms of the display of moral virtue. The pursuit or practice of moral virtue is held as intrinsic to the conception of a person. The position here may thus be schematized as: for my p, if p is a person, then p ought to display in his conduct

---

[342] Behrens K. *Two "normative" conceptions of personhood.* Quest 25: (2013), p. 105-107.

[343] Masolo Dismas, *Self and community in a changing world.* (Bloomington: Indiana University Press, 2010), p. 138.

[344] Metz T. *Human dignity, capital punishment and an African moral theory: toward a new philosophy of human rights.* Journal of Human Rights 9(2010), p. 81-99. http://dx.doi.org/10.1080/14754830903530300.

[345] Gyekye K. *Beyond cultures: perceiving a common humanity, Ghanaian philosophical studies.* (Accra: The Ghana Academy of Arts and Sciences 2004), p. 109.

the norms and ideals of personhood. Thus, when a person fails to exhibit the expected moral virtues in his conduct, he is said not to be a person[346].

It is not enough to be a human being; more is expected from an African moral perspective, one ought to be a good person. A human being is here naturally construed as having an ability to form a good character. Metz corroborates this view when he observes that:

> Personhood, selfhood, and humanness in characteristic sub-Saharan worldviews are value-laden concepts. That is, an individual can be more or less of a person, self, or human being, where the more one is, the better. The ultimate goal of a person, self, or human in the biological sense should be to become a full person, a real self, or a genuine human being, i.e., to exhibit virtue in a way that not everyone ends up doing[347].

What captures our attention in the above quote is that as much as everyone is believed to have the moral capacity to exhibit some virtues, not everyone ends up doing so. In other words, some people fail to reach the status of being moral paradigms. In fact, in this regard Menkiti states: "One conclusion appears inevitable, and it is to the effect that personhood is the sort of thing which has to be achieved, the sort of thing at which individuals could fail"[348]. Thus, a society will be composed of those who have failed to live a truly human life and those who have succeeded.

---

[346] Metz T. *Human dignity, capital punishment and an African moral theory: toward a new philosophy of human rights.* Journal of Human Rights 9(2010), p. 83. http://dx.doi.org/10.1080/14754830903530300.

[347] Menkiti, On *the normative conception of a person*, p. 326.

[348] Darwall S. *Two kinds of respect. Ethics* 88: p. 36-37. (1977) http://dx.doi.org/10.1086/292054.

And those who have failed will be blamed and those who have succeeded will be praised[349].

If it is true, that this idea of one leading a genuine human life is an essential part of African moral thought, it appears to be taking us in a direction that is different from that of impartiality as suggested by Wiredu. When we make a moral judgement that one is a person, we are praising her for internalizing sociomoral norms of a society and when we say she is not a person we are blaming her for failing to internalize these norms to inform her character. At the heart of this judgement is the recognition of an individual's effort. We are praising or blaming her for a certain moral exertion; her moral judgement singles her out individually as a (moral) achiever or not. Community approval is a response to her (own) achievement; she made it, morally speaking. It is her achievement and not that of a community the community just recognizes and acknowledges and praises her. This partialist reading of personhood finds expression and support from a singularly unexpected source: Wiredu argues that:

> What, then, in its social bearings, is the Akan ideal of personhood? It is the conception of an individual who through mature reflection and steady motivation is able to carve out a reasonably ample livelihood for self, family, and a potentially wide group of kin dependents, besides making substantial contributions to the well-being of society at large. The communalistic orientation of the society in question means that an individual's image will depend rather crucially upon the extent to which his or her actions benefit others than him/herself, not, of course, by accident or coincidence but by design. The implied counsel, though, is not one of unrelieved self-denial, for

---

[349] Wiredu, K. *Moral foundations of an African culture. In: Wiredu K & K Gyekye* (eds) Person and community: Ghanaian philosophical studies, 1. (Washington DC: The Council for Research in Values and Philosophy, 1992), p. 200.

the Akans are well aware that charity further afield must start at home[350].

This route is one which is supposed to shake Wiredu from his slumber of defending an untenable position of impartiality. It is obviously at odds with his moral principle of sympathetic impartiality we suspect he is not aware of this tension. Wiredu is very clear that one becomes a good person as a result of some personal exertion to improve one's life. In this sense, a journey to moral perfection is a personal project, a partialist consideration, within the incubator of social context[351]. It is important to note also that Wiredu appears to be suggesting that one owes immediate duty to self-development then to one's family and, if possible, one can benefit a wide group. Then the observation that 'charity further afield must start at home' rubber- stamps the partialist reading of an African moral tradition as much as one has a duty to the community at large, that duty must be interpreted within the prism of partiality, which prioritizes one's personal projects, family, friends and so far, as is possible one can extend one's reach and help to the community at large.

One possible objection against partiality might be that this reading of African ethics is individualist, whereas African thought is dominantly construed as communitarian. In this light Metz observes that one "finds contemporary African thinkers railing against Western "brash competitiveness," "single-minded commercialism," unbridled individualism," and "morally blind, purely economic logic," instead tending to favor certain kinds of cooperatives"[352]. Furthermore, Gessler Nkondo, commenting on ubuntu, refers to "the supreme value of society, the primary importance of social or communal interests, obligations and

[350] Menkiti, On *the normative conception of a person*, p. 327.

[351] Metz T (2012) *Developing African political philosophy*: moral-theoretic strategies. Philosophia Africana 14, p. 61-83. http://dx.doi.org/10.5840/ philafricana20121419.

[352] Nkondo G. *Ubuntu as public policy in South Africa: a conceptual framework. International Journal of African* Renaissance Studies 2(2007), p. 88-100. http://dx.doi. org/10.1080/18186870701384202.

duties over and above the rights of the individual"[353]. This position is sometimes captured as the ontological priority of the community over the individual[354]. The objection here is that the idea of partiality leans towards an individualist interpretation of African culture and moral thought, which is supposedly at odds with an African culture and moral thought that emphasizes the slogan of a community first.

We think, first of all, that it is important that we clarify two senses of the claim that African ethics is not 'individualist'; much of the criticism in this direction conflates this distinction. On the one hand, one can use the notion of 'individualism' to make a descriptive claim about how persons come to form their identities, and the role played by social relations in this process[355]. This is a descriptive claim about the relationship between an individual and a community[356]. On the other hand, one can make a claim about the location of moral value as internal in the individual[357], and this in environmental ethics is typically contrasted with 'holism', which locates value in the group[358].

For the first kind of 'individualism' one is making claims that are anthropological or about social-customary arrangements, specifically, contingent facts about how to organize society and formations of individual identities. In this light, Wiredu observes,

---

[353] Menkiti, On *the normative conception of a person*, p. 324.

[354] Louw D. *Ubuntu and the challenges of multiculturalism in post-apartheid south Africa.* (Utrecht: Centre for Southern Africa 2004), p. 423.

[355] Wiredu K. *Social philosophy in postcolonial Africa: some preliminaries concerning communalism and communitarianism.* South African Journal of Philosophy 27: (2008), p. 336. http://dx.doi.org/10.4314/sajpem.v27i4.31522.

[356] Behrens K., *African philosophy, thought and practice and their contribution to environmental ethics.* (Johannesburg: University of Johannesburg, 2011), p. 18.

[357] Metz T (2010) human dignity, capital punishment and an African moral theory: toward a new philosophy of human rights. Journal of Human Rights 9: p. 81-99. http://dx.doi.org/10.1080/14754830903530300.

[358] Wiredu K. *Social philosophy in postcolonial Africa: some preliminaries concerning communalism and communitarianism.* South African Journal of Philosophy 27: (2008), p. 335.

African societies are 'communitarian' in the sense that they prioritize what we owe to each other in terms of obligations. Then, he is quick to remind us that some cultures are individualistic and some communitarian; all this talk is a matter of degree[359]. These corrective and moderate understandings of community by Wiredu, we suspect, are strongly influenced by his colleague Kwame Gyekye. Gyekye argues for what he calls 'moderate communitarianism'. His first and foremost aim is to reject what he calls 'extreme communitarianism' insofar as it does not have space for human rights – rights are things that belong to individuals qua individual[360]. His moderate view balances the ideal of individuality (dignity) and that of community (common good)[361].

Through regards to the latter, it calls for a common good, and with regards to the former it demands that individuals be given certain rights that belong to them naturally and it further calls for enough space for individuals not to be wholly consumed by a community, thus to pursue their own projects and such like. we observe that Gyekye also conflates the two senses of 'individualism' as adumbrated above, but on the whole is correct to defend a space for an individual and her rights, without jettisoning her social obligations. we therefore observe that something like moderate communitarianism that balances individual interests and collective interests is compatible with partiality.

Furthermore, with regards to the second sense of 'individualism' as a claim about the location of moral good in the individual, it is interesting to note with Metz that much of African ethics is actually individualist insofar as it locates the good in

---

[359] Gyekye K. *Beyond cultures: perceiving a common humanity*, p. 39.

[360] Gyekye K. *Beyond cultures*, p. 41.

[361] Metz T (2010) human dignity, capital punishment and an African moral theory: toward a new philosophy of human rights. Journal of Human Rights 9: p. 81-99. http://dx.doi.org/10.1080/14754830903530300.

A CRITIQUE OF KWASI WIREDU'S HUMANISM AND IMPARTIALITY

some (internal) individual property, be it life or dignity or self-realization. In fact, Metz shows that the literature is dominated by individualist interpretations of ethics: out of six, only two principles of right action base morality on some relational property, the rest base it on some individualist consideration, be it dignity, life, utility or perfection[362]. It is therefore simplistic and not obviously true to claim that African ethics are not individualist. A friend of impartiality might further argue that partiality is incompatible with reported hospitality and kindness of Africans to complete strangers, which appears to be a consideration that is best explainable by impartiality. The partiality we defend here has resources to respond to this concern. Partiality as a substantive claim does not entail that we should not help strangers, it is merely asserting that we owe more to those close to us than those not. Thus, to advocate partiality is not tantamount to rejection of hospitality to strangers. To advocate partiality is not to deny the equality of human beings; it is rather to deny that equality of human beings amounts to same treatment of all human beings without any positive discrimination. Metz responds to this charge of incompatibility between partiality and hospitality to strangers by pointing out that "Ubuntu similarly defends the value of partiality we owe more to family than to non-family but it also emphasizes the obligations we owe to strangers, simply in virtue of their humanity".

The fact that Africans prioritize extant and close relationships more than non-close and possible relationships does not mean that we ignore or become cold to the humanity of others when in need. The fact of their humanity is sufficient ground to respond to them accordingly. It is for this reason that Ramose postulates permeable boundaries, and this postulation makes an African conception of partiality rich since it allows us to extend beyond family web and other special relationships, wherever possible. The insight here is that we can never fully respond to the

---

[362] Metz T (2010) human dignity, capital punishment and an African moral theory, p. 89.

plight and unfortunate condition of strangers and wayfarers on our doorstep in need until we have exposed ourselves fully to the plight of those close to us. We can never say we love humanity until we have been true to it with those close and special to us. Hence charity begins, but note, it does not end there.

Conclusion

In this discussion, we have critically reflected on Wiredu's moral theory at two levels, as a meta-ethical theory (humanism) and as a theory of right action (sympathetic impartiality). We problematized one of the stubborn features of African moral features that renders morality in terms of human interests or any other (human) feature. We suggested that a more promising moral theorization must take us in the direction of non-anthropocentrism. This is where moral theorization should be going. Unfortunately, as things stand in the literature, much of it is humanistic. we also rejected humanism to open up a space for a robust philosophical ethics in the African tradition given that humanism is not as firmly grounded as Wiredu would have us think. we have also problematized impartiality as a central feature of African moral theorization; we did this so we can have extensive philosophical works that do more research on African ethics in this regard. The debate between partiality and impartiality has not been extensively considered in the African moral tradition; we have suggested some useful places to start such an investigation.

Bibliography

BEHRENS K., *African philosophy, thought and practice and their contribution to environmental ethics.* Johannesburg: University of Johannesburg, 2011.

BEHRENS K., Two *"normative" conceptions of personhood.* Quest 25:(2013) 103-118.

DONNELLY J., (1982) *Human rights and human dignity: an analytic critique of non-western conceptions of human rights.* The American Political Science Review 76: 303-316. http://dx.doi.org/ 10.2307/1961111.

GYEKYE K., *Beyond cultures: perceiving a common humanity, Ghanaian philosophical studies.* Accra: The Ghana Academy of Arts and Sciences, 2004.

IMAFIDON E., On *the ontological foundation of a social ethics in African traditions.* In: Imafidon E & J Bewaji (eds) ontologized ethics: new essays in African meta-ethics. New York: Lexington Books, 2013.

LOUW D., *Ubuntu and the challenges of multiculturalism in post-apartheid south Africa.* Utrecht: Centre for Southern Africa, 2004.

MANYELI L., *A re-reading of gyekye's moderate communitarianism.* Lwati: A Journal of Contemporary Research., 2010.

MASOLO D., *Self and community in a changing world.* Bloomington: Indiana University Press, 2010.

MBITI J., African *religions and philosophy.* New York: Doubleday 1970.

METZ T., Human *dignity, capital punishment and an African moral theory*: toward a new philosophy of human rights. Journal of Human Rights 9(2010) 81-99. http://dx.doi.org/10.1080/14754830903530300.

METZ T., (2012) Developing African political philosophy: moral-theoretic strategies. Philosophia Africana 14: 61-83. http://dx.doi.org/10.5840/ philafricana 20121419.

METZ T., Two *conceptions of African ethics in the work of D.A. Masolo.* Quest 25: 141-161. 2013.

RAMOSE M., *African democratic tradition: oneness, consensus and openness*: a reply to Wamba-dia Wamba. Quest 6: 62-83.1992.

SHUTTE A., *Ubuntu: an ethic for a New South Africa.* Pietermaritzburg: Cluster Publications, 2001.

SUMNER L. W., *Welfare, happiness, and ethics.* Oxford: Clarendon Press, 1996.

WAMALA E., *Government by consensus: an analysis of a traditional form of democracy*. In: Wiredu Kwasi. (ed) Companion to African philosophy. Oxford: Blackwell Publishing, 2004.

WIREDU K., (2005) On the idea of a global ethic. Journal of Global Ethics 1: 45-51. http://dx.doi.org/10.1080/17449620500106636.

WIREDU K., *Moral foundations of an African culture*. In: WIREDU K & GYEKYE K. (eds) Person and community: Ghanaian philosophical studies, 1. Washington DC: The Council for Research in Values and Philosophy. 1992.

WIREDU K., *Cultural Universals and Particulars: An African perspective*. Indianapolis: Indiana University Press, 1996.

WIREDU K., Reply to English/Hamme. Journal of Social Philosophy 27: 234-243. http://dx.doi.org/10.1111/j.1467-9833.1996.tb00248.x 1996.

WIREDU K., *Society and democracy in Africa*. New Political Science 21: 33-44. http://dx.doi.org/10.1080/07393149908429850l999.

WIREDU K., *Social philosophy in postcolonial Africa: some preliminaries concerning communalism and communitarianism*. South African Journal of Philosophy 27: 332-339. http://dx.doi.org/10.4314/sajpem.v27i4.31522, 2008.

INDEX

Preface and Acknowledgments 7

Oriare Nyarwath
Kwasi Wiredu and the Development of
Contemporary Philosophy in Africa 9

Munguci D. Etriga
Conceptual Decolonization: Wiredu's Seminal Work 29

Mwenda Godfrey
African Philosophy and African Education:
Implications of Wiredu's Conceptual Decolonization Project
on Africa's Educational Policy on Indigenous Languages 59

Nelson Shang
Conceptual Decolonization of the African:
In Search of a New Mentality for African Development 89

Anselm Kole Jimoh
Wiredu's Idea of Conceptual Decolonization and
the Decolonization of Epistemic Inquiry in Africa 111

John Mundua
Kwasi Wiredu, Jürgen Habermas and Alasdair Macintyre:
Universals and Moral Relativism 135

Ochieng' G. Ojwang'
Philosophy and the Political Problems of Human Rights in Africa:
A Reflection on Kwasi Wiredu 167

Crispin Ong'era Isaboke
One Moral Obligation One Universal Morality:
A Critique of Kwasi Wiredu's Cultural Universals and Particulars 211

Oliver Babirye Najjuma
A Critical Analysis of Kwasi Wiredu's Compatibility
of Religion and Morality 225

Sabas Kimani
A Critique of Kwasi Wiredu's Humanism and Impartiality 247

DOMUNI-PRESS
publishing house of DOMUNI Universitas

« Le livre grandit avec le lecteur »
"The book grows with the reader."

Domuni Universitas

Domuni Universitas was founded in 1999 by French Dominicans. It offers Bachelor, Master and Doctorate degrees by distance learning, as well as "à la carte" (stand-alone) courses and certificates in philosophy, theology, religious sciences, and social sciences (including both state and canonical diplomas). It welcomes several thousand students on its teaching platform, which operates in five languages: French, English, Spanish, Italian, and Arabic. The platform is accompanied by more than three hundred professors and tutors. Anchored in the Order of Preachers, Domuni Universitas benefits from its centuries-old tradition of study and research. Innovative in many ways, Domuni consists of an international network that offers courses to students worldwide.

To find out more about Domuni:

www.domuni.eu

EXTRACT FROM THE CATALOGUE

Jean-François ARNOUX,
Et le désert refleurira.

Sabine GINALHAC,
Désir d'enfant. L'éclairage inattendu des récits bibliques.

Pierrette FUZAT,
Un nom au bout de la nuit. Le combat de Jacob.

Patrice SABATER,
La terre en Palestine/Israël.

Marie MONNET,
Emmanuel Levinas. La relation à l'autre.

Apollinaire KIVYAMUNDA,
Maurice Zundel, une biographie spirituelle.

Juliette BORDES,
Viens Colombe. Saint Jean de la Croix.

Joseph MARTY,
Christianisme et Cinéma.

Michel VAN AERDE,
Le père retrouvé

Monique-Lise COHEN, Marie-Thérèse DESOUCHE,
Emmanuel Levinas et la pensée de l'infini.

Claire REGGIO,
Le christianisme des premiers siècles.

Ameer JAJE,
Diaconesses. Les femmes dans l'Église syriaque.

Jean-Paul COUJOU (sous la direction de),
L'État et le pouvoir.

Françoise DUBOST,
L'Évangile des animaux.

Markus JOST,
La Bible à l'école d'Ignace de Loyola et de Menno Simons.

Paul TAVARDON, ocso,
Trappistes en terre sainte. Des moines au cœur de la géopolitique.
Latroun, 1890-1946 (T.1).

Paul TAVARDON, ocso,
Trappistes en terre sainte. Des moines au cœur de la géopolitique.
Latroun, 1946-1991 (T.2).

Marie MONNET (sous la direction de),
La source théologique du droit.

Nilson Léal DE SA,
La vie fraternelle.

Apollinaire KIVYAMUNDA,
Maurice Zundel. La relation à Dieu.

Lara LOYE,
Fraternités.

Bernadette ESCAFFRE,
Vocations. Quand Dieu appelle.

Raphaël HAAS,
Pleine conscience. Bouddhisme et christianisme en dialogue.

Augustin WILIWOLI,
Axel Honneth. Lutter pour la reconnaissance.

Louis FROUART,
Pascal. Cœur, Corps, Esprit.

Emmanuel BOISSIEU,
Platon. Une manière de vivre.

Emmanuel BOISSIEU,
Kant. Une philosophie de la liberté.

Marie MONNET,
Dieu migrant.

Thérèse HEBBELINCK,
L'Église catholique et les juifs (T.1 et T.2).

Béatrice PAPASOGLOU,
Qu'est-ce que l'homme ?

Augustin WILIWOLI SIBILONI op,
Ce que les philosophes disent du vivre-ensemble.

François MÉNAGER,
Yves Bonnefoy, poète et philosophe.

Nicole AWAIS,
L'art d'enseigner le fait religieux.

Thérèse M. ANDREVON,
Une théologie à la frontière (T.1 et T2).

Michel VAN AERDE,
Venez vous reposer. Antidotes spirituels au burn-out.

Agnès GODEFROY,
Bien vieillir, dans les pas d'Abraham.

Olivier BELLEIL,
Résolution des conflits dans l'Église primitive.

Anton MILH op & Stephan VAN ERP,
Identité et visibilité. Conflits de générations chez les Dominicains.

Denis LABOURE,
Astrologie et religion au Moyen Âge.

Jorel FRANÇOIS,
Voltaire, philosophe de la religion.

Augustin WILIWOLI SIBILONI op,
La reconnaissance. Réparer les blessures.

Jean Baptiste ZEKE,
Loi naturelle et post-humanisme.

Emmanuel BOISSIEU,
Paul Ricœur. Un inconditionnel de l'amour.

Ameer JAJE,
Le chiisme. Clés historiques et théologiques.

Jean-René PEGGARY,
*L'aube d'une pensée américaine. L'individu chez H.
D. Thoreau.*

Jean-François ARNOUX,
*Comme un feu dévorant. Flammèches d'une lecture incarnée
de la Bible.*

Olivier BELLEIL,
L'autre dans l'islam coranique.

Sœur Agnès DE LA CROIX,
Miroir juif des évangiles.

Jean-Michel COSSE,
Au centre de l'âme.

Jean-Paul BALDAZZA,
Antoine. Un saint d'Orient et d'Occident.

Ameer JAJE,
Marie dans l'islam.

Olivier PERRU,
Le corps malade.

Jesmond MICALLEF,
Trinitarian Ontology.

Abel TOE,
Pauvreté et développement au Burkina Faso.

Jude Thaddeus MBI AKEM,
Le développement en Afrique.

Claude LICHTERT,
Lire la Bible ensemble.

Jorel FRANÇOIS,
Voltaire, philosophe contre le fanatisme.

Bruno CALLEBAUT,
Les Évangiles. Leurs origines, leurs exégèses.

Claude LICHTERT,
*La parole pour sortir de soi. Dieu et les humains
aujourd'hui : parcours biblique.*

Heriberto CABRERA REYES,
*Effondrement, apocalypse ou renaissance ? Théologie en
temps de crise.*

Patrick MONJOU,
Comment prêcher à la fin du Moyen Âge ? (T. 1 et T. 2).

Robert PLÉTY,
À la découverte du Rabbi de Nazareth (T. 1).

Robert PLÉTY,
À la rencontre du Rabbi de Nazareth (T. 2).

Jules KATSURANA,
Guide pour la Prévention de la violence sexiste.

Jacques FOURNIER,
La Trinité, mystère d'amour.

Louis D'HÉROUVILLE,
Marie-Madeleine, femme pascale.

Olivier PERRU,
*Martin-Stanislas Gillet (1875-1951). La peur de l'effort
intellectuel.*

Paul-Marcel LEMAIRE,
Vivre l'Évangile.

John Jack LYNCH,
Judith, Sarah and Esther. Jewish heroines.

Paul NYAGA,
Moral Consistency with Lonergan's Thought.

François FAURE,
Emmanuel Mounier : La personne est son engagement (T. 1).

François FAURE,
Emmanuel Mounier : Montrer, sans démontrer (T. 2).

Olivier-Thomas VENARD, Gregory TATUM,
Conversations sur Paul. « Supportez-vous les uns les autres ».

Isaac MUTELO,
Muslim Organisations in South Africa.
Political Role Post-1948.

Stephen Musisi KASOZI,
Issues of Constitutionalism. A case study of Uganda.

Pierre Dalin DOMERSON,
La gestion des biens de l'Église. Enjeu pastoral.

Philippe ANDRÈS,
Notre-Dame de Rocamadour. Du Moyen Âge à nos jours.

Oliver BARRETT,
Ecological Crisis. In Catholic Social Teaching.

Augustin WILIWOLI SIBILONI,
Négociation des conflits sociaux.

Alfred DIBAN KI,
Ubuntu et vie chrétienne.

Claude VALENTIN,
99 Questions sur l'Humanitaire.

Philippe MONTOISY,
Le chien militaire et la Première Guerre mondiale.

Alice NEPVEU-BARRIEUX,
La marine dans l'Ancien Testament.
Représentations et enjeux.

Marie MONNET,
En chemin.

Christophe-Marie MOGHA NGAMANAPO MUDAKA,
L'éducation en crise. Analyse philosophique.

Caroline FERRER,
Saint Jérôme dans la collection Fesch en Corse.